INVENTING THE AMERICAN WOMAN

An Inclusive History

SECOND EDITION

Volume 1: To 1877

GLENDA RILEY
Ball State University

Harlan Davidson, Inc.
Wheeling, Illinois 60090-6000

Library of Congress Cataloging-in-Publication Data

Riley, Glenda
    Inventing the American woman : an inclusive history / Glenda
Riley. — 2nd ed.
        p.   cm.
    Includes bibliographical references and indexes.
    Contents: v. 1. To 1877 — v. 2. Since 1877.
    ISBN 0-88295-922-0 (v. 1) — ISBN 0-88295-923-9 (v. 2)
    1. Women—United States—History.   2. Sex role—United States—
History.   I. Title.
HQ1410.R55   1995
305.4' 0973—dc20   94-39761
                                                               CIP

Cover design: DePinto Graphic Design

Manufactured in the United States of America
99 98 97 96   4 5 BC

CONTENTS

REFERENCE
CONTENTS IN BRIEF

Volume 2, Since 1877

INTRODUCTION
Gender Expectations Across Cultures

Since the first edition of *Inventing the American Woman* appeared in 1986, the study of women's history has penetrated the curriculums of most American high schools, colleges, and universities. The widespread response to *Inventing*, as well as subsequent requests for its revision and updating, further demonstrate the tremendous thirst that Americans have developed for knowledge concerning the nation's women and their historical experiences.

Like the first edition, this one presents an overview of the history of women in the United States. Intended for use as an introductory textbook supplement in U.S. history or a core text in women's history courses, it combines factual knowledge with a thesis intended to provoke discussion and further thought. More specifically, this volume tracks the evolution of gender expectations and social constructs concerning the essence of womanhood that have played, and continue to play, a critical role in directing and shaping American women's behaviors, responses, and dissatisfactions.

American Indians were the first to establish gender expectations in what is today the United States, but when European settlers reached early America they disregarded or rejected native peoples' ideas regarding women. Instead, European settlers established their own beliefs which soon became dominant and reflected the thinking of a society that argued for the acceptance of certain enduring "truths" regarding women. A real American woman supposedly was, among other things, a devoted mother, a domestic individual who labored most happily and productively within her own home, an unusually virtuous person who had to remain aloof from the corruption of politics, and a weak-minded, physically inferior being who needed guidance from wiser and stronger people, namely men. Once established as principles, these tenets were embodied in a series of intricate images and prescriptions that defined and limited women's roles. In other words, people invented an ideal American woman.

On one hand, this model of womanhood might be judged innocuous. Generally, white middle- and upper-class women best fulfilled its mandates. In turn, it rewarded and honored them. If they remained domestic and unassertive, such women could expect the plaudits of family members, friends, and clergy. Often, such women felt grateful and even revered; they gained satisfaction from meeting their society's expectations of women. For other groups of women, especially Native Americans, black, Spanish-speaking, and Asian women, as well as women employed outside their homes and poor women, this model simply appeared irrelevant.

On the other hand, the model should not be underestimated as a form of social control, for it provided a comfortable substitute for careful thought. People generally found it was easier to believe that both women and men had a well-defined "place" than to deal with the full complexities of human society and personality. Such thinking also helped perpetuate an economic system based upon the usually greater physical strength of men, who for centuries had performed the heavy labor involved in hunting, farming, and manufacturing, while women often remained behind to bear and raise children and perform lighter tasks. And it reinforced a political system in which men made more of the public decisions and women more of the private, or domestic ones.

Gender expectations and social constructs also kept in force power imbalances. Prevailing beliefs regarding women translated into sanctions, which in turn undergirded policies and legislation regulating families, schools, churches, politics, and the workplace. Too often, these resulting prescriptions robbed all women of the opportunity to cultivate their talents and deprived the developing nation of women's nondomestic skills and labor. Such constraints frequently caused women's education and socially acceptable literature to be narrow, often puerile, and limiting to the mind. And they encouraged women's clothing and pastimes to be impractical, sensuous, and physically restrictive.

Consequently, during the 1600s, 1700s, and early 1800s, thousands of women resisted being molded into the idealized American woman. Although middle- and upper-class women were generally the first to speak against and challenge tenets of American womanhood, women of other social classes soon expressed their discontent as well. Typically, women dissidents drew upon women's culture and its varied resources both to help them endure the system and to reform it. At the same time, such forces as early industrialization, urbanization, and national expansion not only tested customary prescriptions but demonstrated their unsuitability to a modernizing society.

By the mid-1800s, the idealized American woman sustained open attack. Women's participation in women's rights activism, reformism, religious revivalism, and paid employment all helped erode the model. During the late 1800s and well into the twentieth century, such other developments as Progressivism, world wars, civil rights, contemporary feminism, and the emergence of double-income families forced many Americans to continue to rethink their beliefs, recasting their ideas in a mold that better fits the reality of all kinds of women in the present-day United States, including professionals, poor women, lesbians, full-time homemakers, divorced women, and those of color.

Now, as the United States moves into the twenty-first century, its people will continue to struggle with, and redefine, expectations of women and societal constructs regarding them—and increasingly those affecting men as well. Understanding the historical development of both the nation and its women is essential to these undertakings. Thus, this book considers women and the changes they experienced during various epochs of American history. At each chapter's conclusion is a list of suggested readings to provide the interested reader with additional factual information, varied interpretations, and methodological perspectives regarding women's issues and themes for particular eras.

About terminology: A special attempt has been made in this text to respect sensitivities regarding the labels and language that carry great freight in such issues as racism, sexism, ageism, and classism. Some of the relevant style choices and definitions observed include referring to so-called minorities as *peoples of color*; virtually interchangeable references to *African Americans* and *blacks;* use of the term *Anglos* to mean white Americans; and preferred use of the term *Chicanos/Chicanas* for *Mexican Americans* and *Latinos/Latinas* for the broader group of Americans with heritage from any Spanish-speaking country. Upper-case *Native Americans* is used interchangeably with *American Indians* or, where unmistakable, *Indians*. Especially in precolonial and colonial context, the term *native Americans* (lower-case *n*) identifies indigenous Spanish-speaking as well as American Indian peoples. Except where hyphens are truly necessary to avoid misreading, this text also prefers not to hyphenate groups of people, even when such compounds as African American and Asian American are used as adjectives. Such choices in terminology and style remain an especially important effort in a book that braves generalizations regarding the complex historical experience of so many people—in this case, over half the people of the United States.

This book ultimately is about more than American women's past. By implication it is also about their collective present and future, periods that will witness the emergence of a long overdue development—a reinvented, and far more inclusive, American woman.

Women in Early America
to 1763

1

Women's history in early America is the saga of different types of women who shared a continent but not a culture. The first American women were American Indian (today also called Native American) women, who lived in North America anywhere from ten thousand to as much as twenty thousand years before Europeans arrived. During the late 1500s, Spanish-speaking women migrated to the southeastern and southwestern parts of what later became the United States. Then, sometime around 1608, other European women, largely English, reached the newly established American colony of Virginia. Over a decade later, in 1619, the first African women stepped foot on the Virginia shore. Although each of these groups had its own ideas about how women should behave, European beliefs increasingly influenced the thinking of most colonial Americans during the 1600s and 1700s, and thus also helped shape the expectations, policies, and laws colonial Americans formulated and applied to women.

NATIVE WOMEN

Among Eastern Peoples

The many tribes of American Indians who inhabited the continent of North America for thousands of years before Europeans arrived developed rich cultures, including complex economic and religious life, intricate social structures, agricultural techniques, and technology. Generally, during the 1600s and 1700s, eastern families lived in homes made of hide, woven mats, bark, or poles. Furnishings consisted of floor mats, beds of hide and fur, cooking utensils of iron and copper, and pottery ornamented with geometric designs. Inside these homes, women cooked over open fires, allowing the smoke to exit through openings in the roofs. Women also made thread from bark, grass, or animal sinew; fashioned clothes from textiles and animal skins; wove baskets and mats; and crafted bowls and pots. The elaborate designs these native women created for clothes and pots, as well as the games and rituals they devised, indicate that they enjoyed a modicum of leisure time. Most native women could also divorce and remarry without loss of honor.

Because virtually all these native groups venerated women's reproductive and nurturing capacities, they assigned women the role of primary producers of foodstuffs. Among the agricultural Algonquians, who lived along the northeastern coast, women supplied about 90 percent of the food by farming. Observing these women, colonist William Wood claimed that native women's output exceeded that of "English farmers," and that at harvest the women gathered large crops, dried them in the sun, and conveyed them "to their barns, which be great holes digged in the ground in the form of a brass pot, sealed with rinds of trees, wherein they put their corn, covering it from the inquisitive search of their gourmandizing husbands, who would eat up both their allowed portion, and reserved seed, if they knew where to find it." In addition, Algonquian women fished, gathered wild plants, processed and stored food, produced household goods, and aided in hunting.

Native women also wielded influence beyond their homes and fields. They routinely acted as businesspeople and entrepreneurs, offering for sale or barter crops, furs, textiles, and baskets. Women could also rise to the position of leader, commonly called *sachem* or *werowance* among eastern peoples. Although the office of leader was usually inherited, it was retained only by keeping the respect of group members, for they supported the leader with contributions of food. One such woman ruler led the Appamatucks against the English settlers in 1611, while a woman named Quaiapan served as sachem of the Narragansetts during the 1660s and 1670s.

Native women also served as shamans, or priests. In this role, they acted both as religious leaders and medical practitioners. In some bands, women performed as both shaman and war leader, a position that carried with it much power and respect. During the 1660s and 1670s, for example, a woman named Weetamoo led approximately 300 Pocasset Indian men in warfare.

In about one-third of these native groups, women also gained authority as a result of the social structure which included one or more of the following characteristics: matriarchal (women ruled the families and tribes); matrilineal (lineage descended from the mother); or matrilocal (a bride brought her groom to live in her mother's house). As a case in point, the northern Iroquois—the Mohawk, Oneida, Onondaga, Cayuga, and Seneca of New York—assigned to men the tasks of hunting, warfare, and diplomacy, and to women the responsibility of running the social and

political life of their villages. Iroquois women could select chiefs, participate in politics, initiate warfare, and change spouses without fear of ret-
ribution. In addition to this semimatriarchy, the Iroquois were
matrilineal, with mothers and daughters forming the primary kin relationships.

In Other Regions

Farther west, other American Indian women lived in ways that differed according to tribe and region. Among the Ojibway of present-day
Minnesota, for example, mutual respect between spouses and shared
child-raising characterized the family unit. To make a living, women
farmed and men hunted, but it was the women who parceled out both
grains and meat, deciding who would get what size portion. Women and
men cooperated in such other tasks as canoe-building, fishing, and trading furs, maple sugar, and wild rice. Because Objiway women had ownership rights over the foodstuffs they produced and the furs they processed,
they were the ones haggling with the first white traders and settlers in
Minnesota.

Thousands of other native groups existed in what would become the
United States. These included the Hopewell culture in the Ohio River
Valley, the hunting-gathering tribes of the Great Plains, and the fishing
peoples of the far Northwest.

In areas today known as Arizona, Colorado, Utah, and New Mexico
also lived a variety of native groups, including the Anasazi, who built
multistory apartment dwellings of adobe on rock ledges and in crevices of
cliffs. As early as 1085, they had completed what is today called Pueblo
Bonito, which, after one hundred years of work, contained over six hundred rooms. Unlike most other Indian groups, Anasazi men cultivated the
crops, while women remained in the villages, called *pueblos* by Spanish
explorers. In the villages, women processed and prepared food, cared for
families, and produced textiles, baskets, and pottery, including water jars,
storage vessels, and cooking utensils.

At the beginning of the 1600s, approximately fifty thousand Anasazi
Indians lived along the Rio Grande and the present-day New Mexico–Arizona border. Women gathered, prepared, and preserved food, cared for
children, crafted pottery, spun and wove cloth, and raised turkeys. They
also built houses with plastered walls, which they then owned, for
matrilineal descent and matrilocal residence were widely observed. As
Spaniards entered the area they hired Indian women, especially as interpreters, cooks, domestic servants, and construction workers. The Spanish
men and Indian women also cohabited or married, thus creating a mixed-
blood population (called *Mestizos*).

By the 1600s and 1700s Spanish-speaking women resided primarily in
the area that later became Florida, and in the Trans-Mississippi region, in
territory that became Arizona, California, New Mexico, and Texas. Some

of these women had migrated to, and settled in, these areas, but many others were native-born. In Florida, Spanish women had arrived nearly fifty years before Anglo women and subsequently produced native daughters and granddaughters. In the West, however, most Spanish-speaking women of the time were already native to North America. These were women of Spanish descent living in the Spanish colony of Mexico, as well as the *Mestizo* women of Spanish and American Indian ancestry.

In fact, many Mexican women helped colonize for Spain the region that later became the American West. The rolls of expeditions and other colonial documents indicate that women colonists existed and that a significant number headed their own households. During the late 1700s, widow Doña Inez Luz led a family of two recently widowed daughters and four young grandchildren to Mexico's northern frontier, while military wife Doña Teresa Varela assumed responsibility for two sons, two daughters, their spouses, a grandchild, an unmarried son, and twenty-two servants. Most of the towns in which these women lived depended upon agriculture and livestock, as well as the presence of the military to regulate Indians or reconquer them after a rebellion.

Spanish-speaking women's lives, too, varied according to group and area. For instance, in California, some lived on extensive *ranchos*, which included a *hacienda*, numerous outbuildings, and many acres, while in New Mexico they often lived in simpler adobe homes. Some of the women who resided in Santa Fe, established as the capital of New Mexico in 1609, ran small businesses. By the early 1700s, a number of middle- and upper-class New Mexican women also owned and controlled land, either with their husbands or individually. They participated in the judicial system by testifying as witnesses and initiating court proceedings, often without their husbands' assistance or knowledge. A growing number were literate enough to sign their names on their testimony and other documents.

In addition, for a variety of factors such as increasing female longevity and more male casualties of war, the number of widows increased during the 1700s. According to Spanish law, widows could inherit land, while their daughters inherited estates on an equal basis with their brothers. Thus, numerous widows and some of their daughters owned businesses and influenced public affairs.

Contact Between Natives and Colonists

During the American colonial period, 1607 to 1776, most contact between native peoples and European settlers occurred within the boundaries of the American colonies or areas adjacent to them. Thus, when most European explorers, adventurers, and settlers arrived they encountered Indians rather than Spanish-speaking people. These new arrivals judged Native American women from their own particular experience. Some colonists developed a positive view, especially those who married native women and created families (their mixed-blood offspring were called Métis), or those who traded with native women, giving them needles, machine-woven textiles, kettles, tea, stockings, and shoes in exchange for baskets, hand-produced textiles, and furs.

Other colonists viewed native women as beautiful and exotic Indian princesses who could help them conquer native peoples. The most famous example of such an Indian princess was Pocahontas. This native woman, originally named Matoaka, was the daughter of Powhatan, an Indian ruler in early Virginia. According to unsubstantiated legends, in 1607 Pocahontas intervened with her father to save the life of Captain John Smith of Jamestown.

During following years, the young woman performed many acts of kindness for various Jamestown settlers. In 1613, Pocahontas met John Rolfe, the colonist responsible for introducing the cultivation of tobacco to Jamestown. When she agreed to marry Rolfe, ministers instructed her in Christianity and baptized her Rebecca. After the couple's marriage in 1614, they lived in Jamestown and had one child. In 1616, John Rolfe and Pocahontas went to England, where Pocahontas was presented at court and touted as an Indian "princess." In 1617, Pocahontas died and was buried in England.

Colonists also viewed in a favorable light other Indian women who proved useful to European settlement. For instance, Mary Musgrove, a part-Creek woman, became an Indian leader in colonial Georgia; Kateri Tekakwitha, a Mohawk convert to Catholicism, stood as a symbol to unconverted Indians; and Nancy Ward, a Cherokee leader, befriended settlers on many occasions. In addition, Mary Brant, a Mohawk woman, was a consort of Sir William Johnson, superintendent of Indian affairs for the northern colonies, in the late 1700s.

On the other hand, numerous European settlers developed a negative view of native women, envisioning them as degraded beasts of burden. Disparaging accounts came from missionaries, trappers, traders, travelers, and settlers throughout the 1600s and 1700s. Because the majority of such sources regarded native people as primitive savages to be Christianized, exploited, removed, or exterminated, their accounts frequently tended to magnify, and even create, negative aspects of Indian life.

Also, these observers were usually European males from a non-nomadic, agricultural background and thus unaccustomed to a division of labor in which women did the village and agricultural work, while men engaged in hunting, fishing, and fighting. Consequently, Europeans regularly described Indian women in disparaging terms, calling them slaves or "squaws." One typical account of native women written by a missionary in the early 1600s characterized Indian women as "poor creatures who endure all the misfortunes and hardships of life." According to this missionary, Indian women were little more than the servants of Indian men. Such damaging characterizations bequeathed a very unattractive picture of Indian women to subsequent generations of Americans.

Perhaps the system of sexual segregation among most coastal Algonquian groups misled colonial observers regarding the supposedly "degraded" position of native women. Women often ate separately from men, performed their own dances, and spent their menstrual periods in special huts. Although the Europeans failed to understand it, such divisions did not signal women's unimportance or subordination. In fact, among most tribes, sexual harassment of women and other abusive behavior was virtually unknown, while rape, when it did occur, constituted a capital offense.

As contact between Native Americans and colonial Americans increased during the 1700s, some colonists gave more balanced reports of native women. For instance, Roger Williams, the religious leader and champion of Indian rights who founded Rhode Island, noted that native women and men worked together on such tasks as clearing a field for cultivation or harvesting a crop. In addition, a female prisoner-of-war during the 1700s reported that native women's chores were not as severe as those performed by white women.

This growing contact between natives and colonists generally proved unfavorable for Indians. As early as the 1630s, plague and smallpox epidemics ravaged coastal Algonquian language groups, including the Wampanoags and Narragansetts in New England and the Powhatans in Chesapeake Bay. By the mid-1600s, the mere 10 percent of Indians who survived the diseases introduced by Europeans gradually lost their skills and came to depend upon such European goods as textiles and weapons. Most colonists believed this was God's will. As one colonist said, in God's plan "some are mounted on horseback, while others are left to travel on foot . . . some have the power to command, while others are required to obey."

At the same time, colonists often benefited from their relations with Native Americans. Indian men gave their services as laborers, guides, and teachers of hunting and other skills, while Indian women served as spouses, companions, traders, craftspeople, and skilled agriculturalists. Among many other contributions, the Indian corn called maize facilitated the survival and expansion of the American colonies. Indian culture and arts gave many forms of beauty and originality to the infant white civilization, while the Indians' love of liberty and fierce independence helped shape the colonists' conceptions of freedom.

Unlike Indians and American colonists, Spanish-speaking peoples and American colonists, at least in this early period, seldom clashed. Numbers of Spanish-speaking peoples were relatively small in what would become the American Southwest; their settlements were scattered along the California coast and through present-day Arizona, New Mexico, and Texas. Also, few American colonists ventured beyond the Appalachian Mountains and the Mississippi River. Those who did were usually ship-captains, sailors, explorers, soldiers, traders, and merchants. Through exploration and trade, a few Spanish-speaking women adopted American goods and clothing styles, while some intermarriage occurred. Little of what transpired, however, could help predict the future enmity that would develop between the two groups.

COLONIAL WOMEN

The Arrival of European Women

In 1607, the English sent a shipload of men to settle in Virginia. Hopeful that they would find rich natural resources similar to those discovered by Spanish colonizers in South America and French colonizers in Canada, these Englishmen looked to the new land with optimism.

Their hopes were soon shattered. After almost destroying themselves in their futile attempts to discover precious metals and other riches, these first English colonists at Jamestown turned to agriculture. They began to grow crops to feed themselves and then raised tobacco for export to England. It soon became apparent to both them and the mother country that colonization in Virginia would succeed only if it were based on long-term settlement by families who could provide a market for English goods.

Of course, such family-based colonization required the presence of women. Not only were their childbearing abilities essential to the success of the English colonies in North America, but their contributions as laborers, religious and social forces, and wives were also crucial.

A few European women entered the colonial scene in North America very early. A woman named Anne Forest and her maid, Anne Buras, arrived in 1608. Other women probably completed the hazardous journey as well, but the first significant number of women landed in Virginia in 1619. By their own consent, these women were sold as wives. Two years later, three more ships arrived with fifty-seven potential wives, including teenager Jane Dier, twenty-five-year-old widow Marie Daucks, and twenty-eight-year-old, never-married Allice Goughe.

Between 1619 and 1622, Virginia officials auctioned off more than 150 "pure and spotless" women for eighty pounds of tobacco and other goods. Although the London Company of Virginia obviously recognized the need to send women to Virginia if colonial markets and social stability were to develop in the near future, by the mid-1600s men in Virginia still outnumbered women six-to-one.

In November 1620, a group of religious dissenters against the English Anglican Church landed north of the fledgling settlement at Jamestown. According to the passenger list of the *Mayflower*, eighteen women and eleven girls were among those who landed at Plymouth in what became Massachusetts. Only four of the women lived until the following spring, while all eleven of the girls survived that first harsh winter. As a result of the defection from the church and of the Plymouth Company's interest in promoting the increase of families in their colony, more women soon followed, but it was not until 1700 that the sex ratio began to equalize in Massachusetts.

As other colonies gradually established themselves, their founders also recognized that women constituted an important group of settlers, both economically and socially. Lord Baltimore of Maryland encouraged the immigration of women because he believed that, "it is time to plant with women as well as with men; that the plantation may spread into generations." This policy seemed especially critical for Maryland, which by the 1650s had approximately six hundred white males and less than two hundred females.

Despite the pressure on women to migrate to America, men continued to outnumber women. Throughout the South during the 1600s, the imbalance stood at as much as five or six men to one woman. This continuing shortage of women throughout colonial America spurred a growing demand for their importation. While some women came to the colonies as wives and daughters, many others came as potential wives. Besides those who migrated by their own consent, other women came as kidnap victims of agents who saw potential gain in selling women as wives. Hundreds of others arrived as petty criminals sentenced to deportation by governments eager to decrease their prison populations while increasing those of their colonies.

A large number of women also came to America as indentured servants, that is, people who sold their labor for a term of from four to seven years in return for their passage, support during their indentures, and a small amount of cash and clothing at the end of their terms. These were usually single women between the ages of eighteen and twenty-five. Perhaps as many as half of female colonists came as indentured servants, the earliest going to the southern colonies, and later indentures to the middle and New England colonies. During the 1600s, approximately one-third of colonial families employed an indentured servant, who was considered part of the household. Although these servants engaged primarily in domestic tasks, they occasionally performed field work as well.

Violations of an indenture were crimes that could lead to severe punishments. Both running away and pregnancy evoked an extension of service. The latter was common since indentured women were prohibited from marrying until the end of their terms. In Maryland alone, one-fifth of indentured women were charged with "bastardy." A Virginia law passed in 1692, however, indicated that many of these pregnancies were due to "dissolute masters" who had "gotten their maids with child." Despite such stains on their reputations and perhaps children to raise, virtually all female indentures married at the end of their terms and often married well because of the continuing need for wives.

Women's Status

Europeans brought with them the social, economic, and political beliefs and systems that they had known back home. These included traditional western European and English conceptions of gender roles, which assigned to men the heavy labor, including farming and manufacturing, and to women child-rearing and lighter domestic labor. In addition, most colonists were Christians and, as such, esteemed women but did so primarily in their roles as wives and mothers. In addition, unlike American Indians, colonists tended to view women as both separate and inferior.

From the perspective of most colonists, however, female settlers had the best lives of any women in the world. One pointed out that colonial women lived in a "Paradise on earth for women" because they could marry if they so desired. George Alsop of Maryland even declared that "no sooner are they on shore, but they are courted into matrimony, which some of them had they not come to such a market with their virginity, might have kept it until it had been mouldy." Like most people of that day, Alsop assumed that all women desired marriage and would experience fulfillment and satisfaction once they entered into it.

During the seventeenth century, the unbalanced ratio between men and women put pressure on women to marry while yet in their teens. In his 1692 guidebook for women entitled *Ornaments for the Daughters of Zion*, Puritan minister Cotton Mather wrote that "for a woman to be praised, is for her to be married." During the eighteenth century, however, women usually married between the ages of twenty and twenty-three. Throughout this era, nine out of ten women married at least once.

Those women who remained single usually suffered discriminatory treatment because people considered them unproductive. Society expected unmarried women to join their nearest male relative's household and serve as unpaid help. An unmarried woman performed domestic chores, especially spinning, thus the term spinster. Single women, however, enjoyed a legal status known as *feme sole* that gave them a few legal privileges, including the control of their personal property and the right to engage in business.

Those women who married entered a legal state known as Civil Death or marital unity. This status, derived from English common law and religious tradition, denied legal existence to a married woman. Sir William Blackstone's *Commentaries on the Laws of England in 1765* put forth the tenets of marital unity. By marriage, the husband and wife became one person in law; that is, during the marriage, the very being or legal existence of the woman was suspended or at least incorporated and consolidated into that of the husband.

In theory, then, a married woman had no legal existence apart from her husband. Men, who married on average between the ages of twenty-five and twenty-eight, were liable for the support of their wives and children, had to leave two-thirds of their estates to their families, and were responsible for their wives' crimes and debts. In one case, a Boston court fined a wife for physically abusing her husband, but he had to pay the fine imposed upon her.

Moreover, married women could not sign contracts, own property, vote on civil or religious matters, or retain and control their own earnings. For instance, when in 1697 Hannah Duston of Massachusetts killed ten Indians in a daring escape from captivity, her husband collected her reward. This restricted legal status, known as *feme covert*, reflected the widespread belief that women were best represented by their fathers, brothers, and husbands, who had superior knowledge of the world and would speak for women's best interests.

In daily life, however, colonists relaxed some of the limitations on women. Few colonists would benefit from impairing the activities or the effectiveness of women, for women often possessed skills critical to family survival, could handle weapons as well as men, and effectively ran the family farm or other enterprise during men's frequent absences for business or military engagements. William Byrd, a Virginia planter, described one especially dynamic woman of his acquaintance with due respect as "a very civil woman who showed nothing of ruggedness or immodesty in her carriage, yet she will carry a gun in the woods and kill deer, turkeys, and shoot down wild cattle, catch and tye hogs, and perform the most manful exercises as well as most men in these parts."

Local courts of equity played a key role in this expansion of women's rights. Because judges recognized that men did not in practice always represent women's needs fairly and that women often suffered distress under the law, they frequently modified legal codes and laws through their decisions, thus granting American women a number of privileges not enjoyed by English women. During the 1600s and 1700s, some courts even tried to protect married women's property. As early as 1646, the Massachusetts General Court ruled that a "wyfe" must formally consent to her husband's sale of their property. Over a century later, in the 1764 case of *Davey v. Turner*, the Pennsylvania Supreme Court ruled that married women, or *feme covert*, had to consent formally to the sale or transfer of a couple's property. This was an attempt to protect the property and dower rights that women brought to marriage.

Through other court decisions, some colonial women won the right to enter contracts, control their own earnings, and own property. For instance, in 1643, Deborah Moody of Long Island received a colonial land grant. Another resident of New Netherland, Cornelia Schuyler, later obtained a holding of thirteen hundred acres. In the South, Elizabeth Digges possessed a large plantation, 108 slaves, and a lavishly furnished mansion, while Margaret Brent owned over one thousand acres of land. Brent became such a powerful and respected landholder in Maryland that after Governor Leonard Calvert's death in 1647, she executed his will. Moreover, Brent asked for two votes in the Maryland legislature—one for herself as a freeholder and one as the governor's representative—but the legislature denied her request.

Women also owned land during the 1700s. Quaker Elizabeth Haddon migrated to New Jersey in 1701 to take over the family holding and serve as a missionary to Indians. Even after Haddon married itinerant minister John Estaugh, she continued to develop her estate, Haddonfield, and exercise as much power and influence as any male landholder of the period. At the same time, Catharyna Brett of New York personally managed her inherited property, and expanded her holdings, including building a lucrative gristmill.

Women could enlarge their prerogatives in other ways as well. For instance, women could protect their dowries and family property through prenuptial agreements. Especially among well-to-do southern planters, fathers tried to safeguard their daughters' dowries by helping negotiate premarital contracts. Such agreements provided that married women could control their own dowries, whether the dowries consisted of money, slaves, or land, and that the dowries would pass to the children at the mothers' death. This guarded a family from the husband's mismanagement, malfeasance, and bankruptcy. It also gave wives a modicum of income should their husbands become stingy or abusive.

In addition, deaths of spouses created opportunities for women. Widows often took over a family business or trade after their husbands' death. During the 1600s, death ended approximately two-thirds of marriages before they reached the tenth anniversary. This large number of widows not only ran farms and plantations, but also worked as shopkeepers, merchants, blacksmiths, gunsmiths, and tavern-keepers. As unmarried women, or *feme sole*, widows could own property, sign contracts, and conduct their own business affairs.

Moreover, daily practice allowed both single and married women more autonomy than appeared possible in codes of law. Early American women actually exercised a wide variety of rights and engaged in a large number of nondomestic activities and enterprises. Among other things, they taught school in their homes and were paid in kind (in goods), dispensed charity from their own back doors, sold or bartered surplus products, occasionally voted in local and school elections, and, in the absence of jails, took prisoners into their homes for a fee.

Women's Work

Virtually all women colonists assisted in the family business, whether it be farm, plantation, or shop. They served as unpaid household labor, working both as domestic artisans in the home and as laborers in chicken houses, barns, and sometimes the fields. Governor William Bradford of Plymouth observed that when the Pilgrims landed "the women went willingly into the fields and took their little ones with them to set corn."

Throughout the 1600s and 1700s, women continued to work in the fields during periods of labor shortages. Although they often performed such male-defined tasks as field work, men only infrequently reciprocated by performing women's domestic chores. Gradually, as a region became more settled, women's work increasingly focused on houses and gardens, while men's tasks centered around barns and fields.

Women performed extensive domestic tasks, often under difficult conditions. It was women's responsibility to put to good use the raw materials generated by the men through planting or hunting. Women served as domestic manufacturers as they transformed these raw materials into finished products. In this capacity, women artisans were to their families what factories later were to industrialized societies.

Of all the goods that women produced, food required the most continuous attention. Women raised chickens, milked cows, and tended vegetable gardens. Then they prepared and processed food. This involved butchering, cooking, smoking, salting, drying, pickling, and preserving— all processes demanding a great deal of time and expertise. In addition, women manufactured soap from grease and lye, as well as candles from tallow.

Women performed these tasks over open fires. In warm weather, they moved outdoors to cook, wash clothes, and make enough soap and candles to last the winter. During the rest of the year, women worked indoors, hauling water from rivers, wells, or rain barrels for cooking, as well as for washing clothes and bathing. They had to heat each bucket of water over the fire, which they continually stoked, and then wash the plank floors with the dirty water or haul it away.

Women also executed numerous other tasks. They combed wool and hackled flax that they then spun into thread. Next, they wove the thread into cloth, colored it with their own homemade dyes, and sewed it by hand into clothing. Although women spent untold hours at their spinning wheels and with their knitting needles, they also served as nurses, doctors, and morticians for their families, friends, and neighbors. In addition, they were accomplished herbalists and apothecaries who produced a large variety of efficacious medicines. During the eighteenth century, they also bore an average of eight children, taught their children early school lessons, and trained them as laborers. "On the side," these women brought in cash by selling butter, eggs, beeswax, thread, and other goods that they produced.

This brief description of colonial women's domestic work does not begin to do justice to the breadth and complexity of women's duties. Even during the late 1600s and early 1700s, when New England shops sold various kinds of goods, women's work remained extremely taxing. And in the South, the romanticized *grand dame* of the plantation was in reality a hardworking manager, supervisor, hostess, accountant, teacher, and medical practitioner, responsible for a large plantation community. Moreover, thousands of women colonists also worked outside their homes for wages.

In the labor-scarce colonial economy, women could easily work at other jobs besides their domestic duties. Such employment enhanced women's economic importance in the family and gave them skills to fall back upon if they chose to leave. Moreover, not all husbands exercised their right to control women's earnings. Thus, colonial women labored as butchers, gunsmiths, journalists, midwives, millers, nurses, printers, proprietors and managers of taverns and boardinghouses, shipbuilders, silversmiths, tanners, teachers, and upholsterers.

Women learned their trades through apprenticeships. Like young men, they served apprenticeships with local craftspersons, tradepersons, or in family households. A young colonial woman would be apprenticed between the age of eleven to thirteen for a term of service as long as ten years. Female apprentices were cared for, trained in such skills as silversmithing or upholstery or taught such domestic crafts as spinning and sewing. They were also taught to read and sometimes to write. Women acquired other skills through their fathers, brothers, or husbands who practiced a trade in or near the family home. As these men frequently sought the aid of the women of the family, they provided the opportunity for women to learn and become proficient in the trade also.

Other colonial women pursued professions. Midwives delivered most babies. Some local governments licensed midwives, while others informally recognized their competence. These women, who were usually mature and experienced, held respected positions within their communities and were revered as friends as well as medical practitioners. They would guide an expectant mother through pregnancy, attend her during the birth, and sometimes even remain with her until she could resume management of her household. Midwives also trained other women, passing along their own knowledge and skills through apprenticeships.

Women physicians existed as well; during King Philip's War (1675–1676), a Mrs. Allen served as an army physician. Some years later, another woman doctor advertised in a New England newspaper that she "follows the midwife and doctress business; cures burns, salt rheum, canker, scaldhead, fever sores, rheumatism, and the piles."

In addition, despite their exclusion from formal training, a few women were able to turn their artistic skills into paid employment. Henrietta Deering Johnston, who migrated to Charles Town (later Charleston,

South Carolina) with her husband around 1706, helped support her family by drawing pastel portraits. After her husband died at sea in 1716, she continued to do portraiture, supporting herself in her widowhood.

Other women pursued a variety of business activities. During the 1660s, Margaret Philipse of New York engaged in business, especially as a shipper of furs. Beginning in 1662, Alice Thomas profitably ran a brewhouse in Boston, although she frequently landed in court for committing such crimes as selling liquor to Native Americans.

Between 1720 and 1770, women ran 10 percent of the businesses in New England. For instance, Quaker women on Nantucket Island developed into shrewd traders. With their husbands away a good deal of the time on whaling or trading voyages, women ran the family farms, sold dry goods produced from their own flax and wool to passing trade ships, and supplied the ships with necessary provisions. A French visitor to Nantucket in the 1770s wrote that Nantucket men, "full of confidence and love, cheerfully give their consent to every transaction that has happened during their absence and all is joy and peace."

About the same time, Betsy Ross, a successful upholsterer in Philadelphia, employed several young men in her business establishment on Elfreth's Alley. Although Ross is usually characterized as a grandmother who created the American flag from scraps kept in her sewing basket, Ross was a well-known and respected entrepreneur who brought her considerable skills to bear on the question of a suitable American flag.

Women's Personal Lives

The surprising complexity of these women's lives indicate that the history of female colonists before 1776 does not easily lend itself to generalization. Still, similarities existed in the lives of colonial women, whether they lived in the South of the 1660s or in the New England of the 1700s. Whether she was married or single, the central focus of a white colonial woman's life was her household and family. A typical colonial household might include a married couple, their children, and perhaps an unmarried aunt, uncle, or grandparent. Perhaps as many as one-third of these households also included an indentured servant, hired field workers, or a number of black slaves.

Although the family was patriarchal (families and groups ruled by men), patrilineal (family lines descended from the father), and patrilocal (married couples live in the groom's father's house) in structure, women were valued and protected within it. Colonial laws also compelled husbands to support their wives and to be faithful to them (although men were penalized less severely for adultery than were women). Both failure to provide and adultery were punishable offenses. Husbands' physical punishment of wives was also controlled by law. In 1641, for example,

Massachusetts prohibited a husband from abusing his wife "unless it be in his own defense upon her assault."

In this family structure, spouses generally divided labor according to gender, with women dominating the home and men the fields or other place of business. But the family organization was not necessarily a dictatorship. Rather, colonists usually described marriage as egalitarian. A wedding sermon in Boston in 1750 stated women "are not made of the head to claim superiority, but out of the side to be content with equality." Courts and community opinion, especially in New England, cautioned husbands to extend honor and respect to their wives.

Sexual intimacy was also an important part of colonists' married lives. Men, especially among the Puritans, were expected to satisfy the sexual needs of their wives. In Massachusetts and Connecticut, failing to do so, whether through impotence or neglect, was cause for divorce. While believing in sensuality within marriage, most colonists strongly opposed adultery. Courts punished such "inconstancy" with fines, whipping, the pillory, or even death. Legislation in Massachusetts Bay prescribed for the crime of adultery the punishment of whipping and the wearing of the "capital letters A.D. cut out in cloth and sewed on their uppermost garments."

Still, some colonists strayed or committed such sexual crimes as seduction. This constituted a lesser offense than adultery and one not always unpleasant or violent. A more-than-willing Virginia woman of the 1600s was so pleased with the outcome of her seduction of a man that she swore to give him "as much cloth as would make him a sheet." Rape, however, was usually a violent, demeaning violation. One disinclined Massachusetts woman of the same era reported that a man flung her down in the street; another, that her master caught her by the wrist and forcibly "pulled her against the side of the bed."

Because sexuality and childbearing played a prominent role in the lives of colonists, women by necessity devoted a large amount of time to pregnancy and childbirth. Wed in 1685, Sarah Stein Place, a typical New England woman, bore her first child in 1686 and her eighth in 1706. Such frequent pregnancies were likely to take a colonial mother's life in one out of every thirty cases. Those colonial women who survived could expect to bear their last child at age thirty-nine and to live until age forty-nine. They would spend almost twenty years with an infant at their sides and almost forty rearing their children to adulthood.

Until the mid-1700s, expectant women depended upon midwives rather than doctors to deliver their babies. The word midwife comes from an English term meaning "with women"; birthing remained exclusively a female affair during these years. The midwife's primary function consisted of assisting the mother to deliver naturally. She might use herbal teas, wine, or liquor to lessen the pain, but she avoided mechanical devices and drugs.

Throughout the colonial period, women prepared for childbirth by abandoning corset stays, wearing flat shoes, and refraining from carriage rides. Common advice also cautioned women to avoid "sudden frights, strong passions, [and] ungratified longings" to protect her unborn child. Guidebooks advised expectant mothers to pray and to contemplate the possibility of death.

As the day of the birth approached, the mother-to-be's own mother, aunts, sisters, friends, and midwife joined her. They laid out linen, readied basins and towels, told bawdy jokes to lighten the tension, walked the expectant mother about to relieve the pain, and held her by the arms as she delivered her baby through a low stool with an open seat. They then helped care for the mother and newborn babe while celebrating its birth with a feast. They admitted the father only briefly, and barred other men from the chamber for several weeks. After friends and family dispersed, the new mother returned to her regular round of duties and chores.

Not all of the colonial woman's waking hours focused on family and work, however. One leisure-time activity was the production of handiwork and practice of a craft, especially during the 1700s when some women had slightly more time for such activities. Women's needlework skills resulted in finely stitched samplers, bed rugs, coverlets, pillow shams, and other textiles. Women also hooked, embroidered, and appliqued rugs. They painted watercolors and embroidered pictures, portraits, and mourning pictures, which recorded family deaths. They painted stoneware crocks, worktables, sewing boxes, and dishes. And they stitched a large variety of quilts, many of which chronicled births, deaths, marriages, and other significant family events. Surviving examples of women's work include a finely crafted bed rug created by Phoebe Billings of Massachusetts during the early decades of the 1700s, a colorful crewel-worked bed ensemble designed by Mary Bulman of Maine during the 1740s, and a detailed over-mantle painting by Sibyl May of Connecticut during the 1750s.

Colonial women pursued other activities as well. By giving handouts from their doors or in their kitchens, or by working through church groups, women engaged in welfare. They cared for widows, orphans, criminals, the disabled, and the poor in a day when social institutions such as hospitals and prisons were virtually nonexistent. In addition, women participated in church functions. Although denied full participation and the right to hold office, most women attended religious services and ceremonies. Only The Society of Friends, or Quakers, extended to colonial women a reprieve from the doctrine of St. Paul that demanded the silence of women in church. Because Quakers believed in spiritual equality of women and men, and in a lay ministry that included both women and men, they proffered to women a degree of equality. This included participation in church governance, especially through "women's meetings," instituted in 1681.

Some women also pursued education. Basic education for women included mainly the "three r's"—reading, writing, and 'rithmetic—and by the mid-1700s, at least in New England, the illiteracy rate for women began to decline. But advanced education for women usually led only to such female "accomplishments" as needlework, singing, and playing the pianoforte. In the South, some daughters acquired education through the common practice of allowing young women to sit in on sessions given by tutors hired to instruct young men.

At first, colonial women also strove for political involvement. They occasionally voted in early town meetings or spoke out in local gatherings, but increased settlement brought with it consolidation of political power in male hands. By the mid-1600s, in most areas of the colonies not only the vote but also office-holding, judgeships, jury service, and public debate were restricted to men.

A similar process occurred on the edges of society. Along the colonial frontier that slowly pushed southward and, by the mid-1700s, westward toward the Appalachian Mountains, women found that their labor, childbearing abilities, and other important contributions were valued but not rewarded by inclusion in such aspects of public life as education and politics. On the North Carolina frontier, for example, women worked alongside their men doing the heavy labor involved in clearing forested land for farms, planting crops, constructing homes and barns, and raising stock. Frontierswomen received appreciation for their domestic skills as well as their abilities outside of the home, yet, as settlement progressed, traditional ideas of women's work and roles soon returned.

For women discontent with this system, or with their particular mates, divorce was sometimes available. Wives with grievances could sue for divorce in most New England colonies and some Middle colonies. Puritan colonists preferred to keep couples together and often fined troublesome spouses or ordered them to "live happily together," but they also believed that some marriages could not be saved. Thus, a Massachusetts court granted the first divorce to a Mrs. James Luxford in 1639; in five years, another couple divorced. During the early 1700s, a growing number of women obtained divorces and did so at a greater rate than did men. Still, authorities continued to remind women that they should act passive and accepting. In 1712, Benjamin Wadsworth, a Puritan minister, stated that a wife "aught to be under the husband's government."

By the end of the colonial period, Massachusetts alone had granted over one hundred divorces. Courts accepted the grounds of bigamy, nonsupport, desertion, adultery, and, because Puritans believed in childbearing, impotence. Although judges often ordered alimony for wives or restored their dowries to them in cases where husbands caused marriages to end, such awards were erratic and difficult to enforce. If a woman was at fault in the marital breakdown, she received nothing; by her behavior she had forfeited all rights to conjugal support. After a divorce, women usually returned to their families, but frequently assumed *feme sole* status, so they could manage their own affairs.

Connecticut granted even more divorces than did Massachusetts, although its population was smaller. The first Connecticut divorce occurred in 1655 when Goodwife Beckwith claimed that her husband had disappeared. Connecticut courts also established the first formal list of grounds in the American colonies: adultery, desertion, and male impotence, or in the words of the legislation, a husband's failure to perform his "conjugall duty."

In southern colonies, courts refrained from giving divorces. They adhered to English law, which stated that only Parliament could grant divorces, and gave instead limited divorces called separate maintenance agreements. Chancery courts granted these to wives who demonstrated that their husbands treated them in cruel or irresponsible ways. A separated couple lived apart, but, because the husband had caused the marriage to disintegrate, he continued to provide the financial support he had pledged at the time of marriage. Other couples, especially in newly settled areas, simply announced in the newspapers that they had decided to part and were no longer responsible for each other's debts, crimes, or offspring.

Because women divorced and separated in growing numbers, and the majority of widows chose not to remarry, women headed a large number of households. According to a guidebook published in 1750, *A Wedding Ring Fit for the Finger*, this was perfectly acceptable, for "when the great light goes down, the lesser light gets up." In other words, although a wife was subject to her husband when he was present, she could "be sovereign in his absence."

Defying Gender Expectations

Despite this complex portrait of colonial women, the customary image presents them in prim white caps and serviceable dresses, quietly caring for their homes and families. At least in part, this notion originated with the many guidebooks written to shape women's behavior. In the 1660s, for example, well-known minister Cotton Mather lectured the colonial woman regarding the domestic skills she needed to "enable her to do the man whom she may hereafter have, good and not Evil, all the days of her life." Mather added that because women were more godly and religious than men, and, in his view, had "more time to employ in the more immediate service of their souls than the other sex is the owner of," they should also serve as spiritual caretakers of their husbands. He explained that "the curse in difficulties both of subjection and child-bearing," was in fact a blessing for "God sanctifies the chains, the pains, the deaths."

Perhaps it was women's very assertiveness and nondomestic activities that prompted so many colonial writers and speakers to energetically promote restrictive rules and prescriptions for colonial women, for, although Mather and others supported a model for women that emphasized such characteristics as passivity, virtue, and domesticity, not all colonial women took his advice to heart. For instance, women asserted themselves by running away from fathers or husbands whom they found overly restrictive or abusive. Colonial newspapers during both the 1600s and 1700s carried many advertisements for runaway women, and church records included many orders for their return. Because of the labor shortage, women could easily find employment in other towns, where rudimentary communications assured them anonymity. Few seem to have responded to either the newspaper advertisements or church directives by returning to their fathers or husbands.

Furthermore, women participated in military engagements, both against American Indians and during periods of civil unrest. When civil war erupted in Virginia in 1676, women joined the fray. More lower-class than middle- and upper-class women acted as spies, couriers, and suppliers of food, medicine, clothing, and gunpowder during Bacon's Rebellion. The lower-class women flouted colonial ideas regarding female behavior to carry intelligence, deliver gunpowder, and even offer to fight. Presumably, lower-class rebellious women felt less bound by gender expectations than did upper-class Loyalist women, for the latter typically played the more customary female roles of helpmeet, letter writer, and nurse.

Moreover, when the religious revival movement known as the Great Awakening erupted in the colonies during the 1730s and 1740s, women flocked to revival meetings in numbers equal to, or greater than, those of men. Revivalism offered women more opportunity for social interaction and self-expression than more traditional and formal religious services. A proliferation of meetings, ministers, and sects diffused authority and created an opportunity for women to assert themselves. Women helped to judge members for admission, to select ministers, and to organize religious services. During the 1760s, Sarah Osborn of Newport, Rhode Island, spoke to hundreds of people in her home each week on religious matters.

In addition to eschewing passivity, women sometimes left virtue behind as well. North Carolina court records reveal that two young women received reprimands for swimming nude with two young men in the Chowan River. The most common crime to appear in North Carolina records was fornication, defined then as engaging in sexual relations before marriage. Moreover, single women often chose their own mates and did not hesitate to elope when thwarted by their parents. Once wed, dissatisfied women sought sexual alliances outside of marriage and illegitimate children were not unusual; when widowed, many women chose to remain single rather than to remarry.

Cases of individual women reveal that domesticity also lacked allure in some women's eyes. Clearly, a discrepancy existed between the model established for colonial women and the reality that many achieved. Colonial poet Anne Bradstreet is an early illustration of a woman who grappled with conflict between the image and her own desires. After immigrating to Massachusetts Bay with her husband, Simon, in 1630, Bradstreet pursued her household duties and bore eight children, but also demonstrated her talent as a poet and writer.

Bradstreet was aware of women's accepted roles and duties, for many sermons, statements, and books clearly spelled them out. Two such books, *A Good Wife, God's Gift* and *Marriage Duties*, both appeared as early as 1620. Also, if women deviated from the accepted rules, they soon felt the sting of public censure. The venerable and respected governor of the Massachusetts Bay Colony, John Winthrop, declared in 1645 that Anne Hopkins, wife of the governor of Connecticut, had "fallen into . . . the loss of her understanding and reason, by occasion of her giving herself wholly to reading and writing many books." Winthrop added that "If she had attended her household affairs, and such things as belong to women, and not gone out of her way and calling to meddle in such things as are proper for men, whose minds are stronger," Hopkins might have kept her sanity.

Yet Bradstreet felt compelled to go on with her writing, often after a long day's work as the ideal wife and mother. In 1642, she expressed her bitterness regarding the censure that her work drew. "I am obnoxious to each carping tongue," go the lines of one poem, "who says my hand a needle better fits." She concluded: "If what I do prove well, it won't advance/They'll say it's stolen, or else it was by chance." In 1650, when a book of her poems, *The Tenth Muse Lately Sprung Up In America*, appeared anonymously in London as a result of her brother-in-law's efforts, Bradstreet was soon identified as its author. Her brother, however, took offense and minced no words when offering his opinion of her activities. "Your printing of a book, beyond the custom of your sex, doth rankly smell," he stated in a public letter to her published in London. Despite her discouragement over this episode and her increasing acceptance of the idea that "men can do best, and women know it well," Bradstreet continued to write. Six years after her death in 1672, Bradstreet's works appeared in a compilation titled *Several Poems Compiled by a Gentlewoman in New England.*

The well-known religious dissident, Anne Hutchinson, also stepped beyond the bounds of her domestic world, thus contributing jarring notes to the ongoing debate regarding the nature of women. Like Bradstreet, she was cognizant of prescribed behavior for women. Hutchinson, a Biblical scholar, was also fully conversant with St. Paul's admonition that women should "keep silent in the churches." Yet after her arrival in Boston with her husband William in 1634, Hutchinson increasingly fueled a religious controversy.

Hutchinson believed and taught that individuals could communicate with the spirit of Christ and interpret Biblical teachings and sermons for themselves. Such teaching created a social problem because it stressed the individual's ability to feel God's grace within, a tenet that minimized ministerial guidance and encouraged women to think and question. Because such beliefs threatened the power of the authoritarian Puritan ministers in Massachusetts, church officials condemned Hutchinson's ideas as antinomian heresy, meaning anti-authority, both political and religious. Governor Winthrop, fearing the disruption Hutchinson was causing, also denounced her, calling her a woman of "a nimble wit and active spirit, and a very voluble tongue, more bold than a man."

Despite these attacks, Hutchinson continued to defend herself and to teach her religious beliefs. Hutchinson attracted numerous followers, both women and men. Prominent and affluent merchants and craftspeople who felt constrained in their businesses by church rules supported her. Her views also appealed to a number of women who seemed restive and in search of a way to express themselves. Yet Hutchinson was not just a rebel and an agitator. She was also exemplary in fulfilling her prescribed obligations as a woman. She was a devoted wife, the loving mother of fifteen children, and a beloved midwife and nurse.

Despite Hutchinson's stature and the wide respect accorded her, church authorities feared her teachings and the growing factionalism in the community that her ideas encouraged. Charging Hutchinson with both religious heresy and behavior unfitting a female, the authorities called her to trial in 1637 and 1638, telling her that "you have rather been a husband than a wife, and a preacher than a hearer." Because Hutchinson had stepped out of her "place" and challenged home, church, and state, Massachusetts courts excommunicated her from the church and banished her from the colony. Along with many of her followers, Hutchinson left Massachusetts Bay and settled in Rhode Island, where she continued her resistance. She later moved to New York where, in 1643, American Indians killed her, two of her sons, and three of her daughters because of a tragic misunderstanding regarding payment for the land Hutchinson occupied.

Neither Hutchinson's punishment nor her death marked the end of the antinomian controversy or of women's resistance to restrictions on their lives. In 1638, Massachusetts courts ordered a number of other women dissenters whipped or cast out of the church. In 1641, authorities excommunicated Ann Hibbens for slander and denounced her for resisting the supremacy of her husband, "unto whom God put her in subjection." In 1644, officials also excommunicated Ann Eaton, an opponent of infant baptism, for lying and for stubbornness. Twenty-two years after the Hutchinson affair, one of Hutchinson's major supporters, Quaker Mary Dyer, was judged "troublesome" and hanged in Boston.

A similar problem erupted with the women of Salem, Massachusetts. Here, women who questioned religious and other authorities or acted in ways beyond accepted bounds were branded witches. Throughout the witchcraft trials of the 1650s and 1660s, Salem tribunals ordered women whipped, chained to posts, jailed, excommunicated, and executed. In 1648, for instance, Margaret James was executed for having a "malignant" touch and using suspicious medicines.

In a later outbreak of the witchcraft scare during the 1690s, tribunals condemned as witches many women and a few men in some forty other towns, mainly in New England. Because women were often thought to be evil, partly due to beliefs connected with Eve, they sustained more convictions than did men. Also, like Rebecca Nurse, a seventy-one-year-old woman jailed and then hanged in 1692, these women were usually middle-aged or older, reputed to be contentious, and involved in community affairs. Women who achieved even a modicum of economic success, as well as those who enjoyed real wealth, were more likely to be accused of practicing witchcraft than those who did not. Wives or widows active in commerce and business endeavors sustained an unusually high number of charges and convictions. This suggests that witchcraft convictions punished women whose economic activities diverged sharply from Calvinist beliefs that women should remain quiet, passive, and sequestered within the home.

During the 1700s, as areas of the American colonies grew more settled and "civilized," gender expectations often tightened, at least for white women of the middle and upper classes. Still, some women continued to venture beyond the bounds of their usual domains. In the South, for example, young Eliza Lucas practiced her own brand of noncompliance. Because her father served as governor of Antigua in the West Indies and her invalid mother was incapable of running the family plantations in South Carolina, in 1739 seventeen-year-old Eliza began to manage the family's three plantations in the Charleston area. She taught herself bookkeeping, accounting, and other skills needed to run such an extensive business and learned all she could about the cultivation of rice, South Carolina's major crop.

At her father's urging, Lucas began to experiment with other crops. One of these was the indigo plant, which produced a blue dye very much in demand by the British textile industry. Although neighboring planters thought her an eccentric young woman, she believed that indigo might pull the economy of South Carolina out of the doldrums. Lucas worked in the fields alongside her overseer, studied the involved process of retting the indigo plant into dye, and finally accepted the aid of a knowledgeable indigo maker sent by her father from the West Indies. Because this man thought Lucas unwomanly and feared that her success would undermine his own island's sale of indigo, he quarreled with Lucas and sabotaged the retting equipment.

Despite these difficulties, Lucas finally produced the plantation's first cakes of dye in 1744. Upon observing her success, neighboring planters sought her aid. She graciously gave them both indigo seeds and advice. Eventually, indigo became the second largest export in South Carolina. Also in 1744, after rejecting her father's choices of potential husbands, Lucas chose her own husband, Charles Pinckney, widower of her best friend and twenty years her senior.

Even though she was atypical in many ways, Lucas also embodied the well-bred southern woman. She studied Plutarch, Virgil, French, and shorthand. She participated in the prescribed female activities of teaching plantation children, doing needlework, and playing the pianoforte. And she kept a letter-book filled with charming phrases and interesting observations that is one of the most significant collections in existence kept by a colonial lady.

Women of the North also tested the limits during the 1700s. By 1760, Margaret Cheer had achieved fame as the leading actress on the American stage. Even after her marriage, Cheer traveled with "The American Company of Comedians" until the Continental Congress closed American theaters in 1769. The following year, Ann Catherine Green, the mother of fourteen children, began to publish the *Maryland Gazette*, the only newspaper in Maryland for many years. Noted for her fairness and skill, Green became the official publisher for the colony of Maryland. Thus, legal restrictions and gender expectations notwithstanding, numerous colonial women developed their own talents, skills, and interests.

African Women

Early African Women

The situation of the second group of women to settle in early America was quite different. African women were wrested away from their homelands against their will to provide labor for colonial Americans. Although early generations of slaves left no written documents, colonial records reveal their lives to some degree.

Annals of the London Company show that the first boatload of twenty Africans arrived at Jamestown in August 1619. A Dutch man-of-war, whose crew had seized one hundred African slaves from a Spanish frigate on its way to the Spanish West Indies, brought these twenty survivors to Virginia for sale. The *Treasurer*, an English ship that had sailed with the Dutch ship, had only one slave who had outlasted starvation and ill treatment, a woman her captors called Angela.

These and other early African women came to Virginia as indentured servants, a temporary status that was supposed to end after a period of years. Unlike colonists in the British and French West Indies, colonists in America hesitated to embrace slavery. In fact, the colony of Georgia prohibited the importation of African slaves until 1750. As early as the 1640s, however, a number of colonies, notably Virginia, began to turn indentures into formalized slavery. Virginia court records reveal that black people were sold "for life" and that the status of many black children was that of "perpetual servant." By 1648, Virginia's slave population numbered three hundred.

Slaveholders also preferred to have ownership of their slaves' *future* children. Because no laws insured this as yet, purchasers often stipulated it at the time of sale. In 1652, one Virginia planter signed an agreement stating that he had purchased a young black woman as well as "her issue and produce during her . . . Life tyme and their successors forever."

By 1661, Virginia legalized slavery, sealing at least twenty years of practice into law. Although English common law stated that children followed the status of their fathers, in 1662 Virginia law decreed that all black children would automatically inherit their mother's condition, that "all children born in this country shall be held bond or free according to the condition of the mother."

The Virginia legislature also took a stand against interracial unions, established at first primarily by white male colonists with African slave women. Virginia's 1662 law stated that any "Christian" who engaged in "fornication with a Negra man or woman, he or she offending shall pay double the fines imposed." Other colonies soon followed suit with laws supporting black slavery and forbidding miscegenation. By the mid-1700s, every colony prohibited cohabitation between the races and imposed fines, whippings, imprisonment, and banishment on those who refused to comply. Still, from the beginning, interracial unions occurred, creating a new group of Americans called mulattoes or Black Creoles.

African women reflected both the social class diversity of Africa and its ethnic variance. These women represented every class from royalty to commoners, and came primarily from the West African coast ranging from Senegambia to Angola and around the "horn" of the continent to the island of Madagascar. Slave women were taken captive from such tribes as the Dahomey, Ashanti, and Mandingo, and such countries as Sierra Leone, Gambia, and Cape Verde.

In their African homes, these women had served as wives, mothers, traders, farmers, political leaders, and even warriors. During the passage from Africa to the American colonies, they became "trade goods," for along with gold, ivory, and grain, merchants exchanged African women for iron, guns, gunpowder, whiskey, and foodstuffs. In the process, these women endured lack of food and medicine, exposure to weather at sea, branding on the breast or face, and sexual assault. Crowded conditions meant they usually slept together on their sides spoon-fashion, often shackled by the ankles. Because slaves often lay in feces, urine, and vomit, disease was rife. Mortality rates ranged from 10 to 50 percent.

Understandably, mutiny commonly occurred on slave ships. Women joined the mutinies, or frequently attempted suicide, fasting to the point of starvation. If they reached the West Indies or the American colonies alive, women submitted to numerous examinations, including rough gynecologic ones, and sale as slaves. At first, buyers preferred strong young men for use as field laborers. In South Carolina in the mid-1700s, for example, men sold for upwards of 250 English pounds, while women brought approximately 200 pounds. Although buyers gradually recognized African women's potential as breeders of future slaves, women continued to be brought to the colonies in lesser numbers than men. This imbalance frequently left African women bereft of female networks and all the more subject to sexual abuse by white and black men.

African Women's Work

Once in the American colonies, black women fell outside the colonists' notion that women should be first and foremost wives and mothers. Partly due to acute labor shortages, colonists preferred to view African women as workers and producers of additional slave laborers. Also, partly due to Christian teachings equating darkness with evil, Christian colonists thought of black people as more corrupt than, and thus inferior to, themselves. Because black men and women were inferior, the argument went, Providence clearly meant them to perform brute labor and work for other supposedly superior people.

Consequently, black women typically endured heavy workloads, broken families, and a short life expectancy created largely by inferior nutrition and a lack of immunity to unfamiliar diseases. Women's poor health and the depression and alienation they experienced under slavery suppressed the incidence of fertility. Still, slave owners expected women to produce as many children as possible. In 1639, a person visiting Samuel Maverick, who was the son of an Anglican minister and reportedly New England's first slaveholder, claimed that Maverick forced his slaves to cohabit. The visitor noted that Maverick "commanded" an African slave in his household to "go to bed" with his female slave against her will, and added that Maverick's slave woman had once been "a Queen in her own Country."

In addition to producing future workers, women provided cheap labor. In the New England and Middle colonies, they worked on farms, usually tending stock and cultivating crops, or in farmhouses as domestic servants, washwomen, and nursemaids. By 1690, women constituted a minority of the four hundred black people residing in Massachusetts. One of these was Tituba, from Barbadoes, bought by Reverend Samuel Parris to work as a domestic servant. Along with her husband, John, Tituba managed the Parris household. Parris also hired Tituba out to a local weaver and John to a tavern-keeper, thus insuring himself a source of income.

Tituba often passed dark winter evenings by telling the children and several bound girls (indentured servants) tales of her native land, including stories about talking animals and magic. Unfortunately for Tituba, witchcraft had become a frightening concern in Massachusetts during the early 1690s. When some of her listeners performed strange acts, including barking like dogs, people suspected Tituba of practicing witchcraft. Several of the girls duly accused Tituba and, after Parris beat her, Tituba confessed. In 1692, Tituba became one of the first three women accused of witchcraft in Salem, Massachusetts. A local court convicted Tituba and jailed her for thirteen months. Subsequently, Parris sold Tituba and she disappeared from the historical record.

The New England and Middle colonies did not always treat slave women in such unenlightened ways. Not all colonists believed in the limitations the slave system imposed upon black people. As early as 1704 a white reformer in New York City, Elie Neau, organized at Trinity Church the first school for slaves in the American colonies. Puritans established a number of similar schools in New England, while Quakers did so in Pennsylvania and New Jersey. Some educated black women subsequently gained public notice. In 1746, Lucy Terry Prince, educated by her owner, became the first black poet in America. Prince's poem, "A Slave Report in Rhyme," described a battle between American Indians and colonists at Old Deerfield in Massachusetts and was later published in 1855.

In the southern colonies, slave women served as midwives, nurses, apothecaries, cooks, seamstresses, weavers, and dairy maids. Still, 89 percent of slave women labored in the fields. They transferred their agricultural skills from African fields to those of the American colonies, where they tended tobacco, wheat, corn, rice, and indigo. Women worked alongside men, clearing the fields for planting, sowing, weeding, and harvesting. On some plantations, women did separate jobs from men; for example, women hoed and men plowed. But on others, or in time of emergency, women performed the same tasks as men, including plowing. In between, women undertook a variety of gender-differentiated tasks, including caring for and butchering livestock, filling ice houses, spinning cotton, weaving cloth, and cooking. If slack times occurred, the owners of slave women might rent them out for extra income.

Other slave women worked in plantation and farm houses, helping care for the families who raised crops. Such work could bring benefits in the form of scraps of food or clothing, but it also required long hours waiting in dark hallways and pantries, days spent standing on the rough brick floors of kitchens and washhouses, or nights sleeping on straw mats near children's beds. Nor were mistresses of large houses necessarily easier to work for than male overseers in the fields. Instances of brutal and abusive mistresses were rife.

Neither did slave women have much hope for their children's futures. During the 1600s and early 1700s, southern slave children sometimes received basic education because planters' wives and daughters often believed it their duty to teach their slaves elementary reading and writing. On some plantations, rudimentary schools even provided classes for slave children. Education soon disappeared, however, for planters argued that slaves were uneducable and any schooling a waste. Other slave owners who feared that teaching slaves to read and write would help them foment rebellions also actively opposed the educating of slaves.

Slave women also saw their families splintered by sale and death. Slave women usually managed to form new families with different mates or lived with their children. Often, women established their primary bonds with daughters and other women, forming female networks that served as both support and work groups. From women came an effort to conserve what remnants of African culture they could, including birthing practices and the growing of such crops as groundnuts and yams. Too, women devised new folkways to replace those lost in passage, including marriage rituals and work songs used in the fields. The typical slave woman, then, acted in a self-reliant and independent manner.

White Fears and Black Resistance

Gradually, a growing number of native-born slave women came to adulthood. These women spoke English, developed immunities to local diseases, and were able to bear more children. As a result, natural increase among the slave population began to occur during the 1720s and 1730s. By 1740, according to some investigators, a total of 23,958 slaves lived in northern colonies, while 126,066 resided in southern colonies.

As the number of black people in America increased, so did whites' fears regarding them. Colonists increasingly viewed blacks as troublemakers who ran away or rebelled. Indeed, according to public notices and newspaper advertisements, both slave men and women often ran away. Slaves also frequently revolted. In 1708, for example, a number of Newton, Long Island, slaves rebelled and killed seven white people. In punishment, authorities hung three slave men and burned one slave woman. The colony also passed a law allowing the courts to sentence rebels to death in any manner to maintain "public tranquility." Outside the American colonies, harsh penalties occurred as well. In 1732, a slave plot in Louisiana led to the hanging of a slave woman.

Other slaves used arson as their weapon against slave owners. In 1740, a Charleston, South Carolina, court condemned a slave woman to death for the crime of arson, while in the following year a Charleston, Massachusetts, court ordered Kate, slave of Francis Varambaut, executed for setting fire to a house and intending to burn the entire town. Later, in 1766, when another Massachusetts court sentenced to execution a woman who burned to the ground her owner's house, tobacco house, and outhouse, the prosecutor noted that slaves had already burned two other tobacco houses, full of tobacco, that winter.

Such rebellions led to increased constraints on the slave population. Worries about runaways and rebellions eventually led to the formal prohibition of education for, and written communication between, black people. Denied a written outlet for their thoughts and used to the custom of oral history from their African or Caribbean homes, black Americans relied on oral tradition to chronicle their history. When excluded from churches, where owners believed slaves would meet and plan rebellions, slaves held their own religious observances, often based upon African traditions. And when, on the owner's theory that they could sell unmarried slaves with less upset, slaves were refused access to formal marriage and separation, they held their own ceremonies and relied on their own communities for sanction.

By the close of the American colonial period in the 1770s, one appraisal estimates that 48,460 black slaves lived in the New England and Middle colonies, while 411,362 lived in the South. Although the slave women among them played a vital role in the colonial economy, their contributions were frequently overlooked and undervalued. Nor did their lives fit the white colonists' model of womanhood. Black women, especially those in the New England and Middle colonies, observed and understood prevailing gender expectations, but few were able to fulfill them. Rather, black women often had to be assertive and strong. Although they did cook, sew, and care for their families, they also performed heavy labor, resisted their oppressors, and filled leadership roles. In numerous ways, then, the reality of slave women's lives diverged from the social ideals of the culture at large regarding what women's lives "should" be.

Free Black Women

A slightly different situation existed for free women of color. Women in both rural and urban areas obtained their freedom by working their way out of slavery, by receiving it from their owners as a gift, or by receiving it as a bequest in an owner's will. In the New England and Middle colonies, legal quests for a slave's emancipation sometimes succeeded as well. In 1766, a forty-six-year-old mulatto named Jenny Slew sued for her emancipation. Because Massachusetts was one of the few states that allowed slaves to bring suit (slaves were usually regarded under the law as property rather than persons), Slew successfully argued her case. She claimed that she had been born free because her mother was white. When the judges divided on the case, Slew won her freedom. In addition, the court awarded her four pounds and court costs. After attorney John Adams listened to the hearings, he wrote "this is called suing for liberty; the first action that ever I knew of the sort, though I have heard there have been many."

Free blacks sometimes chose to stay with former owners as paid domestic servants, or they hired themselves out as domestics, farm labor, or in other service jobs. Some, especially in cities, started their own small businesses, including selling fruits and vegetables from pushcarts. Mary and Anthony Johnson of Northampton County, Virginia, were two successful free people of color. They arrived in separate ships in 1621 and 1622, then met on a plantation where Mary was the only woman. At some point, they obtained their liberty, married, and raised four children. They owned a 250-acre plantation and their grown son John a 450-acre plantation, which they sold when they moved to Maryland during the 1660s.

Other examples of free women of color could be found in Philadelphia, where a number of wealthy Quaker professionals and merchants emancipated their slaves during the 1700s, especially after 1740. Although the majority of free black women worked as domestic servants, washwomen, and nursemaids, many of them could read, write, and figure sums. Other free black women ran small businesses or owned property. One of these, Jane Row, held real estate in Philadelphia and in Southwark, and owned two slaves. Another, a widow, owned a lot and several buildings in Spring Garden in Philadelphia. Unlike many slave women in Pennsylvania, these free women of color lived with their families and could establish homes, raise their children, and, if they chose to do so, borrow from the ideal American womanhood that white colonists advocated.

The process of inventing the archetypal American woman had only begun during the colonial era. Still, gender expectations and social constructs regarding women exerted increasing force on women in early America through public opinion as well as through policy and law. Although the model excluded the numerical majority of American women, its tenets had already begun to define their lives in both subtle and not-so-subtle ways. Although Sarah Harrison of Surry County, Virginia might mutter "no obey" at her 1687 wedding to James Blair, many other women assumed and accepted prevailing male prerogatives.

Suggestions for Further Reading

Anderson, Karen. *Chain Her by One Foot: The Subjugation of Women in Seventeenth-Century New France*. London: Routledge, 1991.

———. "Commodity Exchange and Subordination: Montagnais-Naskapi and Huron Women, 1600–1650," *Signs* 11 (Fall 1985): 48–62.

Anderson, Marilyn J. "The Best of Two Worlds: The Pocahontas Legend as Treated in Early American Drama," *The Indian Historian* 12 (Summer 1979): 54–59, 64.

Barker-Benfield, G. J. "Anne Hutchinson and the Puritan Attitude Toward Women," *Feminist Studies* 1 (1972): 65–96.

Benson, Nancy C. "Pioneering Women of New Mexico," *El Palacio* 85 (Summer 1979): 8–13, 34–38.

Berkin, Carol Ruth. "Within the Conjurer's Circle: Women in Colonial America," 79–105, in *The Underside of American History*, edited by Thomas R. Frazier. 3d ed. New York: Harcourt Brace Jovanovich, 1978.

Berkin, Carol Ruth, and Mary Beth Norton, eds. *Women of America: A History*. Boston: Houghton Mifflin Co., 1979. Parts I and II, except section 3.

Brown, Jennifer S. H. "Métis, Halfbreeds, and Other Real People: Challenging Cultures and Categories," *History Teacher* 17 (November 1993): 19–25.

Buffalohead, Priscilla K. "Farmers, Warriors, Traders: A Fresh Look at Ojibway Women," *Minnesota History* 48 (Summer 1983): 236–44.

Castañeda, Antonia I. "Spanish and English-Speaking Women on Worldwide Frontiers: A Discussion of the Migration of Women to Alta California and New Zealand," 283–300, in *Western Women: Their Land, Their Lives*, edited by Lillian Schlissel, Vicki L. Ruiz, and Janice Monk. Albuquerque: University of New Mexico Press, 1988.

Córdova, Teresa, et al. *Chicana Voices: Intersections of Class, Race, and Gender*. Albuquerque: University of New Mexico Press, 1990. Section III.

Dearborn, Mary V. *Pocahontas's Daughters: Gender and Ethnicity in American Culture*. Section 1. "A Case Study of American Indian Female Authorship," 12–30. New York: Oxford University Press, 1986.

D'Emilio, John, and Estelle B. Friedman. *Intimate Matters: A History of Sexuality in America*. New York: Harper & Row, 1988.

Demos, John. *A Little Commonwealth: Family Life in Plymouth Colony*. New York: Oxford University Press, 1970.

———. *Entertaining Satan*. New York: Oxford University Press, 1982.

Dewhurst, C. Kurt, Betty MacDowell, and Marshal MacDowell. *Artists in Aprons: Folk Art by American Women*. New York: E. P. Dutton, 1979.

Dye, Nancy Schrom. "History of Childbirth in America," *Signs* 6 (Autumn 1980): 97–108.

Evans, Sara M. *Born for Liberty: A History of Women in America*. New York: Free Press, 1989. Chapters 1, 2.

Foote, Cheryl J., and Sandra K. Schackel, "Indian Women of New Mexico, 1535–1680," 17–40, in *New Mexico Women: Intercultural Perspectives*, edited by Joan M. Jensen and Darlis A. Miller. Albuquerque: University of New Mexico Press, 1986.

Friedman, Jean E., William G. Shade, and Mary Jane Capozzoli, eds. *Our American Sisters: Women in American Life and Thought*. 4th ed. Lexington, MA: D. C. Heath, 1987. Chapters 1–3.

Gragg, Larry. *The Salem Witch Crisis*. New York: Praeger, 1992.

Green, Rayna. "The Pocahontas Perplex: The Image of Indian Women in American Culture," *The Massachusetts Review* 16 (1975): 698–714.

Gregory, Chester W. "Black Women in Pre-Federal America," 53–70, in *Clio Was a Woman: Studies in the History of American Women*, edited by Mabel E. Deutrich and Virginia C. Purdy. Washington, DC: Howard University Press, 1980.

Gutiérrez, Ramón A. *When Jesus Came, the Corn Mothers Went Away: Marriage, Sexuality, and Power in New Mexico, 1500–1846*. Stanford: Stanford University Press, 1991.

Hall, Gwendolyn Mildo. *African in Colonial Louisiana: The Development of Afro-Creole Culture in the Eighteenth Century*. Baton Rouge: Louisiana State University Press, 1994.

Hernández, Salomé. "Nuava Mexicanas as Refugees and Reconquest Settlers," 41–69, in *New Mexico Women: Intercultural Perspectives*, edited by Joan M. Jensen and Darlis A. Miller. Albuquerque: New Mexico Press, 1986.

Hewitt, Nancy A. *Women, Families, and Communities: Readings in American History*. Vol. I. Glenview, IL: Scott, Foresman, 1990. Section I.

Higham, John. "Indian Princess and Roman Goddess: The First Female Symbols of America," *Proceedings of the American Antiquarian Society* 100.1 (1990): 45–79.

Hubbell, Jay B. "The Smith-Pocahontas Story in Literature," *The Virginia Magazine of History and Biography* 65 (July 1957): 275–300.

Hull, N. E. H. *Female Felons: Women and Serious Crime in Colonial Massachusetts.* Chicago: University of Chicago Press, 1987.

Kamensky, Jane. "'Words, Witches, and Women Trouble: Witchcraft, Disorderly Speech, and Gender Boundaries in Puritan New England," *Essex Institute Historical Collections* 128 (October 1992): 286–309.

Karlsen, Carol F. *The Devil in the Shape of a Woman: Witchcraft in Colonial New England.* New York: W. W. Norton, 1987.

Kerber, Linda K., and Jane De Hart. *Women's America: Refocusing the Past.* New York: Oxford University Press, 1987. Part I.

Kessler-Harris, Alice. *Women Have Always Worked: A Historical Overview.* New York: McGraw-Hill, 1982.

Koehler, Lyle. *The Search for Order: The "Weaker Sex" in Seventeenth-Century New England.* Urbana: University of Illinois Press, 1980.

Lang, Amy S. *Prophetic Woman: Anne Hutchinson and the Problem of Dissent in the Literature of New England.* Berkeley: University of California Press, 1987.

Leavitt, Judith Walzer. *Brought to Bed: Childbearing in America, 1750 to 1950.* New York: Oxford University Press, 1986.

Lindemann, Barbara S. "'To Ravish and Carnally Know'—Rape in Eighteenth-Century Massachusetts," *Signs* 10 (Autumn 1984): 63–82.

Main, Gloria L. "An Inquiry Into When and Why Women Learned to Write in Colonial New England," *Journal of Social History* 24 (Spring 1991): 579–89.

McDaid, Jennifer Davis. "'Living on a Frontier Part': Virginia Women Among the Indians, 1622–1794," *Virginia Cavalcade* 42 (Winter 1993): 100–111.

Medicine, Beatrice. "North American Indigenous Women and Cultural Domination," *American Indian Culture and Research Journal* 17 (1993): 121–30.

Monroy, Douglas. *Thrown Among Strangers: The Making of Mexican Culture in Frontier California.* Berkeley: University of California Press, 1990.

Norton, Mary Beth. "The Evolution of White Women's Experience in Early America," *American Historical Review* 89 (June 1984): 593–619.

———, ed. *Major Problems in American Women's History.* Boston: D.C. Heath, 1989. Section I.

Ortíz, Roxanne Dunbar. "Colonialism and the Role of Women: The Pueblos of New Mexico," *Southwest Economy and Society* 4 (Winter 1978/79): 28–46.

Pinckney, Elise, ed. *The Letterbook of Eliza Lucas Pinckney, 1739–1762.* Chapel Hill: University of North Carolina Press, 1972.

Pleck, Elizabeth. *Domestic Tyranny: The Making of American Social Policy against Family Violence from Colonial Times to the Present.* New York: Oxford University Press, 1987.

Porterfield, Amanda. *Female Piety in Puritan New England: The Emergence of Religious Humanism.* New York: Oxford University Press, 1991.

———. "Women's Attraction to Puritanism," *Church History* 60 (June 1991): 196–209.

Ransome, David R. "Wives for Virginia, 1621," *William and Mary Quarterly* 48 (January 1991): 3–18.

Riley, Glenda. *Divorce: An American Tradition.* New York: Oxford University Press, 1991.

Rock, Rosalind Z. "'Pido y Supllico': Women and the Law in Spanish New Mexico," *New Mexico Historical Review* 65 (April 1990): 145–59.

Rubinstein, Charlotte Streifer. *American Women Artists from Early Indian Times to the Present.* Boston: G. K. Hall and Co., 1982.

Ryan, Mary P. *Womanhood in America: From Colonial Times To The Present.* 3d ed. New York: New Viewpoints, 1983. Chapter 1.

Salmon, Marylynn. *Women and the Law of Property in Early America.* Chapel Hill: University of North Carolina Press, 1986).

Scholten, Catherine M. "On the Importance of the Obstetrick Art: Changing Customs of Childbirth in America, 1760–1825," *William and Mary Quarterly* 34 (July 1977): 426–45.

Sklar, Kathryn Kish, and Thomas Dublin. *Women and Power in American History: A Reader.* Vol. 1. Englewood Cliffs, NJ: Prentice Hall, 1991. Selections 1–6.

Smith, Daniel Scott, and Michael S. Hindus. "Premarital Pregnancy in America, 1640–1671: An Overview and Interpretation," *Journal of Interdisciplinary History* 5 (1975): 537–70.

Spruill, Julia Cherry. *Women's Life and Work in the Southern Colonies.* New York: W. W. Norton and Company, 1972.

Stevenson, Brenda K. "Slavery," 1045–54, in *Black Women in America: An Historical Encyclopedia*, edited by Darlene Clark Hine. Vol. II. Brooklyn, NY: Carlson Publishing, Inc., 1993.

Thickstun, Margaret O. *Fictions of the Feminine: Puritan Doctrine and the Representation of Women.* Ithaca, NY: Cornell University Press, 1988.

Ulrich, Laurel Thatcher. *Good Wives: Images and Realities in the Lives of Women in Northern New England, 1650–1780.* New York: Oxford University Press, 1983.

Watson, Alan D. "Women in Colonial North Carolina: Overlooked and Underestimated," *North Carolina Historical Review* 58 (January 1981): 1–22.

Wertz, Richard W., and Dorothy C. Wertz. *Lying-In: A History of Childbirth in America.* New York: Free Press, 1977.

White, Richard. *The Middle Ground: Indians, Empire and Republics in the Great Lakes Region, 1650–1815.* Cambridge: Cambridge University Press, 1991.

Woloch, Nancy. *Women and the American Experience.* New York: Alfred A. Knopf, 1984. Chapters 1–2.

Republican Motherhood
Resistance, Revolution, and Early Nationhood, 1763 to 1812

2

A widespread desire for self-govern-
ment had been evolving for many
years due to the economic, social,
and political differences between England and its colonies in North
America. After almost a decade of
overt resistance, on 2 July 1776, the
Continental Congress voted to fight
for the independence of the American colonies from England. When
Congress released the news on 4
July, Loyalists, who backed the English, felt apprehensive and disheart-
ened, while Patriots, who supported
the new American government,
were joyful. The years of upheaval
would have far-reaching effects, including changes in American ideas,
law, and policies regarding women.

Colonial Women

The resistance phase of the emerging revolution began in 1763, the
year in which the French and Indian War ended. Dissatisfied colonists
registered chronic complaints concerning the provisions of the treaty that
followed the French and Indian War, as well as the many pieces of legislation that Parliament passed in an attempt to control Britain's unruly
American subjects. The usual historical account of the resistance period is
marked by such names as Samuel Adams, Thomas Hutchinson, Thomas
Jefferson, and Thomas Paine, as well as such organizations as the Stamp
Act Congress, the Sons of Liberty, and the Continental Congress.

These accounts omit the many contributions of female Loyalists and
Patriots, usually Anglo (meaning white) women who threw their energies
into supporting or opposing the British. Although women were regarded

as apolitical beings, the furor soon drew women into political issues. They had to side with or against their menfolk, buy British goods or boycott them, refuse to send goods to the front or generously supply Patriot soldiers, and decide whether to flee America or stay and see the conflict to its end.

Loyalist women advocated the cause of Great Britain. While lower- to middle-class Loyalist women spoke and marched for British causes, middle- to upper-class Loyalist women took a more customary female approach, acting with proper decorum, patience, and willingness to compromise. Through their purchases, conversations, letters, and articles, they tried to convince opponents of the Crown to remember that they all were British subjects.

Somewhere between these two extremes was Loyalist Margaret Draper, who, after her husband's death in 1774, began to publish her husband's newspaper, the *Massachusetts Gazette and Boston News-Letter*. For the next two years, Draper edited this newspaper, the oldest in the colonies, and in its pages, staunchly defended British actions and policies. When the British evacuated Boston in 1776, Draper, like other Loyalists, fled the country, locating first in Halifax, Nova Scotia, and later in England. When American Patriots took over Boston, they seized Draper's property, but the British government rewarded her allegiance with a lifetime pension.

Because Patriot women increasingly formed a numerical majority, Loyalist women found themselves in a minority, often cut off from the support of former friends and sometimes even that of family members. Such Patriot women gradually rejected "female" restraint in order to demonstrate their disapproval of, and resistance to, British rule. As a case in point, Sarah Jay, daughter and wife of Patriots, wrote in an early letter, "What have I to do with politicks?" But in a subsequent letter, she excused herself for her growing political passion: "I've trangrss'd the line . . . by slipping into politicks, but my country and my friends possess so entirely my thoughts that you must not wonder if my pen runs beyond the dictates of prudence."

Two other educated women, Mercy Otis Warren and Abigail Adams, also wives of Patriot leaders, took their voluminous correspondence public. First, Warren and Adams discussed political events not only with each other but also with a number of men involved in the protest movement. Then, after Warren's and Adams's questions elicited serious and often lengthy replies, they read the exchanges to a group of people interested in discussing the issues. This debate is believed to have provided the basis for the Committees of Correspondence, agencies for communicating insurrectionist ideas and actions from colony to colony.

Other Patriot women contributed to the resistance by willingly boycotting the importation of many of their favorite goods, especially tea.

Women formed anti-tea leagues, in which they experimented with brewing herb teas from raspberry, sage, and birch leaves. The most popular home-grown tea, called Liberty Tea, utilized the leaves of loosestrife plants, members of the primrose family that commonly grew in the fields and roadsides of New England.

Patriot women further supported nonimportation by refusing to purchase British textiles. Instead, they produced their own cloth and remade their families' old clothes. In 1768, a New York newspaper described the "glorious example" of two Newport women who "spun fully sixty yards of good fine linen cloth nearly a yard wide, besides taking care of a large family." By the time the Revolution began, women had become expert at "making do." In 1777, one woman told a British officer: "I have retrenched every superfluous expense in my table and family. Tea I have not drunk since last Christmas, nor bought a new cap or gown since your defeat at Lexington: and, what I never did before, have learned to knit, and am now making stockings of wool for my servants: and this way do I throw in my mite for the public good." She concluded that, "I know this, that as free I can die but once: but as a slave I shall not be worthy of life."

Besides supporting boycotts and nonimportation, women Patriots assisted in political action against the British. They joined the Daughters of Liberty, who, along with the Sons of Liberty, held bonfire rallies, distributed anti-English propaganda, and hung tax collectors in effigy. Behind the Boston Tea Party of 1773 was a woman, Sarah Bradless Fulton, who initiated the plan and helped in its execution.

Other Patriot women organized active demonstrations on their own. In 1774, Penelope Barker convinced fifty-one women in Edenton, North Carolina, to sign an agreement boycotting British goods until the British government repealed the tax on tea. Although these women justified their actions on the basis of their inability to remain "indifferent on any occasion that appears nearly to affect the peace and happiness of our country," they met with unsparing ridicule, especially from British observers.

Such derision seldom deterred Patriot women. Three years later, in 1777, several Massachusetts women forcibly opened the warehouse of a merchant who was hoarding goods in order to sell them later at inflated wartime prices. It was reported that "a number of females, some say a hundred or more, assembled with a cart and trunks, marched down to the warehouse and demanded the keys, which he refused to deliver." One woman then grabbed the merchant by his neck, pushed him into a cart, and seized the keys. After opening the warehouse, the women hoisted out hogsheads of coffee and drove off with them while a large group of men stood by in amazed silence.

Patriot women also pressured men in other ways to defy the British. Some young women refused to dance with or court men who had not declared their anti-English sentiments. Some wives denied their husbands "conjugal rights" until they swore opposition to Great Britain. And a large number of women encouraged their husbands and sons to volunteer as members of the Continental Army.

Indian and Black Women

Native American, slave, and free black women made their own decisions regarding colonial resistance to the British. Whether they allied with or against American colonists sometimes depended upon the women's connections to individuals or communities, but in other cases, women chose the side they thought might improve their own status.

As a result, some American Indians backed the Americans and some the English. The Senecas of New York, for example, supported the British, largely because American Patriots refused to guarantee the Seneca possession of their territory after the war's end. The Cherokee and two Iroquois tribes, however, joined the British to protest Anglo-American settlement of their lands.

Black women divided as well, according to which opponent they thought would be most likely to abolish slavery. In 1775, Lord John Murray, Earl of Dunmore and Royal Governor of Virginia, promised to emancipate those blacks who fought for the British. Others upheld the Patriot cause, often providing such critical assistance as conveying intelligence and nursing the wounded. Of course, black women who worked for the Patriots also hoped for emancipation in return for their allegiance.

Once fighting began, the presence of British armies encouraged slaves to escape their owners. The British often harbored runaway slaves and granted them liberty as a means of weakening the efforts of Patriots, especially those in the South. These former slaves frequently escaped in family groups that included women and children. Over half of the twenty-three slaves who fled Thomas Jefferson's Virginia plantation during the war were women and girls.

THE AMERICAN REVOLUTION, 1776–1783

Rhetoric of Revolution

Both female and male imagery frequently appeared in the flood of essays, pamphlets, articles, and sermons that flowed from American pens. Numerous commentators described such republican qualities as virtue and sacrifice as feminine characteristics. At the same time, however, John Adams characterized a true republic as "great, manly, and warlike," while he stated that a republican government demanded "manly" public sacrifice and participation.

A similar contradiction existed in depictions of Great Britain. On the one hand, Britain represented an uncaring mother, who had turned her face away from her child, the American colonies. On the other, some accused Britain of exhibiting the worst attributes usually associated with men: greed, lust, and violence.

Clearly, both the new American republic and Great Britain had some supposedly female aspects and some male. This would also prove true of American women. They were "feminine" in the sense that they deplored war, feared the death of their men, and wished to behave as apolitical as conventional wisdom portrayed them. But women could act "masculine" as well; they wanted freedom from outside control, would fight if they had to, and could operate in the political arena when necessary. Consequently, while some women viewed themselves as weak and passive nonparticipants, many more threw their energies into helping one side or the other.

Loyalist Women

On one side stood Loyalist women who continued to support the British during the American Revolution. As a consequence of their allegiance to Britain, many women lost their livelihoods and property. Grace Growdon Galloway, wife of attorney Joseph Galloway who had served as speaker of the Pennsylvania Assembly between 1766 and 1774, saw her Loyalist husband branded a traitor and her own estates seized by the Patriots. Later, in 1782, South Carolina passed a Confiscation Act which not only impounded Loyalists' property but banished some Loyalists from the state.

After the war, special commissions in each state judged how much Loyalists should receive in compensation for their homes, lands, and businesses. The commissions also tried to resolve the significant question of whether married Loyalist women could, as women, make political decisions on their own. Certainly, Lucy Flucker Knox knew her own mind. In 1777, Knox had written her husband that she enjoyed making her own choices and had no intention of resuming a subordinate status when he returned: "I hope you will not consider yourself as commander in chief of your own house . . . there is such a thing as equal command."

But most people believed that women should be excused for their actions because they had simply obeyed their husbands. In South Carolina, women manipulated this belief to their advantage. In more than sixty-five cases, women sought from the courts redress for the effects of the Confiscation Act, asking either for the return of their property or damage awards. Most of these female plaintiffs claimed, and the court believed, that they had been passive, innocent victims of war. The attorney of Jane Linwood argued that "as a Lady," she could not "be deemed Guilty of any Act inimical to the American Cause." The widespread assumption that women were apolitical saved Jane Linwood's property; in 1784 the court removed the Linwood's name from the confiscation list.

Patriot Women

On the other side of the revolutionary cause were Patriot women. Even as men debated the pressing issue of whether women could be political beings, women's actions proved that they could indeed act in highly political ways. Women who supported the Patriot cause simply assumed they were part of what one revolutionary called "the people." They also believed that, like men, they were struggling for liberty, "everyone's birthright."

For Patriot women, pushing their men toward the front lines meant great sacrifice. As a case in point, free black Lucy Terry Prince of Northfield, Massachusetts, encouraged her two eldest sons to enlist and served with the militia although she and her husband, Abijah, would have to work the farm alone. In other cases, women had to run the family farms and businesses by themselves, as well as selling produce to supplement their husbands' irregular soldier's pay.

Despite the hardships, most women responded without hesitation. When Abigail Adams's husband, John, urged her to "rouse your whole attention to the family, the stock, the farm, the dairy" in his absence, she became an expert farm manager. It was her hope that, in time, she would have the "reputation of being as good a farmeress as my partner has of being a good statesman."

While maintaining their families and farms, women Patriots also organized women's associations that devoted untold hours to sewing clothes, rolling bandages, and preparing foodstuffs. Among these were a number of unnamed black women, one a free black domestic servant who gave most of her meager wages to the war effort, while another gave soup and bread to imprisoned patriots.

Women also spent huge amounts of time and energy organizing charity fairs and other events to collect money for food, clothing, and sanitary supplies such as bandages for the army. In a fund-raising broadside printed in 1780, a Philadelphia woman explained that women of the newly organized Ladies Association were motivated by the "purest patriotism" in aspiring "to render themselves really useful." Among other feats, these women raised $7,500 and supplied 2,005 shirts. In 1781, George Washington publicly praised the Ladies Association of Philadelphia, which included Benjamin Franklin's daughter Sarah Franklin Bache, for their fund-raising efforts. They had "embellished" the American character, Washington stated, "by proving that the law of country is blended with those softer domestic virtues" of women. He added that these women deserved "an equal place with any who have preceded them in the walk of female patriotism."

Women not only supplied food and other goods, but also destroyed them rather than permitting them to fall into the hands of the British. Implementing a scorched earth policy, women gladly demolished their own food supplies for the American cause. Catherine Schuyler of Albany,

New York, burned fields of wheat to keep them from the enemy. Other women even helped ravage their own homes. Determined to rout English soldiers from her home, Rebecca Motte of South Carolina personally handed flaming arrows to colonial soldiers who aimed them at her home. Motte quietly proclaimed, "I am gratified with the opportunity of contributing to the good of the country."

None of these activities seem to diverge too far from the usual realm of female activities, but women also engaged in heavier work usually thought of as male tasks. Women collected lead, melted it down, and produced the shot used by the Patriot army. Women manufactured and assembled arms. And they converted their businesses to wartime production. A Mrs. Proctor of Salem, Massachusetts, transformed her tool factory into a Patriot arsenal, while a woman blacksmith known only as Betsy lent her expertise regarding cannon and other arms to the Patriot cause. At the same time, the women traders on Nantucket Island defied the British blockade of the American coast to supply the rebels.

Other women became involved in the Patriot cause because of their technical skills. In 1775, Mary Katherine Goddard had been appointed postmaster of Baltimore and was probably the first woman to fill such a post. By the time of the Revolution, she was a successful and respected businessperson in Baltimore. As a leading Baltimore printer and publisher of *The Baltimore Journal*, Goddard received the government contract to print the official version of the Declaration of Independence in 1777. As an avowed feminist, Goddard recognized the historical importance of this occurrence; she placed her name rather than the usual printer's initials at the bottom of the document.

Yet other women aided the Revolution by acting as saboteurs and spies. For instance, in 1778 Phoebe Fraunces, General George Washington's black servant, stopped a British plot to murder Washington. Similarly, Lydia Darragh, a Quaker woman in Philadelphia, eavesdropped at the door of a room in her home, which British officers had taken over for meetings. When she heard attack orders read, she penetrated the British lines on the pretense of getting flour milled. Darragh located an American officer to whom she entrusted her secret. A few days later, Darragh placidly observed a British officer's dismay at finding American cannon mounted and prepared to receive his attack. "We have marched back here like a parcel of fools," he fumed.

Courageous women disguised as men thwarted yet other attacks. In Massachusetts, a group of women dressed themselves in their husbands' clothes and carried pitchforks to guard a nearby bridge. Here they forcibly unhorsed and searched a British courier. When they discovered dispatches concealed in his boot, they conducted him to the local jail for detention. In South Carolina, Elizabeth Marshall and her daughters-in-law also dressed as men. They, too, accosted a courier and seized his dispatches, thus blocking the passage of essential military intelligence.

Not all this effort supported the cause of American liberty; women had to protect themselves as well. German mercenaries known as Hessians drank and gambled to a degree some women considered dangerous. Lydia Mintern Post of Long Island, forced to house Hessian soldiers, wrote, "we have trying and grievous scenes to go through; fighting, brawls, drumming and fifing, and dancing the night long; card and dice playing, and every abomination going on under our roofs." The presence of foreign troops and decreasing supplies of food also brought the threat of such diseases as smallpox and dysentery to women and their children. Moreover, beginning as early as 1776, British soldiers, frustrated by their inability to put a halt to the rebellion, brutally assaulted women in New Jersey and New York. The faster women could bring the war to conclusion the safer they and their families would be.

Patriot Women at the Front

Women also served at the front, usually in one of three capacities: 1) as camp-followers and wives who accompanied and assisted soldiers and officers, 2) as regular troops fighting with male Patriots, and 3) as irregular troops fighting with militia or in independent women's units.

The first category numbered perhaps as many as twenty thousand women over the course of the war and included some of the legendary women of the Revolution, such as Mary Ludwig Hays McCauley, who worked as a nurse, camp cook, and washwoman. Reportedly, she was known as Molly Pitcher because she carried so many pails and pitchers of water to the men, but it is likely that no real Molly Pitcher existed at all— that Molly Pitcher was a folktale. Mary, however, saw her husband fall and took over his cannon, keeping it in operation for the rest of the Battle of Monmouth in July 1778. Soldiers remembered her as a warm-hearted, energetic woman who swore volubly and chewed tobacco. Not until 1822 did the Pennsylvania legislature reward McCauley's war service with a small pension.

Scores of other women flocked to the camps of the Continental Army, pledging to help in any way possible. Martha Washington, for example, wintered with her husband at Valley Forge. Here, she went from hut to hut carrying food to the sick and consoling the dying. In another instance, Emily Geiger volunteered to carry a message after the male soldiers in camp declined to do so. When a British scout detained her, Geiger ripped up the document and swallowed it. The next day she promptly delivered the message that she had quickly committed to memory. Yet another task that women often performed was combing the battlefields for the dead, whom they identified and gave proper burial.

Of those women who fought as regular or irregular soldiers, less is known. Although Continental Army regulations prohibited the recruitment of women, women could enlist. Their names appeared on company rolls, they drew their pay along with men, and they wore men's clothing.

Women served not only with the Continental Army but with militia units who joined General George Washington's forces or who fought Native Americans along the lines of advancing Anglo-American settlement. One of these was Margaret Corbin who followed her husband to the front, where she served as a nurse, cook, washwoman, and soldier. In the Battle of Fort Washington in November 1776, Corbin's husband fell at her side. Corbin filled his battle post until she was disabled by three grapeshot that permanently cost her the use of one arm. In 1779, she received a small pension, thus becoming the first woman pensioner in the United States.

Other women soldiers felt they received better treatment and more dangerous assignments if thought to be men, so they took male names to conceal their gender. In 1782, Deborah Sampson, generally believed to be a mulatto, enlisted in the Continental forces under the name of Robert Shurtleff. Her unusual height, strong features, and great stamina protected her from discovery until she was hospitalized with a fever and was discharged in 1783. She later wrote that she had "burst the tyrant bonds which held my sex in awe and clandestinely, or by stealth, grasped an opportunity, which custom and the world seemed to deny, as a natural privilege." The U.S. Congress granted Sampson's heirs her pension as a war veteran in 1792.

Women as Propagandists

Women also supported the propaganda efforts of the war, wielding their pens to keep people fighting and shore up American spirits. Phillis Wheatley, a black slave, was one such woman. In 1761, a wealthy Boston merchant, John Wheatley, purchased Phillis as a personal servant. The Wheatleys soon recognized the young girl's nimble mind and gave her opportunities unusual for a slave. Phillis Wheatley became a Latin scholar, poet, and witty conversationalist. One of her most celebrated poems, "Ode to General Washington," was published in the *Pennsylvania Magazine* in 1776. It identified Wheatley as a Patriot and gained her a personal invitation to visit General Washington's headquarters in Cambridge, Massachusetts.

Mercy Otis Warren also wrote patriotic poetry. In addition, Warren was a historian, playwright, and arch propagandist of the Revolution. She turned her talents to political activism by writing three anti-British satirical plays during the war years. In the late 1770s, Warren began her major literary work, the three-volume *History of the Rise, Progress and Termination of the American Revolution*, which finally appeared in 1805. Warren's work indicated that she was not only a supporter of the principle of American liberty but was also an early enthusiast for the cause of female independence. Warren once commented to a friend that women should accept their "appointed subordination" only for the sake of "Order in Families," not due to any inferiority on their own part.

Abigail Adams's Contribution

During much of her lifetime, Warren was a close friend and frequent correspondent of Abigail Adams. Today, Adams is perhaps the best-known woman of the Revolutionary era. Contemporary feminists often quote Adams's letters to her husband, John, while he served in the Continental Congress. In 1776, recognizing that Congress would have to devise a new form of government for the United States, Adams wrote to her husband: "In the new Code of Laws which I suppose it will be necessary for you to make I desire you would Remember the Ladies, and be more generous and favourable to them than your ancestors." She asked that he not "put such unlimited power in the hands of the Husbands" because "all Men would be tyrants if they could." Adams concluded: "If particular care and attention is not paid to the Ladies we are determined to foment a Rebellion, and will not hold ourselves bound by any Laws in which we have no voice, or Representation."

Adams was not asking for a social revolution in gender expectations. She did not argue that women should vote or hold public office. She did not espouse equality for women or an abandonment of their domestic roles. Rather, Adams envisioned a legal system that would protect women from unlimited power in the hands of men.

John Adams responded to his wife's request in a joking manner. He wrote to her that he had heard that the Revolution had "loosened the bands of Government everywhere," even to the point of stirring up American Indians and black slaves. But, he added, her letter was "the first Intimation that another Tribe more numerous and powerfull than all the rest were grown discontented."

In ire at John's reply, Abigail Adams suggested to Mercy Otis Warren that they petition the new Congress regarding the situation of women, but Abigail soon dropped her case with the statement to John: "I can not say that I think you very generous to the Ladies, for whilst you are proclaiming peace and good will to Men, Emancipating all Nations, you insist upon retaining an absolute power over Wives." Her last retort warned him that "we have it in our power not only to free ourselves but to subdue our Masters, and without violence throw both your natural and legal authority at our feet."

Adams's words were courageous yet in a sense empty; in her day women's rights and feminism were not major issues. Also, Adams had few allies to back up her ideas and to help her to mount the revolution of which she spoke. Yet she was still an effective reformer in certain ways. Adams provided a model for other women by proving herself an accomplished business manager and self-proclaimed "farmeress" when John was away, which was a good deal of the time. In addition, she demonstrated that women could develop business acumen. Abigail's wise investments and sound management provided the money to send her sons to Harvard, underwrite John's political career, finance the furnishing of several foreign legations and the newly constructed White House, and support herself and John after his retirement from the presidency. As Abigail's son John Quincy Adams wrote after her death, "her life gave the lie to every libel on her sex that was ever written."

Moreover, Abigail Adams wrote and spoke about the anomaly of slavery. She firmly believed that the slave system destroyed the character of individual citizens and that of society as a whole. In 1797, Adams sent a free black servant boy to evening school. When her neighbors visited to make known their objections, she strongly advocated the principle of "equality of Rights." Arguing that the young man was a freeman, Adams maintained that he had a right to an education. "Merely because his Face is Black, is he to be denied instruction? How is he to be qualified to procure a livelihood?" she asked. As a result of her impassioned defense of the young man's right to an education, Adams's neighbors withdrew their protest.

THE REVOLUTION'S EFFECT ON WOMEN

American Indian Women

During the Revolution, thousands of Native Americans lost their lives, villages, and fields to the ravages of war. Then, as the United States expanded southward and westward after the American Revolution, American Indians learned that the new American government regarded native groups as foreign nations. Congress intended to deal with Indians not as inhabitants of the United States, but as adversaries. The U.S. government duly dispatched troops and negotiated treaties to conquer Indians and possess their lands.

At the same time, waves of Anglo settlers began to flow over Indian lands, whether claimed by the United States or still held by native groups. Oddly enough, Indians themselves facilitated western development by serving as porters, laborers, traders in furs and other goods, guides, bridge builders, explorers of routes, and suppliers of food and other necessary commodities to migrants. The brisk trade settlers conducted with Indians in furs and other goods significantly aided the economic development of the American frontier.

The "seize-and-settle" process usually proved disastrous for Native Americans. In acquiring native land through war or treaty, and in settling the land of these native nations, American agents, officials, lawmakers, and settlers became increasingly impatient with native concepts of communal landholding. Puzzled by the Indian belief that land belonged to everyone and thus could not be transferred to an individual through a piece of paper, settlers resorted to threats and trickery to get Indians to agree to land sales. Convinced of the validity of "private property"—and believing they had a God-given right to the land—settlers pushed Indians farther and farther to the South and West.

In addition, Anglo settlement undercut the position of Indian women. For instance, the American fur trade weakened the status and power of Indian women by utilizing them as poorly paid and low-status interpreters, workers, and liaisons. The "civilization" that the fur traders carried to native women included venereal disease, prostitution, and frequently, abandonment by the men who married them. At the same time, factory-produced goods began to undermine native women's use of items such as textiles and pottery. Moreover, Anglo attitudes regarding the inferiority of women denied Indian women any recognition or reward for the significant role they had played in the development of the fur trade itself.

The importance of Indian women traders to fur-trade societies gradually decreased. Opportunities for women to actively engage in trade, become political leaders of their communities, and serve as shamans or warriors began to decline. In Iroquois society, for instance, a group of female elders had long served as sachems on tribal councils, the most powerful ruling body. Settlers and their government, however, disapproved of such power in the hands of women and now effectively denied it to Iroquois women by refusing to deal with them.

Among the Seneca of New York, women agriculturalists also lost a degree of stature. These women often fell prey first to warfare, then to epidemics and the consequences of trade. During the Revolution, American troops, in reprisal for the Seneca support of the British, destroyed forty Seneca towns composed of communal longhouses as well as Seneca orchards, fields, and crops. Next, smallpox ravaged the tribe, keeping women out of the fields and causing a decline in their numbers. Trade also undercut Seneca women's craft production. Iron scissors and needles made obsolete implements of bone, while textiles replaced fur garments and beads supplanted porcupine quills as decoration. Although Seneca women retained some of their political power, that too began to decline as treaties with the American government reduced the land women controlled. Then, during the 1790s, teachers and missionaries furthered undermined women by encouraging Seneca women to spin and weave, while men took over farming.

In the South, Cherokee societies, in which women held property, kept their children in case of a divorce, and decided whether captives would be adopted or punished, underwent similar changes. As a result of intermarriage with whites and the United States government's "civilization" policy, the Cherokee gradually abandoned matrilineal descent in favor of a patrilineal pattern of inheritance. Cherokee women lost further power by 1800, when a depleted game supply caused Cherokee men to take over the agricultural tasks that had belonged to women.

Native women typically responded to such changes by adapting. Among the Seneca, women replanted their crops, while women of other tribes found new goods to grow or produce. Many also took advantage of the new Anglo trade goods for their own purposes. For instance, many native women used glass beads to construct highly saleable Indian craftwork. Some even learned to copy beads and manufacture them rather than purchasing them. In addition, native women developed new areas of influence in their communities and established female associations, networks, and other bonds to assist each other and enhance women's importance. There is no evidence that native women became subordinate to native men or imitated Anglo society in any other way.

Slave and Free Black Women

When the Revolution ended, black women and men hoped for eventual abolition from their slave status. After the war, the British transported a number of slaves who had joined them to Nova Scotia in Canada. Also, some Americans argued that black slaves who participated in the Revolution on the Patriot side should be rewarded with their liberty. In practice, however, this policy was seldom implemented. A black woman who served an American colonel for forty years made a futile impassioned plea for liberation in 1782, while another black woman who served as a bullet runner for American troops remained a slave until she was nearly eighty years old, at which time she escaped to Canada.

Still, in a burst of enthusiasm, many Americans supported the abolition of slavery. A number of slave owners in the upper South chose to free their slaves. Other Americans began to form antislavery societies. As longtime opponents of slavery, the Quakers stood in the forefront of this activity, organizing their first antislavery society in 1775. Such abolitionist societies, organized especially in Philadelphia and elsewhere in the middle states, sought to convince Americans that the freedom they cherished should also extend to blacks. Using the Declaration of Independence as a basis, the abolitionists claimed that liberty for one and all should transcend distinctions of color.

Several states also passed emancipation provisions. In 1780, the Massachusetts Constitution included a Declaration of Rights stating that "all men are born free and equal." Under this provision some slaves sued for their liberation. In 1781, with the assistance of an attorney, Elizabeth Freeman (also known as Mum Bett) petitioned a Massachusetts court for her emancipation, arguing that the new state constitution guaranteed her liberty. Freeman stated that she had heard a "paper" read that said "all men are born equal, and that every man has a right to freedom." Freeman intended to secure her own freedom and to establish a principle for other slaves as well. The court agreed and issued the first decision which construed a state constitution as inconsistent with slavery. It was a significant but exceptional case. Although Freeman won her freedom, and her case established the principle of inconsistency, it did not result in statewide emancipation.

Clearly, the ideals of freedom and liberty stated in the Declaration of Independence proved troublesome when applied to black women and men. In a society that needed cheap labor and harbored racist beliefs, many Americans thought slavery acceptable. Neither did the new U.S. Constitution, ratified in 1789, ease the situation. On the contrary, the Constitution included three clauses protecting slavery and expressly allowed the importation of slaves into the country for twenty years.

During the 1790s and early 1800s, with the growth of industrialization in the North, black slavery gradually declined in the northern states. With the growth of cotton culture in the South, however, slavery became dominant in the southern states. In 1790, the nation's first census listed 757,181 black people in the United States, of whom 697,624 were slaves. The majority of these lived in the South. Because of the voracious appetite of English textile mills for cotton and Eli Whitney's development, under planter Catherine Green's sponsorship, of a workable cotton gin in 1793, the cotton culture and an accompanying demand for slaves increasingly characterized the South. Thus, by 1800, the black population had jumped to 1,002,037, of whom 893,602 were slaves.

The acquisition of the Louisiana Territory in 1803 brought into the Union additional slave territory. Then, as profits from cotton began to rise, white slave owners intensified their efforts to extract the most labor possible from slave women. Owners usually regarded these women as chattels rather than human beings. They listed slave women in property inventories of plantations by first name, age, and monetary value. On the sale block, auctioneers held women up to public scrutiny much like livestock. One observer at a slave sale reported that a potential buyer "took one of the prettiest women by the chin and opened her mouth to see the state of her gums and teeth, with no more ceremony than if she had been a horse." Women were further dehumanized by having their childbearing and sexual features touted.

Once purchased, slave women labored as nursemaids, midwives, domestic servants, and field hands. On the larger plantations, they served as seamstresses, nurses, poultry-maids, and dairymaids. Since the number of trades and crafts that black women were allowed to pursue was limited compared to those open to black male slaves who worked as blacksmiths, coopers, overseers, and in other similar capacities, more women worked in the fields than did men. The black female field hand was routinely expected to perform domestic tasks as well. One Virginia planter of the late 1700s described a favored slave as "a stout able field wench and an exceedingly good washer and ironer."

After the Constitutional provision abolished the Atlantic slave trade in 1808, owners also began to urge their slave women to conceive and bear as many children as possible. Slaveholders frequently offered prizes, promises of emancipation, and other rewards to slave women who bore ten or more children.

In spite of the indignities and degradation of the slave system, black women held slave families together under extremely difficult circumstances. Although familial ties were extremely important to black slaves, they lived with the constant threat of separation from their kin. To offset the deleterious effects of separation, women formed closed bonds with their remaining children and tried to establish a new relationship with an unmarried slave or one who had lost his wife through sale or death.

Slaves continually protested against their inability to establish families and preserve family units. In 1774, a group of Massachusetts slaves petitioned the state legislature for their liberation, stressing the destructive nature of slavery on family life: "How can a slave perform the duties of husband to wife or a parent to a child? How can a husband leave his master to work and cleave to his wife? How can the wife submit to her husband in all things?"

Other slaves seized their liberty, as did Silvia Dubois, born a slave in New Jersey in 1768. Although her father gained his freedom by joining the Patriots' side in the Revolution, Silvia had to remain a slave but finally struck her mistress and ran away.

Pennsylvania especially provided leadership in attempting to erase the contradictions between the nation's independence and the servitude of some of its citizens. During the Revolution, Pennsylvania passed the Gradual Abolition Law, which fostered an increase in the state's black population. The Census of 1790 recorded 10,301 blacks in Pennsylvania—6,540 freedmen and women and 3,761 slaves. But the state's abolition provisions attracted such an influx of blacks, many via the early Underground Railroad, that the total jumped 176 percent by 1800. Pennsylvania's black population numbered 16,270 by 1800—14,564 free and 1,706 enslaved.

The situation of free black women in Pennsylvania did not markedly improve, however, as a result of the experiment in gradual abolition. Employers frequently turned them away and, when employed, free women of color often worked on farms or as domestic servants for impossibly low wages. They also lived with the ever-present fear of being captured and sold into slavery.

During the postrevolutionary years, a number of black women took matters into their own hands. As early as 1787, free women of color began to work on behalf of such causes as economic autonomy and religious separatism. This early black nationalist movement developed in response to racism and the degraded position of most black Americans. During the postrevolutionary period, the movement especially led to the founding of benevolent societies, including the Free African Society of Philadelphia founded in 1787 and such others as the Benevolent Daughters in 1796 and the Daughters of Africa in 1812. These groups helped black women,

men, and children in need; helped free blacks find employment; sustained black churches and their social-service groups; and helped establish black churches as dynamic forces in black communities.

Other free black women worked for the cause of abolitionism through churches. In the Quaker church, free black women applied for membership, although they sometimes had to sit on back benches during meetings. The number of black women in the Catholic church increased after the Revolution because of the immigration of black Catholics from Haiti. Concentrated mostly in Maryland, black Catholic women began to campaign against slavery using as precedents a number of emancipation cases in the state's history, especially those emancipating mulatto women. By the 1790s and early 1800s, these women also opened schools for black children, educated black women, and began planning for an order of black women Religious.

Despite the difficulties facing free women of color after the Revolution, a number of them proved that economic success could occasionally be achieved. Catherine (Katy) Ferguson, born c. 1774 on a slave ship headed for New York, excelled in business. Ferguson used the proceeds from her catering business to establish in 1793 an integrated school that would endure for forty years. Similarly, Elleanor Eldrige, born in 1784 in Warwick, Rhode Island, and freed with her family because her father and brother had fought on the American side during the Revolution, had by age fourteen learned to spin and weave, making, among other items, exceptional carpets and bedspreads. She worked for Captain Benjamin Green's family until 1812, then went into business for herself, weaving, nursing, and making soap. Still, despite their financial status, these free women of color had fewer rights and freedoms than did their Anglo counterparts.

Anglo Women

Abigail Adams was the most visible, and probably the most vocal, woman of the Revolutionary era, but she did not stand alone. Clearly, many other Anglo women violated the dictates of the female role in order to follow their own interests and convictions. Whether they engaged in political activities, fought alongside men, wrote letters and tracts, or pursued other "unfeminine" activities, their actions challenged the model of American womanhood. Like the many assertive and irrepressible colonial women who had preceded them, women of the war years displayed a high degree of independence of thought and spirit. Not content with the passivity and submissiveness that many Americans believed were inherent female traits, these women defied convention to follow their own desires, talents, and convictions.

In many cases, then, women were able to undertake "male" activities without much public or private censure. It was, after all, a time of national crisis that demanded the relaxation of the usual rules. Women who worked, fought, or wrote to help the cause of independence were usually thought patriotic and loyal to their country, if not to the dictates of their gender roles. Women who neglected the female sphere in order to participate in the larger public realm were indeed Patriots of the first order in many people's eyes.

It would seem logical to expect that these energetic and courageous women might be rewarded with some of the fruits of the Revolution. It also seems reasonable that traditional beliefs regarding the weakness and inferiority of females would fall by the wayside as a consequence of these brave women's deeds. Surely, the postrevolutionary years would allow women to partake of the democracy that was so widely discussed throughout the new nation, especially since women had helped secure it.

In recent years, historians of women have devoted a good deal of time to exploring whether the American Revolution did in fact produce any marked improvements in women's lives. On the one hand, some believe that the Revolution may have had a positive effect on women's lives. The economic and social disruption that it created gave women the chance to take over farms, plantations, businesses, trades, and professions while men carried out war-related duties. It also underwrote divorce for those who wanted to flee unfulfilling or stultifying marriages. The incidence of divorce not only increased, but petitioners employed such terms as "tyranny," "misrule," "injustice," and "happiness of the individual." Reform for women did not consist of rewriting legal codes, granting the vote to women, and developing a strong feminist movement. Rather, it appeared in women's heightened aspirations and the reorganization of family structure.

On the other hand, some historians argue that the American Revolution brought negative results for women. The war pushed America toward industrialism, a system that would move many women into factory jobs that were poorly paid and low in status. Women would thus lose whatever respect and autonomy they had as commanders of their households. Furthermore, the ideology of the new nation demanded that women become "Republican Mothers," whose primary task was to train their sons for future citizenship and their daughters for future domesticity. Neither one of women's new roles—factory worker or Republican Mother—offered women any improvement in their positions.

THE DEVELOPMENT OF REPUBLICAN MOTHERHOOD

Tenets

Before 1776, colonists viewed Anglo women primarily as wives, helpmeets, and ornaments. But colonial Americans did not idealize motherhood; in fact, they often seemed unconcerned about it. Evidently, most people took maternal love for granted and did not consider it a matter that needed direction or guidance. Mothers were so busy with their many chores that they often relied on their husbands or other adult members of the household to care for their children. Also, men worked in or near the home during the years of settlement, so they were able to help rear their children.

After the American Revolution, these casual attitudes changed dramatically. Drawing upon Scottish philosophers and other theorists who had considered women's roles in the polity, American thinkers argued that white women constituted indispensable halves of Republican marriages, as well as being mothers who would raise effective and moral citizens for the new Republic. The new Republic depended upon public virtue; who better to instill it than domestically oriented wives and mothers.

A number of social changes produced this modified perception of women's roles. Many men now worked away from the home, regularly leaving the care of children in the hands of women. The increasing availability of certain factory-produced goods began to alleviate the burden of incessant domestic labor, thus giving women more time for childcare. And women read more than ever before, including the rapidly growing literature on motherhood.

Also, perhaps many women recognized that Republican Motherhood in a way upgraded their inferior status. The potential gain in prestige would also make Republican Motherhood palatable to immigrant women who had little in their backgrounds to prepare them for notions of democracy and republicanism, especially in relation to republican mothering. Representing a growing diversity of cultural experiences, including eastern European, Jewish, and Catholic, immigrant women could identify with a role that granted them increased respect even if they did not yet understand its importance to their new country.

Thus, by the end of the 1700s such topics as discipline and the instilling of morality in young children elicited the attention of American ministers, guidebook writers, and physicians, among others. The Moral Mother, who bore and reared future citizens of the new United States, was now increasingly responsible for protecting virtue and morality among children and in families.

Not only women but men gradually accepted the idea that females were innately more loving and nurturing than males. During these years, white society began to tout mother's love as an inborn instinct and to highly acclaim maternal fondness and tenderness toward children. Americans idealized, romanticized, and sentimentalized motherhood, believing that the future of their new nation somehow depended on it.

Limits of Republican Motherhood

Clearly, the concept of Republican Motherhood applied primarily to white women who were the mothers of future citizens, and even more directly to white women of the middle and upper classes who could devote their full-time energies to childcare. Working, farm, and poor white women seldom had the opportunity to adopt such ideals. Because even white men had to own property to qualify as voters and office holders, few women of the lower classes would rear their sons as the voters and office holders of the future.

Despite this limitation of Republican Motherhood's applicability, thinkers and writers of the time held up such ideals for all Anglo women. One example was writer Hector St. John de Crevecoeur, a New York farmer of French background, who published his impressions of America, *Letters from an American Farmer*, in 1782. He described an ideal wife and mother much like his own wife, always spinning, knitting, or nursing a child. He claimed that American men did not expect a dowry with a wife, for they realized that a "wife's fortune consists principally in her future economy, modesty, and skillful management." According to Crevecoeur, if a farmer were "blessed with a good wife," he had the opportunity to live better than "any people of the same rank on the globe."

Similarly, Thomas Jefferson in his *Notes on the State of Virginia*, which first appeared in published form in Paris in 1782 and in London in 1787, described white women in terms of their industry, ability as helpmates to men, and motherhood. He lauded the beauty of their "flowing hair," "symmetry of form," and fair skin, which revealed "the expressions of every passion by greater or less suffusions of color."

When he turned to Native American women, Jefferson made it clear that they were very different. Because they were not regarded as citizens, Indian women would not raise their sons as citizens of the new Republic, nor mold their daughters as eventual Republican Mothers. In addition, Jefferson noted that Indian women were forced to submit to "unjust drudgery," as was the "case with every barbarous people." They bore fewer children than did white women, for, as "with all animals, if the female be badly fed, or not fed at all, her young perish." To Jefferson, such "obstacles of want" were simply nature's way of limiting "the multiplication of wild animals." He concluded that, when married to a white man and fed properly, exempted from "excessive drudgery," and protected from danger, an Indian woman could bear as many children as did white women.

Jefferson displayed a similar bias when be focused his attention on black women, who were usually regarded as property and never as citizens. After maintaining that black people slept frequently, he explained that an "animal whose body is at rest, and who does not reflect, must be disposed to sleep of course." Jefferson also lamented that the "veil of black" gave black women's faces an "eternal monotony." Phillis Wheatley he dismissed as an example of religious zeal, rather than of talent: "The compositions published under her name are below the dignity of criticism." If the charges against Jefferson of taking his own slave, Sally Hemmings, as his mistress have any foundation in fact, his statements become all the more ironic, for he apparently found a black woman worthy of his companionship.

Jefferson's writings demonstrate that even educated, liberal observers adhered to prevailing gender expectations and models. While he discussed white women largely in terms of their domestic roles, he viewed native and black women primarily in terms of their race. And although the statesman extolled Anglo women's contributions to the nation, he denigrated those of Indian and black women. It is unlikely that ordinary citizens of the time would have been any more informed or open-minded.

Effect of Republican Motherhood on White Families

Republican Motherhood not only provided enhanced status for Anglo women, however. It also created greater expectations of marriage and motherhood for them. Demographic shifts accompanied, and perhaps helped create, these changes. Women now controlled more personal and real property. For those women who wed, the age of marriage gradually rose, while family size slowly declined. During the late 1700s and early 1800s, women of the Virginia gentry began to complain about bearing an average of eight children. Accordingly, they decreased the number of children they bore by marrying later, lengthening the period of sexual abstinence after a birth, and experimenting with birth control devices.

At the same time, birth itself rapidly became a more complicated affair. Dr. William Shippen of Philadelphia led the revolution in birthing techniques. After studying medicine, including midwifery, in London, Shippen returned to Philadelphia in 1762. He brought with him British standards concerning hospitals, medical training, and professionalism. At his urging, the only hospital in America, the Pennsylvania Hospital, in 1763 initiated formal medical training and lectures in midwifery, including the use of obstetrical forceps. By 1807, five medical schools in America offered courses in midwifery to male students. The increasing presence of trained male doctors in the delivery room brought instruments and anesthesia into regular use and the Caesarean section became a common emergency procedure.

Another consequence of the growing emphasis on motherhood was an interest in childcare practices. Manuals such as *Mother's Catechism and Maternal Instruction* appeared in large numbers. The prevailing view of children became less one of a miniature adult in need of rescue from original sin and more one of a pliable and innocent being whose upbringing demanded specialized equipment, toys, and books. Thus, from the concept of motherhood came the concept of childhood.

But not all women married. Because an increase in the number of women in the general population created a more competitive marriage market, the proportion of single women in the U.S. population grew. By 1796, women headed 8 percent of Baltimore's households; one-third of these were never-married women, while two-thirds were widows.

The growing availability of divorce, except in South Carolina, also swelled the number of unwed women. Women successfully sued for divorce in larger numbers than did men. This statistic can be interpreted as a consequence of an enhanced spirit of independence among women, along with their rising expectations of marriage and unwillingness to tolerate anything less than they had anticipated. Certainly, a new ideal of companionate marriage was developing. An anonymous article of the 1790s declared that an ideal marriage was one based on "mutual esteem, mutual friendship, mutual confidence, begirt about by mutual forbearance." Possibly the heightened worth of motherhood raised expectations regarding the contributions of men to marriage and family relationships. And having become ever more emotionally and professionally invested in their children, women were perhaps no longer, for their children's sake, as willing to endure a husband's adultery and alcoholism.

Women who chose not to marry, or were unable to find a mate, or who divorced their spouses supported themselves by working as seamstresses, laundresses, dyers, starchers, lace makers, and mantua makers. They also ran small businesses supplying groceries, dry goods, millinery, hardware, and other goods.

Women in Politics, or Not

The political realm proved a source of frustration for women. They soon learned that the grand statements regarding "freedom and liberty for all" contained in the Declaration of Independence excluded them. They were not part of "the people" after all, nor was liberty their "birthright."

Leaders of the new Republic soon resolved women's place in the new United States of America. John Adams argued that, while women were theoretically part of the new U.S. government, they should exercise their influence in the home rather than in any public political capacity. Adams maintained that women's power lay in their influence over men and children, whom they could steer toward the adoption of "proper" republican values. Adams also wrote to a friend that, like men without property, women lacked decisiveness, while "their delicacy renders them unfit for practice and experience in the great business of life."

Similarly, Thomas Jefferson, the author of the Declaration, believed that "the tender breasts of ladies were not formed for political convulsion." Like John Adams, Jefferson thought that women should remain in the protected privacy of home, while men fought the daily battles in the public and political arenas. Although he carried on extensive correspondence with Abigail Adams, Jefferson remained convinced that neither he nor his fellow citizens were ready for women voters and office holders.

Nor did Jefferson seem to recognize that black slave women on his own plantation confronted and overcame the vicissitudes of a harsh world outside their homes.

As a result of such attitudes, when U.S. voters discarded the Articles of Confederation and ratified the new Constitution in 1789, republican women found that the document included no rights or protection for them. Nor were women released from coverture and the limitations of marital unity. They had no representatives in governing bodies nor any emissaries or planks in the platforms of the first political parties. And their occasional right to vote in some local and state elections was last exercised in 1807 in New Jersey.

Other women, barred from expressing themselves politically, did so personally. While they could not vote or hold office, they could demand the right to choose their own mates or refuse to marry at all. During the 1780s and 1790s, more women in eastern regions chose not to marry rather than select a less-than-suitable mate. Daughters, especially of eastern, well-to-do families, thus exercised their "independence" in the marriage market. Long before the contemporary feminist movement coined the slogan, some women recognized that the personal was political.

Clearly, the many political ramifications of the Revolution and the new nation's government did not extend to women. Some women accepted this situation as inevitable. Like her husband John, Abigail Adams believed that women would be sullied by political participation. She was also a woman who took mothering seriously; she once wrote to her son John Quincy, then a student in England: "I would rather see you find a grave in the ocean you have crossed than see you an immoral, profligate or graceless child."

Improved Female Education

Anglo women gained far more in the realm of education. A corollary of Republican Motherhood, that mother must have some education to raise republican children, soon spurred a reconsideration of women's education. Although the rhetoric of the 1780s and 1790s declared that reason and rationality were masculine qualities and not common among women, at the same time, many Americans believed that women must be better educated for their roles as Republican Mothers.

As women's education became an ongoing debate, it was obvious that most Americans believed that the new republican woman should be rational, competent, and self-reliant. This view did not favor "intellectual" women or the departure of women from the home as their primary sphere. Rather, it emphasized the idea that women's duties in the home had achieved a new significance. One trustee of a southern institution hoped for neither "excessive refinement nor extreme erudition." He simply wanted female students to develop a "rational, well-informed piety."

Some reformers, however, wanted more for women students; they hoped for an education equal to that given men. In her letters to her husband, Abigail Adams explored the meaning of the Revolution for women's education. Adams understood that women's primary duty was to cultivate wisdom and loyalty in their children, thus preserving virtues, especially those supposedly female traits of selflessness and purity, necessary to an independent republic. But how would women train "heroes, statesmen and philosophers," she wondered, if they themselves were not "learned." In 1778, she reminded her husband John of the "narrow contracted Education" of women in the new United States. "You need not be told," she wrote, "how much female Education is neglected, nor how fashionable it has been to ridicule Female learning."

At the same time, Judith Sargent Murray, an author and early feminist, became one of the first Americans to argue publicly for equitable educational opportunities for women. In 1779, writing under the pen name of Constantia, Murray declared that men and women had equal minds that deserved equivalent educations. "Are women deficient in reason?" she asked. "We can only reason from what we know, and if an opportunity of acquiring knowledge hath been denied us, the inferiority of our sex cannot fairly be deduced from thence." If women were "allowed an equality of acquirements" in the area of education, they would "meet on even ground" in their achievements.

Abigail Adams continued to worry about the matter and, by 1787, concluded that women were "rational beings" whose minds "might with propriety receive the highest possible cultivation." Although Adams recognized that an educated woman would "draw upon herself the jealousy of the Men and the envy of the Women," she believed that the only "way to remedy this evil" was "by increasing the number of accomplished women," thus forcing their acceptance by society.

The celebrated Dr. Benjamin Rush of Philadelphia explained it this way: "Let the ladies of a country be educated properly and they will not only make and administer its laws, but form its manners and character." Also, in 1787, Rush presented to the newly established Young Ladies Academy of Philadelphia an address that urged the inclusion of academic subjects in the curriculum, but warned students to act in a "womanly" way so they would not inflame Americans' fear that education would "unsex" women. The course of study of this academy, which claimed to be the first of its kind chartered in the United States, included reading, writing, arithmetic, English grammar, composition, rhetoric, and geography. This curriculum represented a major alteration in ideas regarding women, for prominent men had, for the first time, devoted their time and energy to advocate the concept of a sound education for women.

Still, as Rush's remarks suggested, the academy's founders did not intend it "as constituting an Era altogether new." Instead, strong evidence indicates that the school's founders wanted to lessen women's discontent while improving the education of the mothers of the new country's future citizens. Consequently, women who gave graduation addresses reflected their continuing acceptance of the *status quo*. "I believe I must give up all pretensions to profundity," one stated, "for I am more at home in my female character." Only a few of these women made any mention of equal education and widening the accepted female sphere.

In 1792, a bold new experiment in women's literature, the *Ladies Magazine and Repository*, published in Philadelphia, revealed a similar double-sided approach to women's education. On the one hand, the editors emphasized that women should read such intellectually expanding works as Mary Wollstonecraft's *A Vindication of the Rights of Women* (1792), which argued for female education that would do more than leaving women in a "state of perpetual childhood," prepared only to attract and please men. On the other hand, the editors featured such male writers as Noah Webster and Benjamin Rush who argued that women's education should enlarge only to the point of allowing women to understand Republican ideals.

As a consequence of the growing interest in women's education, a number of schools attracted more female students than ever. The Linden Hall Seminary, which grew out of a Moravian, or United Brethren, day school established in Lititz, Pennsylvania, in 1764, expanded its facilities and programs after the Revolution. By 1790, it enrolled a dozen female students. Applications increased so rapidly that in 1799 one teacher wrote, "We cannot increase our numbers for want of teachers, every one must wait for a vacancy." A renovation allowed the enrollment to expand somewhat, and, by 1804, seventeen female day pupils and fifty-two boarders attended the school. During the 1790s, northern young women could also attend a wide variety of other schools in Philadelphia or Boston, or enroll in such New England small-town schools as Sarah Pierce's Litchfield Academy.

In the South, planter's daughters could select either northern boarding schools or female academies, especially in North Carolina and Georgia. Southern women's academies moved away from superficial education in "female accomplishments" to training in subjects that would contribute to women becoming more effective mothers and more informed citizens. In 1805, a Virginia planter requested that his daughter send a complete account of her academy education: "I wish to know how each day is employed—what proportion is devoted to study, to writing, to cyphering, to reading, to sewing, to amusement, to idleness." Southern women flocked to academies in order to gain, if not equality, at least an improved quality of life as wives, mothers, and plantation mistresses.

The Feminization of Religion

Changes for women occurred in religion as well. The number of women church members far outnumbered men; most congregations had a majority of female members. As church audiences became largely female, ministers found it necessary to "feminize" their message to meet the needs of their listeners. Clergy turned their attention to topics of concern to women, such as the family, public and private morality, the refinement of society, and missionary endeavors. The clergy also stressed the crucial role of godly mothers and the importance of women's morality, thus adding the church's voice to the growing emphasis on motherhood.

Women were quick to seize their opportunities. Beginning in 1776, "Mother" Ann Lee promoted a new sect, Shakerism, known for its female participation and leadership. This Protestant, celibate, and communitarian sect envisioned Lee as the female incarnation of Christ, as well as the female side of a God who had both male and female components. Lee also believed that sexuality constituted the primary barrier to human perfectibility, a message she intended to deliver to humankind. She and her followers became known as Shakers because of a ritualistic dance they performed in which they "shook" off the devil from their hands and feet. Lee died in 1784 of injuries, perhaps inflicted by a mob, but the sect she founded continued to follow her teachings.

When the Second Great Awakening began around 1800, women spurred it onward as members, lay speakers, and exhorters. Revivalist Jemima Wilkinson especially attracted numerous followers with her charisma and exceptional speaking abilities. As a popular and effective preacher, she helped legitimize the highly emotional nature of the Second Great Awakening, and allowed women to express their religious sensibilities freely.

As religious, impassioned, and highly moral beings, these women saw themselves as the inculcators of virtue not only in children but in men as well. They actively recruited men for conversion, an act that implied the superiority of their female religious nature. In an 1810 sermon, one preacher agreed: "We look to you, ladies, to raise the standard of character in our own sex." Women also openly expressed anger against authority, particularly that of ungodly men and controlling ministers, thus venting some of the tensions created by limitations on their lives.

Similarly, in the Catholic church women gained a degree of visibility. Elizabeth Ann Seton, a widow who converted to Catholicism in 1804, founded a community of women Religious in 1809. Located in Emmitsburg, Maryland, Seton's order founded the first Catholic parochial school in the new nation. Later, in 1812, Archbishop John Carroll confirmed the rules and constitution of Seton's Sisters of Charity, making it the first American community of women Religious.

Effect on Women's Literature

The concept of Republican Motherhood also encouraged a number of novelists to write explicitly for women, notably white women. The resulting didactic tales usually ended with a highly moral message directed especially to future as well as present wives and mothers.

The most popular example of the genre was Susanna Haswell Rowson's novel, *Charlotte Temple, A Tale of Truth*, first published in 1794. On the third page, Rowson explained that, as author, she would guide the reader through a "perusal of the young and thoughtless of the fair sex." Rowson intended her tale of Charlotte Temple's involvement with an evil man named Montraville to prove instructive to young female readers. In the novel, after Charlotte marries and is deserted by Montraville, it becomes clear that women have responsibility for their own fall from virtue. By the early 1800s, this cautionary saga of seduction reportedly sold more copies than any other book in the history of British or American publishing to that date.

Such stories reinforced the growing belief that women acted as moral forces and purveyors of virtue in the new American republic. But such literature also created a unified female reading audience that increasingly believed in women's moral superiority over men, and it opened a wider area of employment to female writers.

Women in the Arts

After the Revolution, Anglo women also moved into the arts, competing with male artists by creating conventional works of art. They did so without the benefit of formal training or study abroad because these activities were believed unseemly for women.

Despite these restrictions, several women gained public recognition for their pastel drawing during the late eighteenth century. Ruth Henshaw Bascom of Massachusetts, known for her pastel crayon portraits, reportedly never accepted money for any of her works. Sarah Perkins, a Connecticut pastelist, also produced portraits during the 1790s, but she cut short her work as an artist by taking charge of her seven brothers and sisters at the age of twenty. She later married a widower with five children, and then had four children of her own.

Other women artists worked in the medium of watercolor. Sophia Burpee sometimes combined her watercolors with exquisite embroidery. Ruby Devol Finch executed watercolor paintings, especially of the parable of the prodigal son, as well as miniatures and family records. Like Finch, Mary Parke painted Biblical scenes in watercolors. Susanna Heebner of Pennsylvania also focused on religious themes. Her manuscript illuminations combined religious poetry, moral teachings, and brightly colored decorations.

Probably the best-known female artist of this era was Sarah Miriam Peale. As the youngest daughter of James Peale, a renowned miniaturist and portrait painter, and the niece of acclaimed natural history painter and portraitist, Charles Willson Peale, she had artistic advantages not available to other women. Trained by her father and her uncle, Sarah Peale became an accomplished portrait and still-life artist. Her clients included heads of state and generals, and Peale was the first woman to have her work exhibited at the prestigious Pennsylvania Academy of the Fine Arts.

WOMEN ON THE FRONTIER

American Indian Women

The frontier line continued to push across the Appalachian region and the South, creating a zone where native peoples confronted and resisted Anglo migration. In 1785, the new American government opened the lands beyond the Appalachian Mountains for settlement, and Americans began to migrate, carrying with them gender expectations and laws and policies that affected women.

As among eastern tribes, Indian women who lived along advancing lines of Anglo settlement in the West and the South experienced diminishing roles. A typical story was that of a Mohawk medicine woman named Coocoochee. After undertaking five forced moves across hundreds of miles, she ended up in Kentucky. After her husband died in war in 1790, Coocoochee took refuge with the Shawnees. Here, she acted as a spiritual leader and a Mohawk historian, for she feared that she and her children were the last of the Mohawks.

At the time, however, white society knew little about the deteriorating position of American Indian women. The native women who commanded the attention of Anglos continued to be those who helped them to achieve their ends. Thus, Sacajawea, an Idaho Shoshoni, gained historical fame among whites when she aided the Lewis and Clark expedition as an interpreter and guide between 1804 and 1806. In another case, Marie Dorion, an Iowa Indian, was remembered as the only woman on the famed 1811–1812 expedition to Astoria on the Columbia River and as an Indian who warned whites of a native attack.

Spanish-speaking Women

Growing numbers of Spanish-speaking women were born in, or migrated to, such areas as Florida, the Louisiana territory, and the Southwest during this era. They especially lived in and around Los Angeles, San Antonio, San Francisco, Santa Fe, and Tucson. Others were scattered across the rich valleys and near-desert areas of what later became Arizona, California, New Mexico, and Texas.

Spanish-speaking women were typically Catholic. Especially the Roman Catholic Church stressed family well-being and the collective good above individual gain, as well as emphasizing love of children and the aged, a sense of fiesta and celebration, and holding families together. Thus, women gave their primary allegiance to their families, but even in this patriarchal system, women shared in, or made, family decisions, and according to law, could inherit and hold family property. Of the women who also labored outside their homes, many either volunteered their services or earned wages by teaching, acting as *curanderas* (healers), and working as matrons in the Catholic missions strung across California and into Texas.

Spanish-speaking pioneer women, much like later Anglo pioneer women, contributed greatly to the settlement of *El Norte*, as they called the frontier. These women were well-versed in midwifery, plant medicine, and other domestic skills. Stories of mettle abound as well. After the daughter of Don Jose Dario Argüello, *commandante* of San Francisco during the early 1800s, lost her betrothed in a sea disaster, she led a life of piety and charity, always helping the ill and poor. In 1851, at age sixty, Doña Concepcíon joined the Dominican order. Renamed María Dominica, she became California's first woman Religious and spent the remaining six years of her life in benevolent works.

Anglo Women as Settlers

Frontierswomen fought alongside their men in wresting the land from its native owners and in working to clear the land with oxen, mules, horses, and primitive machinery. Although religion and education offered opportunities for some political participation, the official political realm barred them. These women aided the formation of the new states entering the union after the Revolution—Kentucky in 1792, Tennessee in 1796, and Ohio in 1803. Yet, even in such supposedly egalitarian frontier regions as those along the Cumberland River, women lacked political privileges during the 1780s and 1790s.

As in the East, women adopted those standards of Republican Motherhood that suited their life-styles. Mothers struggled to raise their children as educated "proper," virtuous, and democratic men and women. At the same time, women managed homes, chicken-houses, and dairies—all complex and arduous responsibilities requiring training and skill. They also learned to run farms and handle crises on their own while their men were absent on long trips. Married to hunters, traders, trappers, surveyors, and politicians, women stayed home and minded the family enterprise. Daniel Smith, for example, was gone from his family more than a year when he helped to survey the North Carolina–Virginia line in 1779–1780. Thus, women often tilled the fields, built houses and outbuildings, bred animals, and did a multitude of heavy chores.

Men often recognized women's labor and management abilities in their wills, which commonly left property to wives and assigned them as executrices. When they lost their men, many frontier widows continued to work on their own. It has been estimated that Indian wars widowed almost two-thirds of early women settlers in Tennessee by the 1790s. Yet few left the frontier to live with families in the more settled eastern regions. Widowed in 1781, Leah Lucas stayed on the Cumberland frontier, farming the family land and raising five children.

Other women attained single status by divorcing their spouses. By the early 1800s, it appeared that western divorce rates outnumbered those in the Northeast and the South. With their mobile population, employment opportunities, hastily adopted laws and policies, and emphasis on independence and personal satisfaction, western areas often provided relatively easy divorce. Although the census bureau had not begun to count marriages and divorces, anecdotal evidence suggests that far more women than men took advantage of the availability of divorce in newly settled western sections of the country.

Slave and Free Black Women

Despite myths and media images that present light-haired and fair-skinned women as archetypal western women, frontierswomen also included slave and free women of color. Of the forty-four settlers who founded Los Angeles in 1781, at least twenty-six were black women, men, and children. Other slave and free women of color went West as domestic workers, nursemaids, riverboat cooks, and farm laborers.

In 1787, the Confederation Congress passed the Northwest Ordinance, which, among other provisions, prohibited slavery in the areas that would form the states of Illinois, Indiana, Michigan, Ohio, and Wisconsin. The barring of "involuntary servitude" in this area opened it to free blacks, who worked for fur trappers, traders, soldiers, and farmers, or farmed on their own.

As a growing number of blacks went West, however, other settlers began to fear them, both because of their difference and a growing concern that they would capture the labor market by providing cheap labor. In 1804, the Ohio state legislature enacted the first of a series of Black Laws restricting the rights and mobility of free blacks in the Northwest. Often, neither black men nor women could own property, while exclusion laws barred them from residence in certain towns, counties, and states. Such states as Ohio and Indiana even required that free blacks post a bond of as much as five hundred dollars as an affirmation of their freedom. Still, free blacks continued to migrate in hopes of finding better jobs and less prejudice in the West.

Beginning in 1763, the chaos of resistance, revolution, and early nationhood tested the invented American woman and her "sphere." By 1812, changes resulted in new ideas about white women, especially those of the middle and upper classes. New beliefs included the ideal of companionate marriage, increased respect for motherhood, legitimacy of women's education, and talk of enhanced self-esteem for women. But for Anglo women of the lower classes and for women of color, changing gender expectations generally continued to offer little more than unrealistic ideals.

Suggestions for Further Reading

Akers, Charles W. *Abigail Adams: An American Woman*. Boston: Little, Brown and Company, 1980.

Alexander, Adele L. *Ambitious Lives: Free Women of Color in Rural Georgia, 1789–1870*. Fayetteville: University of Arkansas Press, 1991.

Aptheker, Herbert. *Abolitionism: a Revolutionary Movement*. Boston: Twayne Publishers, 1989. Chapter 1.

Baker, Paula. "The Domestication of Politics: Women and American Political Society, 1780–1920," 85–110, in *Unequal Sisters: A Multicultural Reader in U.S. Women's History*, edited by Vicki L. Ruiz and Ellen Carol DuBois. 2d ed. New York: Routledge, Chapman, & Hall, 1994.

Basch, Norma. *In the Eyes of the Law: Women, Marriage and Property in Nineteenth-Century New York*. Ithaca, NY: Cornell University Press, 1982.

Berkin, Carol Ruth, and Mary Beth Norton, eds. *Women of America: A History*. Boston: Houghton Mifflin, 1979. Part II, section 3.

Bloch, Ruth H. "American Feminine Ideals in Transition: The Rise of the Moral Mother, 1785–1815," *Feminist Studies* 4 (June 1978): 101–26.

———."The Gendered Meanings of Virtue in Revolutionary America," *Signs* 13 (Autumn 1987): 37–58.

Bogdan, Janet. "Care or Cure: Childbirth Practices in Nineteenth Century America," *Feminist Studies* 3 (June 1978): 92–99.

Boydston, Jeanne. *Home and Work: Housework, Wages, and the Ideology of Labor in the Early Republic*. New York: Oxford University Press, 1993.

Buel, Joy Day, and Richard Buel, Jr. *The Way of Duty: A Woman and Her Family in Revolutionary America*. New York: W. W. Norton & Co., Inc., 1984.

Chambers-Schiller, Lee Virginia. *Liberty, A Better Husband: Single Women in America, The Generations of 1780–1840*. New Haven, CT: Yale University Press, 1984.

Clark, Ella E., and Margot Edmonds. *Sacagawea of the Lewis and Clark Expedition*. Berkeley and Los Angeles: University of California Press, 1979.

Clinton, Catharine. *The Other Civil War: Women in the Nineteenth Century*. New York: Hill and Wang, 1984. Chapter 1.

———. "Equally Their Due: The Education of the Planter Daughter in the Early Republic," *Journal of the Early Republic* 2 (Spring 1982): 39–60.

Cody, Cheryll Ann. "Naming, Kinship and Estate Disposal: Notes on Slave Family Life on a South Carolina Plantation, 1786–1833," *William and Mary Quarterly* 39 (January 1982): 192–211.

Coker, Kathy Roe. "The Calamities of War: Loyalism and Women in South Carolina," 47–70, in *Southern Women: Histories and Identities*, edited by Virginia Bernhard, Betty Brandon, Elizabeth Fox-Genovese, and Theda Perdue. Columbia: University of Missouri Press, 1992.

Conley, Frances R. "Martina Didn't Have a Covered Wagon: A Speculative Reconstruction," *Californians* 7 (March/August 1989): 48–54.

Dawson, Jan C. "Sacagawea: Pilot or Pioneer Mother?" *Pacific Northwest Quarterly* 83 (January 1992): 22–28.

DePauw, Linda Grant. *Founding Mothers: Women in the Revolutionary Era*. Boston: Houghton Mifflin, 1975.

———. "Women in Combat: The Revolutionary War Experience," *Armed Forces and Society* 7 (Winter 1980): 209–26.

Devens, Carol. *Countering Colonization: Native American Women and Great Lakes Missions, 1630–1900.* Berkeley: University of California Press, 1992.

Dewhurst, C. Kurt, Betty MacDowell, and Marsha MacDowell. *Artists in Aprons: Folk Art by American Women.* New York: E. P. Dutton, 1979.

Dye, Nancy Schrom. "History of Childbirth in America," *Signs* 6 (Autumn 1980): 97–108.

Dye, Nancy Schrom, and Daniel Blake Smith. "Mother Love and Infant Death, 1750–1920," *Journal of American History* 73 (September 1986): 329–53.

Enríquez, Alfredo, and Mirandé Evangelina. *La Chicana: The Mexican-American Woman.* Chicago: University of Chicago Press, 1979.

Evans, Sara M. *Born for Liberty: A History of Women in America* New York: Free Press, 1989. Chapter 3.

Faragher, John Mack. "The Custom of the Country: Cross-Cultural Marriage in the Far Western Fur Trade," 199–216, in *Western Women: Their Land, Their Lives,* edited by Lillian Schlissel, Vicki L. Ruiz, and Janice Monk. Albuquerque: University of New Mexico Press, 1988.

Foster, Martha Harroun. "Of Baggage and Bondage: Gender and Status Among Hidatsa and Crow Women," *American Indian Culture and Research Journal* 17 (1993): 121–53.

Friedman, Jean E., William G. Shade, and Mary Jane Capozzoli, eds. *Our American Sisters: Women in American Life and Thought.* Lexington, MA: 4th ed. D. C. Heath and Company, 1987. Chapters 4–5.

Gelles, Edith B. *Portia: The World of Abigail Adams.* Bloomington: Indiana University Press, 1992.

Gundersen, Joan R. "Independence, Citizenship, and the American Revolution," *Signs* 13 (Autumn 1987): 59–77.

Gutiérrez, Ramón A. "Honor, Ideology, Marriage Negotiation and Class-Gender Domination in New Mexico, 1690–1846," *Latin American Perspectives* 12 (Winter 1985): 13–26.

Hernández, Salomé. "No Settlement Without Women: Three Spanish California Settlement Schemes, 1790–1800," 309–38, in *Southern California's Spanish Heritage: An Anthology,* edited by Doyce B. Nunis, Jr. Los Angeles: Historical Society of Southern California, 1992.

Hewitt, Nancy A., ed. *Women, Families, and Communities: Readings in American History.* Vol. I. Glenview, IL: Scott, Foresman, 1990. Part II.

Hoffman, Ronald, and Peter J. Albert, eds. *Women in the Age of the American Revolution.* Charlottesville: University Press of Virginia, 1989.

Jensen, Joan M. "Native American Women and Agriculture: A Seneca Case Study," 70–84, in *Unequal Sisters: A Multicultural Reader in U.S. Women's History,* edited by Vicki L. Ruiz and Ellen Carol DuBois. 2d ed. New York: Routledge, Chapman, & Hall, Inc., 1994.

Kerber, Linda K. "'I Have Don . . . much to Carray on the Warr': Women and the Shaping of Republican Ideology After the American Revolution," *Journal of Women's History* 1 (Winter 1990): 231–43.

———. *Women of the Republic: Intellect and Ideology in Revolutionary America.* Chapel Hill: University of North Carolina Press, 1980.

Kerber, Linda K., Nancy F. Cott, Robert Gross, Lynn Hunt, Carroll Smith-Rosenberg, and Christine M. Stansell. "Beyond Roles, Beyond Spheres: Thinking about Gender in the Early Republic," *William and Mary Quarterly* 46 (July 1989): 565–85.

Lasser, Carol. "Gender, Ideology, and Class in the Early Republic," *Journal of the Early Republic* 10 (Fall 1990): 331–37.

Leavitt, Judith Walzer. *Brought to Bed: Childbearing in America, 1750 to 1950.* New York: Oxford University Press, 1986.

Lewis, Jan. "The Republican Wife: Virtue and Seduction in the Early Republic," *William and Mary Quarterly* 44 (October 1987) 689–721.

Lewis, Jan, and Kenneth A. Lockridge. "'Sally Has Been Sick': Pregnancy and Family Limitation Among Virginia Gentry Women, 1780–1830," *Journal of Social History* 22 (Fall 1988): 5–19.

Lothrop, Gloria Ricci. "Rancheras and the Land: Women and Property Rights in Hispanic California," *Southern California Quarterly* 76 (Spring 1994): 59–84.

Nash, Gary B. *Race and Revolution*. Madison, WI: Madison House, 1990.

Newman, Debra L. "Black Women in the Era of the American Revolution in Pennsylvania," *Journal of Negro History* 61 (July 1976): 276–89.

Niethammer, Carolyn. *Daughters of the Earth: The Lives and Legends of American Indian Women*. New York: Macmillan Publishing Company, 1977.

Norton, Mary Beth. *Liberty's Daughters: The Revolutionary Experience of American Women, 1750–1800*. Boston: Little, Brown and Company, 1980.

Perdue, Theda. *Slavery and the Evolution of Cherokee Society, 1540–1866*. Knoxville: University of Tennessee Press, 1979.

Perrone, Bobette, H. Henrietta Stockel, and Victoria Krueger. *Medicine Women, Curanderas, and Women Doctors*. Norman: University of Oklahoma Press, 1993.

Shells, Richard D. "The Feminization of American Congregationalism, 1730–1835," *American Quarterly* 33 (Spring 1981): 46–62.

Smith, Daniel Blake. "The Study of the Family in Early America: Trends, Problems, and Prospects," *William and Mary Quarterly* 39 (January 1982): 3–28.

Soderlund, Jean R. *Quakers and Slavery: A Divided Spirit*. Princeton: Princeton University Press, 1985.

Van Kirk, Sylvia. *Many Tender Ties: Women in Fur-Trade Society, 1670–1870*. Norman: University of Oklahoma Press, 1983.

Ulrich, Laurel Thatcher. *A Midwife's Tale: The Life of Martha Ballard, Based on Her Diary, 1785–1812*. New York: Alfred A. Knopf, 1990.

Wertz, Richard W., and Dorothy C. Wertz. *Lying-In: A History of Childbirth in America*. New York: Free Press, 1977.

Westbury, Susan. "Women in Bacon's Rebellion," 30–44, in *Southern Women: Histories and Identities*, edited by Virginia Bernhard, Betty Brandon, Elizabeth Fox-Genovese, and Theda Perdue. Columbia: University of Missouri, 1992.

Wilson, Lisa. *Life After Death: Widows in Pennsylvania, 1750–1850*. Philadelphia: Temple University Press, 1992.

Woloch, Nancy. *Women and the American Experience*. New York: Alfred A. Knopf, 1984. Chapters 3–4.

Wright, Mary C. "Economic Development and Native American Women in the Early Nineteenth Century," *American Quarterly* 33 (Winter 1981): 525–36.

Zagarri, Rosemarie. "Morals, Manners, and the Republican Mother," *American Quarterly* 44 (June 1992): 192–215.

The Cult of True Womanhood
Industrial and Westward Expansion, 1812 to 1837

3

By the 1810s, a fever of growth and expansion burned its way across the United States. A "boom psychology" encouraged investment in new industries, massive movement of people to American cities from the countryside and from other nations in search of jobs, and thousands of others to cross the Appalachian Mountains toward the beckoning frontier. Even though the customary image of women as primarily wives and mothers endured and even expanded, at the same time, changing activities and growth in paid employment opportunities for women challenged the concept of separate spheres for women and men. Between the beginning of the War of 1812 and the onset of the Panic of 1837, the invented American woman appeared to have become a solid institution, but, in reality, industrial and westward expansion, as well as women themselves, called the model of American womanhood into question.

WOMEN AS WORKERS DURING THE INDUSTRIAL REVOLUTION

Women and Factories

The story of women as factory workers began in 1789, when the first factory for carding and spinning yarn in America was established in Rhode Island. Because most men engaged in agriculture, proponents of the American factory system suggested hiring women, preferably white farm women. These advocates of industry recognized the need to keep men in the fields, producing foodstuffs for nonfarming classes. Besides, it seemed natural for women, who had spun and woven in their homes, to continue their customary work in a new venue.

In his Report on Manufactures of 1791, U.S. Secretary of the Treasury Alexander Hamilton advocated factory employment for women because it made development of the new industrial system possible "without taking men from the fields." He added that factory employment would also render women "more useful than they otherwise would be," while farms would prosper as a result of the income brought in by the "increased industry" of farm wives and daughters.

These arguments multiplied many times over during the following years. One avid supporter of manufacturing argued that "the portion of time of housewives and young women which were not occupied with family affairs could be profitably filled up" by factory work. This view soon expanded to include the claim that a factory was actually a blessing to a community because it furnished employment for women.

Of course, women had always worked; they had labored in cabins, farmhouses, plantation houses, and outbuildings without wages as a reward. Now they shifted their place of employment to the new factories and expected paychecks in return. They did so in large numbers because of the growing need of farm families for cash income during the early 1800s and the increasing availability of factory jobs. Also, the War of 1812 resulted in an upsurge in industrialization that created an expanding demand for workers and offered women not only wages but escape from farm life.

After the War of 1812 ended, the U.S. Congress appointed the first congressional committee charged with investigating the situation of women workers. In 1816, the committee identified 100,000 industrial workers in the United States, two-thirds of whom were female and usually white. The committee's findings also revealed that, among other things, industrialization transformed household production, drew huge numbers of women from their homes into paid employment, and shaped new social classes of women.

During the postwar years, thousands of young farm women in New England left their families to relocate in the new mill towns. The best-known of these factory villages was Lowell, Massachusetts. Here, women workers lived together in company-owned boardinghouses. Often, these "mill girls" sent part of their meager wages home to their families, while their brothers remained on the farm to provide agricultural labor or attended college, paid for by their sister's earnings.

The Lowell women commonly worked twelve to fourteen hours a day, tending two or more machines for about two dollars a week. Although matrons supervised the boardinghouses, factory women possessed a certain amount of independence. They also enjoyed such cultural benefits as libraries and reading and writing for the company-sponsored literary journal, *The Lowell Offering*.

As early as the mid-1820s, however, conditions began to change for Lowell and other factory operatives. Although wages had failed to increase, the work pace had done so. Hours were still long, and working conditions were worsening. Boardinghouses had become overcrowded, and goods in the company stores were increasingly expensive. In 1824, a group of women protested against low wages and bad conditions by walking out of a mill in Pawtucket, Rhode Island. Many other strikes, or "turnouts," followed in other areas. Women workers did not make much progress with these protests. After all, women were expendable because there were always more young women or, by the late 1830s, Irish immigrants willing to fill the places of protesting women. Also, women had difficulty supporting labor organizations on their low wages. And, as women, they were denied knowledge of, and access to, such other important avenues of power as public office-holding.

Despite these growing problems associated with factory employment, women who found it necessary to help support their families continued to enter industrial occupations in large numbers. By 1828, nine out of ten textile workers in New England were female. As immigration increased during the late 1820s and 1830s, a growing number of such women were foreign-born. Because parents of young, unmarried immigrant women routinely expected them to help support their families, almost 60 percent of young, single Irish women worked, with German and other groups following similar employment patterns to a lesser extent. Even in conservative Italian families, daughters often worked to provide temporary relief for an overburdened family budget. In many Jewish families both single and married women worked, sometimes so men could continue the much revered study of the Torah, especially if the men aspired to the respected position of Rabbi.

This diverse female workforce labored primarily in textile factories, cotton mills, the needle trades, and shoe factories. Employers thought of them as "lady operatives" who worked cheaply and could be hired and fired as needed. In other cases, women held atypical industrial jobs. Census data reveal that, among other occupations, women worked as coopers, glass engravers, iron-workers, and tinsmiths. By the 1820s and 1830s, however, the number of women engaged in such occupations began to decline.

Yet other women called pieceworkers labored for wages within their homes. They produced parts that factory workers would later assemble; for this, they earned only "piecework" wages, a minimal fee per part. The country's largest shoe factory, located in Lynn, Massachusetts, depended on the needle skills of such women pieceworkers to bind or to stitch shoe uppers in their homes. Still other women worked at home as seamstresses. After observing Philadelphia seamstresses in 1829, one commentator noted: "It takes great expertness and increasing industry from sunrise to 10 and 11 at night, constant employment which few of them have, to earn a dollar and a half per week."

These types of women workers constituted a new female working class; the market economy drove their lives. Yet, because of the fluidity of the women's labor market and the scattered nature of their work places, these women remained largely isolated from each other as well as from other types of women. They tended to focus on improving their own immediate situations, including obtaining better pay and improved working conditions. Because such issues as education, property ownership, and the right to vote had little relevance to their lives, such women did not form the basis of a women's rights campaign. Instead, they provided a nucleus of the emerging American labor movement.

Women in Nonindustrial Occupations

Yet another group of women earned wages by using their domestic skills in employers' homes. In early America, many families had "hired help," who assisted with domestic tasks and were accepted as part of the family. By the late 1700s and early 1800s "domestics" did the same tasks, but were now seen as servants and assigned specific menial chores performed apart from family members. Free black women and an increasing influx of immigrant women, especially Irish, provided a source of needy, untrained women for the domestic service market.

Domestics toiled at such chores as cooking, food-processing, and childcare. They usually assisted middle- and upper-class women, who could now exchange money for the goods they needed rather than producing them at home. Although pleased to have help, female employers generally treated domestics coolly and paid them poorly. Domestic servants, who lacked an opportunity to organize on their own behalf, were probably the most underpaid of all working women. In 1837, one observer commented that "a woman who goes out to wash works as hard in proportion as a wood sawyer or a coal heaver, but she is not generally able to make more than half as much for a day's work."

A very different type of employed women was the growing number who provided sexual services for pay. In New York and other cities, many destitute seamstresses and servants turned to prostitution as a relatively lucrative pursuit. In New York, one report claims that between twelve hundred and seven thousand prostitutes existed by the 1820s. In Philadelphia of the 1820s and 1830s, thousands of other "disorderly" women walked the streets, parks, and amusement places openly. In Nanny Goat Alley, Ram Cat Alley, and on Baker Street, women solicited business. Especially in New York City and Philadelphia, prostitutes were white and black, overwhelmingly between the ages of fifteen and twenty-five, and largely urban-born. Rather than being arrested for prostitution, these women were brought before the law for vagrancy, theft, or drunk and disorderly behavior. Apparently most urban dwellers regarded prostitutes as a necessary nuisance.

Yet other women, especially heads of households and widows, kept their hand in at operating small businesses, especially those that served other women by supplying millinery, yard goods, or notions. Both white and black women also worked as street vendors, market women, tavern and boardinghouse keepers, and cooks.

One especially successful business woman was Sarah Todd Astor, who helped her husband, John Jacob Aster, parlay her dowry of three hundred dollars into a lucrative fur business, the American Fur Company. While he traveled to locate and trade furs, she managed the business, processed and graded furs, and eventually gave birth to eight children in rooms above their shop. Due to the investment of the profits of the American Fur Company in New York real estate, the Astor fortune was reputed to be the largest in the country at the time of Sarah's death in 1832.

Rebecca Pennock Lukens was another entrepreneur who operated a family business. On his death-bed, Lukens's husband asked her to take over the family iron mill in Pennsylvania. As a Quaker, she was well-educated and had always been encouraged to take an interest in the family metal-working enterprise. Lukens not only saved the mill from bankruptcy but added iron plate rolling to the business, supplying boilers for steamboats and locomotives. Lukens was so successful that she was worth $100,000 at the time of her death in 1854.

Women's Unpaid Labor

Another large component of women labored within their homes without cash wages. Some women, even among the working classes and free people of color, could afford to devote themselves to the care of their families. After all, domestic work demanded full-time attention and energy, while the concept of Republican Motherhood had long assured such women that childcare should be women's first duty.

Because the newly industrializing society measured people's worth by the wage they earned, many Americans overlooked or even denigrated the work such women performed. Despite the lack of pay or recognition, however, thousands of women labored in kitchens, nurseries, dairies, barns, chicken coops, and gardens. Others also worked on the land, either on their own or as "farm wives." Although census takers failed to categorize such women as farmers, women farmers added considerably to the nation's economic growth.

THE NEW LEISURE CLASS

Roots of True Womanhood

Industrialization and accompanying urbanization redistributed millions of Americans. While women had once labored in their homes and their husbands outdoors in the fields, or the two had worked together in a family enterprise, now, especially in the Northeast, large numbers of men moved their work away from the home to factories and cities while their wives remained at home.

Throughout the course of these developments, "woman's place is in the home" became a popular maxim. In addition, it was no longer enough to be a Republican Wife and Mother. Now, such qualities as knowledge of "proper" domestic skills and values, piety, virtue, submissiveness, and enlightened motherhood defined a true woman.

In all likelihood, some Americans felt a pressing need to protect and expand the traditional idea of women as wives and mothers in an era when millions of women left their homes for paid employment. From an economic standpoint, the argument that women's "real" jobs were in their homes also was used to justify low wages and kept female workers segregated in the needle trades and other areas that depended upon cheap labor. Moreover, domestic ideology—or the doctrine of true womanhood—encouraged increased consumption of factory goods by full-time homemakers, as well as holding home-bound women in reserve as an emergency labor supply.

In reality, however, the tenets of true womanhood applied to few American women. Among white, working-class people, for example, women sometimes remained at home, but more often, out of economic necessity, they accompanied their husbands to jobs in factory or city. According to one 1816 estimate, some sixty-six thousand women worked in the cotton textile industry alone. When workers returned home at night, wives and mothers completed domestic chores and childcare as best they could. They were thus among the first women to experience what has since been termed the "double day."

Among the middle and upper classes, both white and black, women often stayed at home. Because men pursued banking, trade, insurance, shipping, and other businesses in cities and away from homes, no longer could women learn trades and professions from fathers, brothers, and husbands. Nor, given their husbands' incomes, did these women need to do so. For the first time, a group of American women experienced leisure. Known by the evolving term "ladies," they had the time to pursue creative homemaking, and to achieve superb domesticity and true womanhood. They could also be symbols for their husbands, who were anxious to prove their own abilities as "bread-winners" by giving their wives leisure time and servants. In addition, such ladies served as undisputed guardians of virtue and morality, thus allowing men to engage in such compromising business practices as selling slaves without fear of tainting their homes and families.

In the South, plantation women also held the status of lady. Supposedly freed from household duties by the presence of slaves, plantation mistresses were to enjoy leisure and pursue such activities as visiting and attending balls. Although these women's supervisory and other duties left them little true leisure time, they often adopted such ideals as domesticity, submissiveness, and service to others. Romantically portrayed in novels and the popular press as southern belles (an extreme model of the invented American woman), Southern women were, in truth, hardworking and competent. Because of the tensions inherent in an economic system based on slavery, as well as many other factors such as love and concern for family honor, they affected an exaggerated coyness and gentility to reflect well on their men. In effect, they had to work hard at not appearing to work hard. Like women in the Northeast, southern women often disliked the restrictions on their lives as well as the slave system with which they lived, but most confided such feelings only to close friends or recorded them in their diaries.

Even though, throughout the nation, middle- and upper-class ladies were the only women with the resources necessary to pursue true womanhood seriously, the concept soon reached the status of a widely held ideology which preached such virtues for all women. Even farm women, mill girls, and poor women began to aspire to true womanhood. But these women found that in reality they could adopt few aspects of such idealized domesticity.

For instance, while middle- and upper-class white women in the Northeast practiced true womanhood in pleasant homes on the periphery of cities, working- and lower-class white families lived in shantytowns, tenements, and slum districts of industrial cities. Disease and epidemics were rife, fire a constant threat, and the crime rate reputed to be the highest in the world. In addition, family violence, including wife and child abuse, was common. Given these dangerous conditions, working women wondered how they could possibly achieve domestic ideals and establish an aura of "morality" in their overcrowded and shabby homes. It was also impossible for them to properly train and rear children who were already engaged in full-time factory labor by the age of seven or eight.

Ladies

In order to help ladies—and other women who aspired to true womanhood—understand their roles and lifestyles, a plethora of prescriptive literature, ranging from guidebooks and etiquette manuals to didactic novels, began to flow from the presses. One popular guide cautioned a lady to keep secret any "learning" she might possess, "especially from the men, who generally look with a jealous and malignant eye on a woman of . . . cultivated understanding." Another book advised women to instill virtue in children, men, and servants. Others urged the need for a woman to marry, both for happiness and economic survival. "Her family is the source of all her joy," one proclaimed.

Extensive discussion ensued regarding what many Americans referred to as the "proper spheres of the sexes." It was generally agreed that men were to provide income and take care of public affairs. Women were to establish homes that would "dispel the gloom and restore the ease and comfort" of men after long days spent coping with weighty matters. Men would rule the public world, while women would preside over the home.

In this system, such fashionable "accomplishments" as playing the piano and speaking French became more important than ever for women who wished to attract a "suitable" husband. One young lady duly learned all the appropriate graces, including how to curtsy and dance. When she was about to wed, her mother told her that she must "please and make [her] husband happy."

In daily living, ladies were expected to enjoy the finer aspects of life. Because household chores and overseeing servants consumed only a portion of their days, ladies sought out a variety of other activities, including dressing lavishly in order to display their husbands' earning abilities and status. Ladies spent hours selecting clothing, which was usually ornate and overdone. Ribbons, flowers, flounces, and ruffles bedecked almost every outfit. Intricate hats and bonnets were absolute necessities, as were gloves, a parasol, reticule (purse), and high-buttoned shoes. These outfits contained as much as 100 yards of material and, in combination with whalebone stays and hoops, weighed fifteen to twenty pounds. When chemise, pantaloons, corset, corset cover, petticoats, and hoops were added, getting dressed was a one- to two-hour project. Once dressed, poring over samples of yard goods, ribbons, or bonnet makings in a favorite shop could consume many more hours.

In addition, Anglo ladies paid considerable attention to their complexions, which they believed should be delicate and pale. They protected their hands and face from the sun and avoided the use of "paints" on their face. A lady's pallor demonstrated her leisure, for paleness indicated little activity. She also avoided exercise other than maneuvering her hoopskirts into carriages and through doorways. Inactivity combined with tight corseting made the fainting couch a necessary piece of furniture for women who often felt weak and dizzy.

Ideal ladies took similar care with their decorum. They avoided discussing politics and current events, speaking only of approved ladylike topics. They used proper language that indicated their modesty: "limb" for "leg" and "female" or "lady" for "woman." European visitors reported that some American ladies were so modest that they even covered piano "limbs" with frilled trousers and draped nude statuary.

Ladies spent their spare time on a variety of activities. Most of them busied themselves with such fancy needlework as embroidery and such craft-work as the making of hyacinth stands and glove boxes. Almost all of them played the piano, sang, studied French, and pursued other female "accomplishments." They read, but limited themselves to "morally improving" works of literature and poetry. They also spent a good deal of time visiting other women during morning calls or afternoon teas. In fact, many women formed close ties with other women. In 1834, author Catharine Sedgwick wrote that strong, affectionate relationships between women were "nearest to the love of angels."

Raising children also required a lady's attention. Once again, the expanding American publishing industry celebrated the importance of American mothers. Authors of advice books and other writers touted mothers as the sole shapers of children's character and exhorted mothers to mold and train their children into virtuous and responsible people. Women were further cautioned to "let thy children be the darlings of thy tenderness." It was widely assumed that women's maternal love, now believed to be innate, would guide women in the proper disposal of their motherly duties.

In reality, most ladies spent few hours with their children, who were with nannies and tutors. When in their mother's company, boys were allowed to run and play certain games, but girls were expected to sit quietly sewing or reading. Children saw their fathers briefly at dinner or bedtime, often in their role as major disciplinarians of the family. The closeness of the colonial American family was clearly unknown to these middle- and upper-class children.

Ramifications of True Womanhood

The belief that women should be wives and mothers, cloistered in their homes, led to limitations for women in certain areas. For instance, newly established medical and law schools barred the admission of supposedly "delicate" women, while practicing physicians and attorneys refused them internships.

By the 1820s, all but three states mandated licenses for medical practitioners, but because licensing examinations covered techniques (such as the use of forceps) taught only in medical schools, women were incapable of succeeding even if they had been permitted to take the tests. Women, however, continued to train through apprenticeships and to practice as doctors and midwives without the benefit of formal licenses, especially in rural areas.

At the same time, numerous licensed doctors and self-styled experts increasingly counseled women that women's reproductive organs determined their physical health as well as their social roles. A malfunction of the uterus, thought to be linked to the entire nervous system, could cause backaches, headaches, insomnia, irritability, and a whole gamut of "nervous" disorders. Female ailments, as they were termed, supposedly determined a woman's emotions and achievements. Common treatments of women's illnesses included cauterizing the uterus, injecting saline into the uterus, and inserting leeches into the vagina.

RESISTANCE TO TRUE WOMANHOOD

Discontent Among Ladies

True womanhood was not as pervasive and powerful as it appeared, even among middle- and upper-class women. Although women generally found the endeavor of being ladies amusing for a few years, a growing number gradually turned to an examination of more serious topics, especially the many reform issues that characterized the 1820s, the so-called "Age of the Common Man." Democratization had spawned demands for widening the suffrage, property, and workingmen's reforms. Soon, ladies, who came together regularly in small groups for social activities, began to discuss what democratization and reform might mean to them.

Other factors also motivated middle- and upper-class women to think and talk about possible improvement in American society and law. The concept of separate spheres itself increased women's discontent. First, many women railed against limitations imposed on them by the idea of women's proper roles. Rather than spending their time in frivolous pursuits, they preferred to develop their own talents and skills. Second, woman's separate sphere caused a group consciousness to develop among middle- and upper-class women, which in turn led them to identify common problems. They saw themselves as a *type* of woman, living under restrictions that kept them from controlling family size, obtaining more than a superficial education, using their unique moral powers in the world outside their homes, or engaging in the arts or business. Third, the growth of companionate marriage made many women loath to release their husbands to the demands of business or the professions.

Little wonder, then, that the leaders of the first women's rights' movement came from the middle and upper classes. Women in general had a long history of social action and reform through such activities as boycotts, charity efforts, and petitions. Such factors as leisure, wealth, and separate spheres had helped create in women dis-ease, discontent, and a willingness to test the bounds of their sphere.

Gynecology and Obstetrics

Among white women, rebellion often began quietly and privately with concerns that dominated and shaped women's lives for most of their adult years—obstetrical and gynecological care. For thousands of women who relied on patent medicines heavy with opium, morphine, or alcohol rather than seek treatment from male physicians, modification of the medical establishment seemed absolutely necessary. Women resisted unenlightened medical practices in obstetrics and gynecology by exploring such cures as diet reform, animal magnetism, and phrenology. They also followed the advice of health reformers who stressed exercise, fresh air, and the consumption of grains.

Moreover, women sought out such unlicensed practitioners as Dr. Harriot K. Hunt, who, after having completed a medical apprenticeship, began practicing as a "female physician" in Boston in 1835. During the late 1830s, Hunt pursued homeopathic, preventive medicine and studied the psychological basis of women's medical problems. Licensed physicians derided Hunt's efforts; in her words, she was "entirely shut out from the medical world." Despite such opposition, she practiced successfully for over four decades.

In addition, women sought ways to control the numbers of children they bore. Although many forms of birth control such as abortions, douches, withdrawal, and condoms date back to ancient times, they were not widely used in the United States. By the 1820s, women were not only asking about birth control but were apparently utilizing various forms, including pessaries (devices to cover the cervix), condoms, withdrawal, and abortion, for the birthrate began to drop, at least among Anglo women in urban areas. This alarmed many Americans who feared population loss. Thus, beginning in 1829, many states began to pass laws against abortion. In 1832, when Charles Knowlton, a Massachusetts doctor, advocated "checks to conception," officials arrested and fined him.

In the matter of birthing, women acted on their fears regarding mother and infant mortality by marshaling anywhere from two to ten other women to help them through their pregnancies and deliveries. Such women helpers often assisted a woman during a difficult delivery, spoke for her when necessary, nursed her through recovery, and performed her household and other duties until she was on her feet. Although doctors tried to limit the number of such helpers in a delivery room, they recognized their importance to the women under their care.

Literature and Publishing

Another important beginning to the evolution of women's rights, especially among Anglo women, occurred in women's literature and publishing. Partly because industrialization had encouraged the development of improved machinery which produced an accessible and inexpensive print media, women's books and magazines began to proliferate. Increasingly, middle- and upper-class women had the education, money, and time to procure and read such journals as the *American Monthly Magazine*, which in 1829 argued that laws prohibiting women from owning property made husbands greedy and wives mean and concealing. Even in the conservative South, ladies could buy and read such reform literature as Mary Wollstonecraft's *Vindication of the Rights of Women*, which maintained that women needed and deserved liberation.

In addition, due to rising income and increased leisure, these women now had the time to pursue women's periodicals, which aimed to improve women's lives and minds with domestic recipes and hints, romanticized stories, and didactic tales. A leading producer of such women's literature was writer and editor Sarah Josepha Hale. After her husband's death in 1823, Hale began a millinery business and, on the side, built a sound reputation as a poet and novelist. After Hale's 1827 novel *Northwood* achieved renown, she founded in 1828 a woman's journal called the *American Ladies' Magazine*. In her first issue, Hale assured men that she intended to help women become more competent in their domestic duties and more agreeable as companions. She would achieve these ends by working for the improvement of "female education," which, in turn, would increase women's effectiveness as the moral and purifying forces of America.

Hale's approach proved appealing to both female and male readers. As a result, her competitor, Louis Godey, bought Hale's *Ladies' Magazine* and persuaded her to join him in Philadelphia. In 1836, Hale left Boston to become the editor of *Godey's Lady's Book*. As editor of *Godey's*, Hale became one of the primary proponents of the concepts of women's sphere and the moral powers of women. In her first issue in January 1837, she explained that *Godey's* mission was to "carry onward and upward the spirit of moral and intellectual excellence in our own sex, till their influence shall bless as well as beautify civil society." Hale soon demonstrated, however, that she planned to work a subtle subversion; she utilized the concept of women's sphere to expand women's activities. During her tenure as editor, Hale used women's imputed moral powers to argue for them as writers, social workers, teachers, Sunday school leaders, ministers, nurses, and doctors. Hale also hired women writers and illustrators, while encouraging the work of other talented women.

Improved Female Education

Among black women, reform emphasis fell more on education. Sarah Mapps Douglass, born a free black in Philadelphia, opened a school for free black children. In 1832, a group of Boston women protested their situations by forming a self-education group, the Afric-American Female Intelligence Society.

Black Catholic women also worked on behalf of education. In Washington, D.C., in 1820, Anne Marie Becroft opened a school for black girls. Nine years later in Baltimore, Elizabeth Lange and several friends established a school in Lange's home for black children. In 1829, Lange also founded the first community of black women Religious, later known as the Oblate Sisters of Providence. Two years later, Becroft left her school in another's care and joined the Oblate Sisters.

Yet another education-minded free woman of color was Marie Bernard Couvent of New Orleans, a former slave transported from Guinea, West Africa, at such an early age that she had no memory of her own parents. Couvent later gained her freedom and married. In 1832, as a widow, Couvent decided that her property would one day support a school for orphans. Couvent, who died in 1837, provided in her will for the "establishment of a free school for orphans of color." Later named Holy Redeemer School, it is now recognized as the oldest black Catholic school in the United States. Like white parochial schools, such black schools offered academic and religious instruction, but also gave vocational training to their students. Such schools sometimes also offered to black Catholic families extension courses in agriculture, health, and home economics.

As editor and reformer Sarah Josepha Hale had long realized, education was also a key issue for Anglo women. As early as the 1810s, advocates of what they termed "improved female education" began to dispute the widely accepted idea that women's minds were smaller and weaker than men's, thus making women uneducable. In 1818, Hannah Mather Crocker, granddaughter of Cotton Mather, stated in *Observations on the Real Rights of Women*: "There can be no doubt but there is as much difference in the powers of each individual of the male sex as there is of the female: and if they receive the same mode of education, their improvement would be fully equal." Other proponents of women's education similarly argued that if women were given "equal advantages" with men, they would soon prove that they were indeed educable.

Critics responded that there was no reason for women to obtain education since they were confined to domestic vocations. What difference would it make if women's minds were equal to men's since women did not need to use them in the same ways? Reformers turned the principles of domesticity to their own ends when they answered that motherhood demanded education if motherhood was to produce salutary adults. While Reformers did not wish to see a woman "emulate the schoolmen's fame," they did believe that a woman's "mental and moral improvement" was necessary for her success as a mother.

Several women tried to resolve this debate by educating women in "serious" subjects. Emma Hart Willard upgraded her Middlebury Seminary to show what women could do with such topics as algebra, trigonometry, history, and geography. In 1819, she appealed to the New York legislature for state aid for women's education. She had come to believe that female education could be equal only if it were publicly supported, as was men's. Not only was Willard's request refused, but a newspaper commented that "they will be educating the cows next." Willard resisted defeat and in 1821 founded the Troy Female Seminary in New York, the first school in the United States to offer a high-school education to women.

In 1826, Scottish-born reformer Frances Wright founded a community called Nashoba in Tennessee to educate black Americans and also began to lecture on the need for public education for all Americans, including women. "Until women assume the place in society which good sense and good feeling alike assign to them," Wright reasoned, "human improvement must advance but feebly." She concluded that, whereas "men establish their own pretensions upon the sacrificed rights of others, we do in fact impeach our own liberties, and lower ourselves in the scale of being."

Catharine Beecher tried to implement this philosophy. Throughout the 1820s, Beecher ran the Hartford Female Seminary with her sister, Mary. During these years, she proposed that schools for women be endowed, argued that teachers' assignments be limited to a few fields, and advocated the training of young women in domestic science and teaching. In the 1830s, Beecher established the Western Female Institute in Cincinnati, where she collaborated with William H. McGuffey on his famous readers. Beecher also joined the temperance movement and wrote extensively about women's domestic sphere, although she herself had decided not to marry.

In the meantime, other reformers concentrated on higher education for women. The Utopian community of Oberlin, Ohio, not only encouraged women to enhance their powers through advanced education but in 1833 founded Oberlin College, the first coeducational college in the nation. Mary Lyon of Massachusetts took a slightly different approach by arguing for separate women's colleges. Dissatisfied with her own meager training, Lyon decided in 1834 to found the first women's college in the United States. She wrote: "My heart has so yearned over the adult female youth in the common walks of life, that it has sometimes seemed as if there was a fire shut up in my bones."

Indeed, Lyon pursued with a fiery zeal her plan for "a residential seminary to be founded and sustained by the Christian public." She personally appealed to women for "five or ten dollars of hard-earned money, collected by the slow gains of patient industry." Although critics condemned her for traveling alone, Lyon persevered, and in 1837, her college, Mount Holyoke, enrolled its first student. The three-year course of study included Latin, science, and anatomy; tuition, room, and board cost sixty dollars a term. When Mary Lyon died in 1849, Mount Holyoke had attained a reputation as an outstanding teacher-training institution.

Other educational reformers added another dimension to the discussion when they raised the issue of women as teachers. As men left teaching for jobs that paid more and offered continuous, year-round employment, American society in general accepted women's entry into teaching in men's stead, for teaching seemed a logical extension of women's domestic duties. In addition, teaching offered good opportunities for women to exercise their supposedly innate moral sense and tenderness.

Despite low pay, little status, and no security, women rushed to fill the space left by men. Most women could live with the drawbacks because they planned to marry and fulfill their domestic destinies rather than fill these jobs for life. Consequently, teaching became classified as "women's work," with all the attendant disadvantages.

Supporters of women as teachers emphasized women's innately high character, capacity for affection that would make students respond to them, and maternal instincts that would allow women to build a greater rapport than would be proper for the "other sex," but pointed out that women still needed adequate training. These supporters issued an early call for improved education not just for women but for women who would serve as teachers of the nation's youth.

Religious Participation

Female evangelism, which continued to characterize the Second Great Awakening throughout the 1810s, 1820s, and 1830s, also helped women's reforms. Because the Awakening welcomed both white and black people, white and free black women participated in prayer meetings, special services, and revivals. In an effort to convert men, women also directed a militant piety against ungodly and unchurched men, yet women converts outnumbered men by three to two.

As women became the majority of congregants, clergy reacted by continuing to feminize their teachings. For example, in response to mothers' protests against the harsh doctrine of infant damnation due to innate human sin, ministers agreed that good Christian nurturing could offset original sin. This growing feminization of religion resulted in an emphasis on introspection and morality. Women learned to assess their own characters and believe in their strengths—two abilities that propelled them toward independence rather than toward domesticity. The stress that religion placed on brotherhood and equality of men before God became, for many women, a sense of sisterhood and equality of women before God.

Women also dominated the Sunday schools that were appearing in many churches. By claiming that their inherent virtue qualified them, rather than men, to instruct children in religious values, women essentially seized positions of power within their congregations. Their roles as Sunday-school teachers effectively allowed women to ignore the Pauline doctrine regarding women's silence in church.

In some sects, women even became preachers. The Freewill Baptists and the African Methodist Episcopal Church especially welcomed women as ministers. It is likely that several hundred women preached during the 1810s, 1820s, and 1830s, while a number achieved a measure of eminence. Harriet Livermore of New Hampshire was one of the best-known white women evangelists and Jerena Lee one of the most widely recognized African American women preachers. Through their devoted and selfless commitment to religion, such women created for themselves and other women a perception of women as capable of religious leadership.

Moral and Other Reform Causes

Female reform societies similarly enlarged women's roles. These groups emphasized the moral influence of women and urged their members to exert active control over the ethics and actions of their friends and neighbors. In 1818, the Colored Female Religious and Moral Reform Society organized in Salem, Massachusetts, while in 1828, the Coloured Female Roman Catholic Beneficial Society established itself in Washington, D.C. In 1834, another group of women reformers founded the New York Female Reform Society dedicated to the credo that "it is the imperious duty of ladies everywhere and of every religious denomination, to cooperate in the great work of moral reform." This society published a journal called *The Advocate* intended to denounce "sin" in all forms; hired several ministers to aid the needy in hospitals, jails, almshouses, and brothels; and stood vigils and prayed outside brothels.

During the 1830s, such female societies proliferated rapidly, encompassing large numbers of women. In 1835, seventy white women founded the Boston Female Moral Reform Society to assist needy women and combat prostitution, and soon attracted hundreds more members through rural auxiliaries. By 1837, the New York Female Reform Society counted 250 auxiliaries and 15,000 members.

Thousands of women also joined the American Temperance Society's crusade during the 1820s and 1830s. They either became members of men's temperance groups, where they soon found their participation strictly circumscribed, or they formed women's organizations in which they could vote, hold office, and set policy. Although white women's groups occasionally accepted black women as members, black women usually worked for the temperance cause within black associations. During these early years, women engaged primarily in exhortation and moral suasion to bring about temperance among drinkers.

Yet other women reformers, especially free women of color, attacked the slave system. As early as 1831, Mary Prince's *The History of Mary Prince, A West Indian Slave* exposed the horrors of Caribbean slavery. In addition, Maria Stewart, a black domestic in Connecticut, began to write and lecture. Stewart spoke to racially mixed audiences of men and women about abolition, colonization, education and employment opportunities for African Americans, and equality between the races. In that same year, free black Sarah Louisa Forten began contributing poems and essays to the abolitionist newspaper, *The Liberator*, while other free black women created the Minerva Literary Association of Philadelphia, a study and reading group that intended to "cultivate the talents entrusted" to its members' keeping and thus "break down the strong barrier" of racial prejudice in the United States.

The following year, 1832, when the Pennsylvania legislature considered a bill that would have required all blacks to carry passes, Sarah Mapps Douglass became a political activist. "One short year ago, how different were my feelings on the subject of slavery!" she exclaimed. But, when racism threatened her own freedom, Douglass determined "to use every exertion" in her power "to elevate the character of my wronged and neglected race." In 1833, Sarah Forten, Forten's mother, and two sisters helped found the Philadelphia Female Anti-slavery Society, after which Forten helped shape the group's policy and tirelessly organized antislavery sewing circles and charity fairs. Sarah Mapps Douglass also actively participated in the Philadelphia Female Anti-slavery Society.

White women championed abolitionism as well. One of the first to do so was author and editor Lydia Maria Child. Widely known for her editorship of *The Juvenile Miscellany*, a children's magazine, and her authorship of *The Frugal Housewife*, a household hint book, Child published the first American antislavery book in 1833. Entitled *An Appeal for that Class of Americans Called Africans*, Child's tract asked for justice and equality for black Americans. She pointed out that the "Negro woman is unprotected by either law or public opinion" and is thus "entirely subservient to the will of her owner." After Child's readers turned against her for her "unfeminine" involvement in political matters, Child became the editor of the *National Anti-Slavery Standard* and devoted the rest of her career to the cause of abolitionism.

About the same time that Child's book appeared, a Quaker teacher, Prudence Crandall, accepted a black student into her Canterbury Female Boarding School in Connecticut. Local authorities warned Crandall that if the young woman stayed, they would "ruin her school." Crandall bravely replied "let it sink, then. I shall not turn her out." When all of Crandall's white students withdrew, she converted her school, with the help of abolitionist editor William Lloyd Garrison, into the High School for Young Colored Ladies and Misses, which opened in April 1833. A storm of protest erupted in the town of Canterbury and a group of irate citizens declared that "the Government of the United States, the nation with all its institutions, of right belong to the white men, who now possess them."

Crandall attempted to carry on with her school, but was jailed during the summer of 1833 under a newly passed law that forbade the teaching of blacks in the state of Connecticut. The abolitionist press aired Crandall's case around the world, and she was finally freed on a technicality. Crandall returned to her school and to the continued harassment of townspeople who threw manure into her well, smashed the windows, threatened the students, and set fire to the building. After mob violence in September 1834, Crandall gave up. Recently married to an abolitionist minister, Crandall moved with her husband to Illinois, where she maintained an interest in reform until her death in 1890.

These initial attempts to help black slaves proved largely ineffectual, but they alerted many women to the need to organize antislavery societies. Beginning in 1832, the formation of the New England Anti-Slavery Society, the Connecticut Female Anti-Slavery Society, and others in numerous states and regions marked the entry of women into the largely male abolitionist movement.

Women's increasing involvement in the abolitionist cause received national attention in the mid-1830s because of the activities of two southern-born women, Angelina and Sarah Grimké. Raised in Charleston, South Carolina, as proper young ladies, both Grimké sisters grew up detesting slavery and resenting the restrictions inherent in true womanhood. In 1821, at age twenty-eight, Sarah moved to Philadelphia and joined the Society of Friends. Angelina followed Sarah to Philadelphia and into the Quaker fold in 1829. Angelina soon joined the Philadelphia Female Anti-Slavery Society, noting in her diary, "I am confident not many years will roll by before the horrible traffic in human beings will be destroyed."

The year 1836 proved a turning point for the sisters. When the American Anti-Slavery Society published Angelina's *Appeal to the Christian Women of the South*, indignant citizens in the South publicly burned copies of the pamphlet, while officials warned Angelina never to return to her home there. Soon, both women began to lecture against slavery. Their willingness to speak to audiences that included both women and men caused a great deal of public indignation. Undaunted, Angelina wrote a second pamphlet in 1837, *An Appeal to the Women of the Nominally Free States*, which argued that as long as slavery existed in the South it hurt the North as well.

The Arts

Some women also tested the boundaries in the arts. Of course, many women continued to produce quilts, rugs, bed coverings, wall hangings, and other artwork in their homes. The teachings of domesticity and true womanhood reassured women that if they created homes of "order and purity" women could exercise "a power that will be felt round the globe." Consequently, many talented women satisfied themselves with needle and thread instead of brush and paint and worked with pieces of cloth instead of on canvas.

Other women refused to accept such teachings and challenged the words of commentators who warned that "art is the most difficult—perhaps, in its highest form—almost impossible to women." Barred from enrolling in art schools and displaying in galleries, women did indeed have a difficult time learning the necessary skills. Women were believed to have a "natural repugnance" to drawing from "life," or in other words, from nude models. According to one minister, "no virtuous and delicate female . . . would desire to abate one jot or tittle from the seeming restrictions imposed upon her conduct."

Several women soon proved him wrong; they taught themselves and became practicing artists. One of the most notable of these was Eunice Pinney, who reared five children while becoming a prolific watercolor artist. Her vigorous and forthright work included landscapes, mourning pictures, and religious, historical, and literary scenes. Ruth Henshaw Bascom also combined domestic duties and art by "taking profiles" with pastel crayons.

A few of these women artists flaunted convention in other ways as well. Deborah Goldsmith, Susan Waters, and S. A. Shute traveled alone from town to town plying the trade of limner, or portrait painter. And Mary Ann Willson lived openly with a Miss Brundage, whom she described as her "romantic attachment," and augmented their income by selling her paintings. Highly original and lively, Willson's works were done with paints made from berries, brick dust, and vegetable dyes.

WOMEN OF COLOR

Applicability of True Womanhood

The concept of true womanhood had little meaning for most women of color, for their lives were configured more by race, religion, and other similar factors than by Anglo ideas regarding domesticity. Of course, some women of color, especially free African American and Spanish-speaking women of the middle and upper classes, already practiced their own version of true womanhood. But many women of color had not even heard about the idealized American woman, while others had little interest. Still others realized that their lives of toil and instability offered little opportunity to develop domestic "virtues," act "feminine," or raise children in "proper" ways.

Even though beliefs regarding true womanhood had little meaning for their lives, its implicit racism often exerted widespread and negative influence on women of color. For one thing, ideals of white womanhood underwrote policies and laws that affected women of color, frequently in a destructive manner. As a case in point, government officials in Washington, D.C., helped destroy the influence of Native American women through mandates that Indian women give up their customary, valued pursuit of agriculture and learn instead to sew, weave, and keep house like the far less prestigious Anglo housewife.

White society also used standards established for white women to judge women of color. Generally, white Americans regarded women of color as coarser in appearance and far less attractive than Anglo women. Because dark skin carried a negative connotation in white culture, only the occasional Indian "princess" or Mexican "señorita" was thought attractive—in an exotic and alien way.

Women of color usually faced a dismaying situation in regard to their actions as well. If a free black woman worked at heavy labor to support her family, critics deemed her unfeminine rather than energetic. And if Spanish-speaking women preferred the ease of low furniture and floor mats in place of upholstered sofas and carpets, Anglo observers thought them undomestic, incompetent, and even lazy.

A third way that the concept of true womanhood impinged on women of color was by disrupting their cultures. As American traders, merchants, and settlers fanned southward and westward over the continent, they not only carried Anglo standards with them, but inculcated them wherever they went. Because the travelers simply assumed that Anglo culture and goods were superior, they did not hesitate to force them on local populations. For instance, in 1821 when American merchants reached Santa Fe in New Mexico they offered to women such American products as whale-oil lamps, what-not stands, and commodes, products that would force women to spend more time caring for their new possessions, doing housework, and acting "domestic" in the approved Anglo sense of the term. The merchants also expected women to learn English, to cook white-style dishes, and to desert their families and religious affiliations to marry or cohabit with them.

American Indian Women

With the white population doubling every twenty-five years, it was clear that Thomas Jefferson's prediction that native peoples could live in peace west of the Mississippi River for many years to come would not hold true. Instead, during the 1810s and 1820s, settlers swept across the Ohio and lower Mississippi valleys, and by the late 1820s, began to cross the Mississippi River, pushing American Indians along ahead of them or destroying Indians and their societies.

In the process, settlers continued to borrow what they could from native peoples and cultures. Indian women served as guides, sexual partners, domestic servants, and teachers of agricultural methods yet seldom received recognition for their ingenuity and expertise. Instead, settlers recognized only those native women who helped them achieve their objectives. One of these, Milly Francis, a Creek Indian woman, received a congressional medal and a small pension for saving a white captive from death at the hands of Creek people in 1817.

Settlers also tended to impose their own ideas upon Native Americans. For instance, during the 1830s, the United States Commissioner of Indian Affairs classified the Cherokee as a hunting society because the men hunted. This view overlooked the fact that Cherokee women had been adept and productive agriculturalists for centuries. The Commissioner's office declared that Cherokee women must be taught to spin and weave while the men must be taught to farm. Not only did this prescription slight women's work, but it forced men to grow crops, long considered uniquely women's prerogative.

Nor were settlers very accepting of natives who took on gender roles associated with the biologically opposite sex. Whites generally reviled those native women who became warriors and spent their lives hunting, fighting, and taking wives. Although Native American tribes ranging from the Creek to the Hopi and the Navaho to the Zuni accepted homosexuality, white settlers and government agents often opposed its existence.

During the 1820s and 1830s, President Andrew Jackson's removal policy forced thousands of Native Americans onto the westward trail. The route Indians traveled between East and West earned the designation Trail of Tears because of the illnesses, deaths, and other tragedies that occurred there. The Five Civilized Tribes, especially the Cherokee, lost not only land, but saw many of their people and much of their culture destroyed in the process of removal.

Indian women frequently responded to destructive policies and treatment by shielding Indian history and customs from the view of Anglos, by fighting alongside native men to stave the Anglo advance, and by refusing to cooperate with removal. Anglo settlers often commented on the ferocity and passion of enraged native women, but they seldom, if ever, speculated that their own policies and attitudes had elicited such reactions. When Anglos found Native American women aggressive rather than accepting, they branded Indian women "hostile" rather than "protective" of their families and cultures.

Native women's culture, however, was both rich and complex. Among other things, they were active farmers, producers, and traders. In Minnesota, trader Jean Baptiste Faribault bartered with Dakota women who brought him tanned furs, maple sugar, and sometimes corn. In exchange, Faribault gave them awls, axes, beads, hatchets, hoes, iron knives, silver ornaments, and tin kettles. These women used such tools as awls to punch holes in leather before stitching it together with deer sinew and decorating the leather with quills or beads and metal tinkling cones.

Slave Women

Most black women found their roles and lifestyles dictated by the slave system. They had little control over their domesticity, childcare practices, or even the moral climate in which they lived. On northern farms and southern plantations, slave women performed a wide variety of taxing jobs, ranging from the unskilled to skilled. In the "big-house" on southern plantations, slave women labored long hours at domestic tasks. Here, or in adjacent outbuildings, they cooked, butchered, preserved, spun, wove, sewed, and knitted. Although these women worked inside and could glean scraps of food and clothing, they also endured constant surveillance, harsh punishment, and isolation from families and friends. They shared the same gender with their mistresses, but race and class differences effectively separated most slave women from their white supervisors. Moreover, mistresses usually expected house slaves to learn white ways of speaking, acting, keeping house, and rearing children, a process of cultural assimilation that sometimes alienated slave women from other slaves.

In plantation fields, slave women planted, cultivated, and harvested crops, especially cotton. Some owners and overseers grouped women, boys, and elderly men into hoe gangs, while they organized robust men into plow gangs. Women made especially adept pickers, bringing in as much as 150 pounds a day. In other cases, smaller planters seldom owned enough slaves to divide them into gender-specific work gangs. According to one slave woman on such a plantation, women's work was difficult to distinguish from men's: "I have done everything on a farm what a man done 'cept cut wheat. I split rails like a man. I used a iron wedge drove into the wood with a maul. I drive the gin, what was run by two mules."

Other slave women worked in skilled positions, including artisans and midwives. One slave woman who was trained as a midwife at the age of thirteen earned substantial sums of money for her owner, but derived no pay or other benefits herself. In her words, "I made a lot o' money for old miss. Lots of times, didn't get sleep regular or git my meals on time for three-four days. Cause when dey call, I always went."

Yet other slave women labored away from plantations. In southern industry, they performed heavy work in cotton and woolen mills, turpentine camps, sugar refineries, food and tobacco factories, hemp manufactories, foundries, saltworks, and mines. They also labored as lumberjacks and ditch diggers, and helped build roads and levees and lay track for southern railroads. In southern cities, slave women worked as chambermaids, nursemaids, hairdressers, seamstresses, domestic servants, and vendors. Usually these women's wages reverted to their owners. Only occasionally were slave women permitted to keep part of their pay or apply a portion to buying themselves out of slavery.

In spite of their large economic contributions to the development of the southern economy, black slave women were generally denied not only wages but privileges and other recognition of their labor. In addition, slave women encountered gender-related difficulties, especially sexual coercion and rape by both white and black men. When children resulted from unions with their masters, slave women usually lacked the time and resources to care for them properly, while children of black unions were sometimes seized at birth or sold away from their mothers as young children. Black women rebelled against such sexual and economic exploitation by avoiding sexual relationships with both white and black men, aborting unwanted fetuses, and committing infanticide to save a child from slavery.

Despite such resistance, women were encouraged to reproduce as frequently as possible. Even though Caribbean and other non-African peoples had become an important source of slaves, the southern agricultural system demanded more hands all the time. Owners sometimes threatened women with beatings, solitary confinement, or sale if they refused to bear children, or promised women extra food, additional clothing, or larger cabins if they did so. Some black women called breeders even brought high prices and elicited special care from their owners. As one slave woman noted, the more children she had, the more she was worth.

In the face of such adversity, slave women usually proved independent and strong. They resisted slavery in both subtle and blatant ways. On the one hand, a woman might steal food, lie, plot against her owners, or feign illness or pregnancy to gain a few days' reprieve from the fields. On the other, a woman might strike an overseer or run away. Newspaper advertisements for runaways indicate that women accounted for 10 to 15 percent of the total. In 1834, the *South Carolina Gazette* carried the following advertisement: "Run away about five weeks ago from Hugh Campbell, a Negro wench named Flora, she has a scar on her forehead." Campbell offered a reward of thirty shillings for the return of Flora, who could expect punishment ranging from whipping and branding to mutilation.

Women also survived slavery by drawing strength from their marriages, which they regarded as a critical part of their lives. Marriages, however, often ended through the death or sale of one spouse or the other. Death ended approximately 45 percent of slave marriages, while sale ended another 32 percent. As one black minister noted, slaves married "until death or distance do you part." As a result of the instability of marriage under slavery, black women often raised their families without the aid of men and devoted much of their energy to maintaining kinship ties and to creating new kin networks when slavery destroyed old ones.

Hard work, poor nutrition, threats to the family under slavery, and resistance to sexual exploitation contributed to a lower birth rate for slave women than for many other groups at the time. Slave women in the upper South carried and bore only an average of five to six children, while women in the lower South bore slightly more. Typically, slave women formed extremely close bonds with their children. Some owners allowed women time off for birth and childcare, but others continued to work women at their regular tasks. Pregnant women even labored in the fields, and, in-between planting or hoeing, new mothers nursed the babies elderly women brought to them in the field. In spite of the barriers, strong mother-child bonds developed, which may have accounted for the fact that fewer slave women ran away than did men. Other women were less fortunate; sale or death denied them the right to raise their own offspring at all.

To preserve their sense of themselves as women, slave women often followed a strict division of labor in their homes. This is the one realm in which true womanhood had the most meaning for them. In one-room cabins with dirt floors, they could pretend to be the women they could not be in the fields or even the big-house. Thus, slave women performed most housekeeping tasks and childcare chores themselves, maintaining their homes with pride and tending their families with care. Like white working women, they put in a double day. But, in their homes, they could also put aside the deferential behavior they displayed to owners and overseers, teach their children respect for their race, and cling to native or other customs.

Free Black Women

Free black women were slightly better off than slave women. Composed of approximately half African American women and half from such Caribbean countries as Haiti and Jamaica, free women of color typically held paid employment. To improve their situations, they formed clubs and organizations, including abolitionist societies. They wrote and published widely, contributing heavily to magazines and to the more than one hundred works of fiction, protest, and autobiography written by free blacks between 1810 and 1860. Free black women also had the right, at least theoretically, to protest against injustice and to use the courts.

Yet most free black women were underpaid and denied opportunities for education or advancement. They held exhausting jobs and sometimes headed households formed by circumstance rather than their own choices. In the South, women, who constituted 53 percent of free blacks, usually lived in cities, where they could procure jobs, join churches and other organizations, or even start small businesses. In the streets of Charleston, South Carolina, for example, women vendors hawked everything from vegetables to fish.

In some cases, southern free black women achieved affluence. In New Orleans, black Creole women owned property and often held respected positions in the community. Some of these free black women were so successful that they even owned slaves who labored on their farms and in their other businesses.

In northern cities, a different situation existed. Factory owners usually avoided hiring free women of color. Thus, approximately two-thirds of free black women sought employment as domestic servants, usually working for white women who believed them docile and passive. White employers usually required black domestics to live in and treated them much like surrogate slaves.

Other northern free black women sewed, or took in laundry, often for the fee of one cent per shirt. Still others engaged in hairdressing, flower-selling, hat-cleaning, or provided additional services, including prostitution. But some were not able to find jobs at all. In 1827, a black newspaper, *Freedom's Journal*, listed forty-three black women paupers in New York City alone.

Like their slave counterparts, free black women worked diligently to cultivate meaningful values and activities in their own lives and those of family members. But, unlike slave women, free women of color had far more opportunity to establish homes, enjoy families, and try to improve their lives. They could also incorporate aspects of domesticity, true womanhood, and piety into their lives. In 1816, for example, Philadelphia women participated in the establishment of the African Methodist Episcopal Church. Such black leaders as Rebecca Cox, Julia A. J. Foote, and Jarena Lee preached the importance of confronting black issues, including civil rights, employment, and education. Lee later explained that during her preaching she felt as if her "tongue was cut loose," and "the love of God, and of his service, burned with a vehement flame" within her.

Throughout the 1830s, free black women also continued to work for racial reform. At a time when Frances Wright and abolitionist Abigail Kelley were among the few white women brave enough to mount the public lecture platform and black lecturers were almost unknown, Maria Miller Steward, a Connecticut free black, lectured publicly on behalf of her people. Other free women of color joined antislavery societies, opened schools, and worked for improved medical care and employment opportunities.

Spanish-speaking Women

In 1819, a number of Spanish-speaking women discovered that they had become American citizens. After the Adams-Onís Treaty, in which Spain renounced all claims to West Florida and ceded East Florida to the United States, women gradually learned that they no longer lived under Spanish law and custom, but those of the United States instead. As a result, those women who enjoyed property and other rights soon lost them.

In addition, thousands of other Spanish-speaking women lived just outside U.S. boundaries, inhabiting Mexico's northern frontier, which reached into Texas, New Mexico, Arizona, and California. Spanish-speaking women in the Southwest were usually Catholic, community- and family-oriented, and used to male authority. Most lived in patriarchal families linked through an intricate system of kinship and godparents. Although daily work roles usually divided by gender, women assisted men in family enterprises. In Texas, women helped men establish great cattle ranches, based upon a Spanish-derived system of land titles. In New Mexico and Arizona, families farmed, traded, or mined, especially copper in Arizona, while in California women helped to trade by sea or worked farms, cattle and sheep ranches, and mines.

In 1821, when Mexico declared its independence from Spain, it appeared that Mexico would rise to wealth and fame. But it proved difficult for people scattered over more than 850,000 miles to develop their holdings and restrain eager Americans. By such routes as the Santa Fe Trail to New Mexico and the Old Spanish Trail to Los Angeles, Mexican lands were well within reach of American explorers, traders, merchants, and settlers.

In 1821, the same year Mexico proclaimed its liberty, Mexican officials opened Texas to Americans who promised to convert to Roman Catholicism and assume Mexican citizenship. Four years later, some 2,000 Americans lived in Texas, including nearly 450 slaves who worked on American-owned cotton plantations. When American settlers in Texas neglected to fulfill their promises and remained American in their loyalties, the Mexican government adopted the Colonization Law of 1830, which forbade further American settlement and prohibited the introduction of any more slaves. In 1836, Americans and Mexicans clashed at the Alamo, and Americans declared Texas an independent republic.

A similar process occurred in New Mexico. Also in 1821, Missourian William Becknell pushed American trade into the Mexican state of New Mexico. Local people welcomed American traders; women appreciated American cooking utensils, household goods, and rich American fabrics and styles. Middle- and lower-class women began to replace their skirts, blouses, and shawls with outfits featuring full skirts, petticoats, and hoops. Soon trade routes linked St. Louis, Santa Fe, and San Francisco, bringing in addition to goods American migrants, some of whom married Spanish-speaking women.

In the Rio Arriba valley, the center of Spanish culture in the Southwest, as many as 75 percent of foreign-born men married local women, usually of the lower and middle classes. Because church marriages were expensive and Spanish frontier society accepted cohabitation, another group married by common law. By the 1830s, the majority of men who married native women listed America as their place of origin and such occupations as trapper, trader, or merchant as their trade. In addition to acquiring wives and families, these men gained certain trade privileges and naturalization as Mexican citizens. Women obtained successful husbands and could bear lighter-skinned children, considered at the time as higher caste than those of dark complexion.

More than two-thirds of husbands stayed with their wives and children, establishing long-term relationships, adopting *tortillas* and *frijoles* as standards of their diets, and learning at least enough Spanish to function on a daily basis. The rest, however, disappeared, leaving their wives and children to support themselves. Thus, although intermarriage aided cultural adaptation of the two groups, it also disrupted kin networks and caused some Spanish-speaking women to mistrust American men.

Other problems also developed between Spanish-speaking residents and Anglo migrants. Legal systems clashed, as in California, where American expatriates favored legal codes that fostered more individualism than did existing Mexican laws. Also, Anglo miscegenation laws now prohibited intermarriage, a long-standing tradition in the region. In addition, as more Anglo women entered the area, they tended to judge Spanish-speaking women by their own standards of domesticity and true womanhood. As a result, Anglo women usually misinterpreted and misunderstood local women's behavior. They sharply criticized local women for their religious practices, or for dancing, drinking, and gambling, all socially acceptable pastimes for women in Spanish frontier society of the time.

As more Americans poured into Texas, New Mexico, and California during the mid-1830s, and in far smaller numbers into Arizona, friction increased. In East Texas, for example, *Tejanos* (Texas Mexicans) withdrew from the Anglo population, forming their own communities. Throughout the Southwest, women, especially of the upper classes, often thought Americans rough, boorish, and dishonest. They increasingly relied upon their own churches, families, and organizations as sources of support. At the same time, Americans frequently judged Spanish-speaking women, especially those of the lower classes, loud, unkempt, and immoral. These vastly overdrawn stereotypes revealed not only the clash of two different cultures but the nativist and racial prejudices of the era that would soon drive these groups even further apart.

WOMEN IN THE WEST

Women on the Trails

During the 1810s, 1820s, and 1830s, settlers poured into the Old Southwest and the Old Northwest, filling areas that became such states as Indiana, Illinois, Missouri, Arkansas, Michigan, Florida, and Texas. By the early 1830s, some settlers crossed the Mississippi River into Iowa and Wisconsin, while by the mid-1830s, some migrants were even beginning to travel the Oregon Trail, heading toward Oregon or California. In 1836,

Eliza Hart Spalding and Narcissa Whitman became the first white women to cross the Rocky Mountains; both entered the Oregon Territory as missionaries.

Men often made the decision to migrate, dictating that wives and daughters pack their things, or ordering slave women to load their goods and themselves into wagons. In other cases, women favored the move; they could appreciate the chance of restored health for a family member in a more favorable climate, the opportunity to recoup a financial disaster sustained by the family, a fortune to be gained from the utilization of natural resources, or the potential of a prosperous future on cheap, available land.

Women found migration attractive for other reasons as well. Some slave women begged to go, especially to California, in hopes of eventual emancipation. Free black women chose migration because they anticipated less prejudice in frontier areas. Army wives chose to follow their husbands to frontier forts. Religious orders of women relocated to serve and educate native peoples. Single women chose to migrate in order to find husbands, procure employment, take up land, or serve as missionaries and teachers. And European women wanted homes where their families could enjoy landownership, practice religious toleration, or escape tyrannical governments.

For many reasons, then, women began the trek with husbands, families, and friends in conveyances that ranged from stagecoaches and railroad cars to the legendary Conestoga wagon. Wagons, either the smaller emigrant wagon or the larger prairie schooner, were popular because they contained abundant space for people and possessions. Men equipped wagons with running gear, trained horses or oxen, and prepared tools, firearms, and stock. Women stitched wagon covers and readied food, clothing, bedding, and medicines.

While these arrangements progressed, people began to prepare themselves for the coming traumatic separation from the friends and family with whom they had spent their lives. After tearful and often prolonged partings, the migrants were on their way. Once on the trail, they were far from alone. Their diaries tell of meeting old friends and neighbors and of making new friends. Women visited with other women and exchanged recipes and bits of useful trail lore. One woman's diary contained frequent references to storytelling, song, music, and merrymaking.

Although loneliness was not part of the trail routine for women, hard work was. Daily living had to continue despite the trail environment. Women cooked meals over campfires, laid beds out under the stars, and washed clothing in streams, while men frequently set up tables, started fires, and even cooked. Because of trail conditions, women's work became more complex and more wearying than it had been before departure. In addition, many trail women were pregnant or nursing infants, which further complicated their numerous trail duties.

Yet women's complaints were not overwhelming. Both free black and white women seemed to draw strength from the tenets of domesticity and true womanhood. Kitturah Belknap, on her way to Iowa in the 1830s, prided herself on her "housekeeping." She took "good earthen dishes" backed up with tinware and "four nice little table cloths" that she made. Belknap supplemented her family's food by buying fresh produce from farms, baking bread that she set to rise on the warm ground under the wagon during the night, and producing rolls of butter by letting the motion of the lurching wagon operate the churn inside it.

Women also utilized the teachings of domesticity to get them through hard times. Black and white, they rallied as wives and mothers, providing strength and support even when the weather was frightful, wagons broke down, oxen died, and people fell ill and died. Women also helped with men's work such as driving the wagon or herding stock at the same time that they tried to protect their children from trail accidents.

Most women recognized that their efforts were crucial to the success of the migration. Any domestic routines that they could establish, any help that they could offer, any support that they could give were all hedges against the disintegration of the undertaking. In addition, most female migrants were farm women who were familiar with the tasks demanded of them. They approached the trail experience as a time of transition, during which they could hone their skills and prepare their minds for what lay ahead. One stated simply, "I never thought about its being hard. I was used to things being hard."

Women as Settlers

When women arrived in their new homes they had mixed reactions. Many reported feelings of dismay regarding native peoples, cold winters, wet springs, hot summers, mosquitoes, and "wild beasts." Some women grew discouraged and gave up. As one explained, "some liked the new country, but others returned to their Native states."

But most women stayed on, whether they liked the area or not. As one woman recalled, "when we got to the new purchase, the land of milk and honey, we were disappointed and homesick, but we were there and had to make the best of it." Another pragmatically wrote to her mother: "I can't say I like the West as well as I do New England yet I think it is better for me to be here."

At the same time, other women felt ecstatic at the sight of green rolling valleys, flowing rivers, and miles of unfarmed land. One young woman claimed not to be disillusioned even when she saw the primitive log cabin that was her new home. In "girl fashion," she explained, "I considered it very romantic."

Most women were less pleased with their first houses, which ranged from the wagons that carried them westward to a corncrib, abandoned outbuilding, lean-to, tar-paper shack, sod hut, or log cabin. But, despite conditions, women turned their energies to converting their first shelters into homes for their families and workplaces for themselves. In the Old Southwest, these housekeepers suffered from scorching sun, oppressive humidity, torrential rains, bugs, and snakes. In the Old Northwest, women often complained of frost on the walls, snowflakes on the blankets and table, and ice on the floors. In some regions, wind was the major problem because it carried dust into clothing, cooking utensils, and food.

Women endured all because they realized that their early homes represented the youth of the frontier and marked a stage that every raw community had to tolerate. So women hung quilts as room dividers, papered the walls with newspapers or painted them with lime, and created household furnishings out of packing crates and rope.

With her workplace established, the frontierswoman turned her energies to producing candles, soap, clothing, foodstuffs, and a wide variety of other domestic goods. All of these products demanded ingenuity, expertise, and incredible amounts of time. In addition, women bore many children, educated them, and trained them as domestic or field laborers. Women were also expert herbalists who served as apothecaries and morticians to their families and friends. And they brought in all the cash that many families would ever see through the sales of their butter, eggs, knitted goods, and other products.

Most frontierswomen found that the worst was over in about two years. They moved into better homes, could buy many items from stores in new towns that rapidly sprang up, and had friends and neighbors to relieve the initial loneliness. Churches and schools also appeared, which gave women other social outlets.

Women also left the fields as soon as they could. They then limited themselves primarily to the house, garden, and barn. Thus, the frontier, contrary to popular belief, did not break down the usual division of labor along gender lines. Rather, frontierswomen perpetuated the same labor system within the family that they had always known.

Nor did the frontier eradicate laws and policies restricting women. When Indiana applied for statehood in 1815, women could not make wills, convey property, or control their own incomes. Indiana became the nineteenth state on 11 December 1816, but nearly thirty years would pass before Indiana adopted legislation protecting married women's property and Hoosiers began to discuss the possibility of women voting.

Similarly, racial prejudice and discrimination went westward with the settlers. In the Old Southwest and adjacent areas, many migrants took slaves with them, intending to raise tobacco or cotton. In 1822, settlers from Virginia brought four slave valets and a woman called Mammy to Missouri. During the first years after arrival, the four black men helped break and farm the land outside the cabin, while Mammy helped inside.

In the Northwest, settlers initially helped each other regardless of race, but as areas became more settled, racial lines reappeared. Although these states and territories legally prohibited slavery, the status of black people often remained unclear. As a case in point, in 1820 officers at Fort Snelling, Minnesota, brought male and female slaves with them. Later, however, a slave woman named Rachel who resided at army posts in Minnesota between 1831 and 1834 successfully sued for freedom in 1835. Fearful of what they called black incursions, some northwestern areas even passed exclusion laws to keep out free black Americans, or denied property and other rights to those who entered the Northwest.

Domesticity and true womanhood also accompanied the migrants. Many of the frontierswomen who managed to leave the fields attempted to reestablish domesticity and other feminine values in their huts and cabins. For example, although hoops often swept skirts into open fireplaces where they singed, women continued to wear them. They also wore sunbonnets to protect their faces from the sun and retain their pale complexions. And they decorated their homes with craft-work and folk art, particularly exquisite quilts that often told a story or recorded family history. Elizabeth Mitchell of Kentucky used her Coffin Quilt to note family deaths by taking labeled coffins from the quilt's border and moving them into the graveyard in its center.

At the same time, however, frontierswomen resisted some of the tenets of domesticity and true womanhood. Especially in the Northwest, they sought education in the country schoolhouses and early women's seminaries, for coeducation constituted an accepted practice in the West from the beginning. Only six years after the Black Hawk Purchase Treaty opened Iowa for settlement in 1833, a Dubuque woman announced the founding of an academy that would provide a "good English education" to both men and women.

Women also rapidly moved into teaching and took paid employment as railway station agents, team drivers, shepherds, store clerks, prostitutes, lawyers, musicians, artists, authors, journalists, and a wide variety of other jobs. And they sometimes voted in local elections and discussed such issues as equality, landownership, and the right of suffrage.

What was the essence of the American woman between 1812 and 1837? In 1835, French visitor Alexis de Tocqueville described the American woman as protected and elevated, while he interpreted the American family as a miniature democracy, with the man as its head and the woman and children as its citizens. Only two years later, however, English writer and traveler Harriet Martineau reported that the American woman's intellect was confined, her morals crushed, health ruined, weakness encouraged, and strength punished, while the family was "a poor institution" in which "one sex overbears the other."

The reason for this apparent contradiction is that no "American woman" existed. Despite the teachings of domesticity and true womanhood, American women remained disparate in race, class, and other characteristics. Nor did they all adhere to the dictates of true womanhood. Along with the twin forces of industrialization and national expansion, women more often challenged than accepted the invented American woman.

Suggestions for Further Reading

Alexander, Adele Logan. *Ambiguous Lives: Free Women of Color in Rural Georgia, 1789–1879.* Fayetteville: University of Arkansas Press, 1991.

Berthoff, Rowland. "Conventional Mentality: Free Blacks, Women, and Business Corporations as Unequal Persons, 1820–1870," *Journal of American History* 76 (December 1989): 753–84.

Billington, Louis. "'Female Laborers in the Church': Women Preachers in the Northeastern United States, 1790–1840," *Journal of American Studies* 19 (December 1985): 369–94.

Blackwood, Evelyn, "Sexuality and Gender in Certain Native American Tribes: The Case of Cross-Gender Females," *Signs* 10 (Autumn 1984): 27–42.

Blewett, Mary H. *Men, Women, and Work: Class, Gender, and Protest in the New England Shoe Industry, 1780–1910.* Champaign-Urbana: University of Illinois Press, 1988.

Boydston, Jeanne. *Home and Work: Housework, Wages, and the Ideology of Labor in the Early Republic.* New York: Oxford University Press, 1990.

Boylan, Anne M. "Evangelical Womanhood in the Nineteenth Century: The Role of Women in Sunday Schools," *Feminist Studies* 4 (October 1978): 62–80.

Braude, Ann. *Radical Spirits: Spiritualism and Women's Rights in Nineteenth-Century America.* Boston: Beacon Press, 1989.

Brown, Irene Quenzler. "Death, Friendship, and Female Identity During New England's Second Great Awakening," *Journal of Family History* 12 (October 1987): 367–87.

Brownlee, W. Elliot. "Household Values, Women's Work, and Economic Growth, 1800–1923," *Journal of Economic History* 39 (March 1979): 199–209.

Carlisle, Marcia. "Disorderly City, Disorderly Women: Prostitution in Ante-Bellum Philadelphia," *Pennsylvania Magazine of History and Biography* 110 (October 1986): 549–68.

Cashin, Joan. *A Family Venture: Men and Women on the Southern Frontier.* New York: Oxford University Press, 1991.

Clifford, Deborah Pickman. *Crusader for Freedom: A Life of Lydia Maria Child.* Boston: Beacon Press, 1992.

Clinton, Catherine. *The Plantation Mistress: Woman's World in the Old South.* New York: Pantheon Books, 1980.

———. *The Other Civil War: American Women in the Nineteenth Century.* New York: Hill and Wang, 1984. Chapter 2.

Cott, Nancy F. *The Bonds of Womanhood: "Woman's Sphere" in New England, 1780–1835.* New Haven, CT: Yale University Press, 1977.

Coultrap-McQuin, Susan. *Doing Literary Business: American Women Writers in the Nineteenth Century.* Chapel Hill: University of North Carolina Press, 1990.

Craver, Rebecca McDowell. *The Impact of Intimacy: Mexican-Anglo Intermarriage in New Mexico, 1821–1846.* El Paso: Texas Western Press, 1982.

Davis, Marianna W. *Contributions of Black Women to America.* Vol. II. Columbia, South Carolina: Kenday Press, 1981. Pages 21–69 (on slavery).

Dewhurst, C. Kurt, Betty MacDowell, and Marsha MacDowell. *Artists in Aprons: Folk Art by American Women.* New York: E. P. Dutton, 1979.

Dublin, Thomas. *Women at Work: The Transformation of Work and Community in Lowell, Massachusetts, 1826–1860.* New York: Columbia University Press, 1979.

———. *Farm to Factory: The Mill Experience and Women's Lives in New England, 1830–1860.* New York: Columbia University Press, 1981.

Dudden, Faye E. *Serving Women: Household Service in Nineteenth-Century America.* Middletown, CT: Wesleyan University Press, 1983.

Ellison, Mary. "Resistance to Oppression: Black Women's Response to Slavery in the United States," *Slavery and Abolition* 4 (May 1983): 56–63.

Epstein, Barbara Leslie. *The Politics of Domesticity: Women, Evangelism, and Temperance in Nineteenth-Century America.* Middletown, CT: Wesleyan University Press, 1981.

Foner, Philip S., and Josephine F. Pacheco. *Three Who Dared: Prudence Crandall, Margaret Douglass, Myritilla Miner—Champions of Antebellum Black Education.* Westport, CT: Greenwood Press, 1984.

Fox-Genovese, Elizabeth. *Within the Plantation Household: Black and White Women of the Old South.* Chapel Hill: University of North Carolina Press, 1988.

Friedman, Jean E., William G. Shade, and Mary Jane Capozzoli. *Our American Sisters: Women in American Life and Thought.* 4th ed. Lexington, MA: D.C. Heath & Co., 1987. Chapters 6–7.

Golden, Claudia. "The Economic Status of Women in the Early Republic: Quantitative Evidence," *Journal of Interdisciplinary History* 16 (Winter 1986): 375–404.

Gordon, Jean. "Early American Women Artists and the Social Context in Which They Worked," *American Quarterly* 30 (Spring 1978): 54–69.

Gordon, Linda. "The Long Struggle for Reproductive Rights," *Radical America* 15 (Spring 1981): 74–88.

Gutiérrez, Ramón. "Honor, Ideology, Marriage Negotiation, and Class-Gender Domination in New Mexico, 1690–1846," *Latin American Perspectives* 12 (Winter 1985): 81–104.

———. *When Jesus Came, the Corn Mothers Went Away: Marriage, Sexuality, and Power in New Mexico, 1500–1846.* Stanford: Stanford University Press, 1991.

Gutman, Herbert G. *The Black Family in Slavery and Freedom, 1750–1925.* New York: Pantheon Books, 1976.

Hagler, D. Harland. "The Ideal Woman in the Antebellum South: Lady or Farmwife?" *Journal of Southern History* 65 (August 1980): 405–18.

Handler, Bonnie. "Prudence Crandall and Her School for Young Ladies and Little Misses of Color," *Vitae Scholasticae* 5 (Spring/Fall 1986): 199–210.

Hardesty, Nancy A. *Women Called to Witness: Evangelical Feminism in the 19th Century.* Nashville: Abingdon Press, 1984.

Harley, Sharon. "Northern Black Female Workers: Jacksonian Era," 5–16, in *The Afro-American Woman: Struggles and Images*, edited by Sharon Harley and Rosalyn Terborg-Penn. Port Washington, NY: Kennikat Press, 1978.

Hewitt, Nancy A., ed. *Women, Families, and Communities: Readings in American History.* Vol. I. Glenview, IL: Scott, Foresman, & Co., 1990. Parts 3–4.

Hine, Darlene. "Female Slave Resistance: The Economics of Sex," *Western Journal of Black Studies* 3 (Summer 1979): 123–27.

Hoffert, Sylvia D. *Private Matters: American Attitudes Toward Child-bearing and Infant Nurture in the Urban North, 1800–1860.* Champaign-Urbana: University of Illinois Press, 1988.

Holland-Braund, Kathryn E. "Guardians of Tradition and Handmaidens to Change: Women's Roles in Creek Economic and Social Life During the Eighteenth Century," *American Indian Quarterly* 14 (1990): 311–44.

Jeffrey, Julie Roy. *Converting the West: A Biography of Narcissa Whitman.* Norman: University of Oklahoma Press, 1991.

Jensen, Joan M., and Darlis A. Miller. "The Gentle Tamers Revisited: New Approaches to the History of Women in the American West," *Pacific Historical Review* 49 (May 1980): 173–214.

Jensen, Joan M., and Sue Davidson, eds. *A Needle, a Bobbin, a Strike: Women Needleworkers in America.* Philadelphia: Temple University Press, 1984.

Jones, Jacqueline. "'My Mother Was Much of a Woman': Black Women, Work, and the

Family Under Slavery," *Feminist Studies* 8 (Summer 1982): 235–69.

Kaufman, Polly Welts. *Women Teachers on the Frontier*. New Haven, CT: Yale University Press, 1984.

Kessler-Harris, Alice. *Out to Work: A History of Wage-Earning Women in the United States*. New York: Oxford University Press, 1982.

———. *A Woman's Wage: Historical Meanings and Social Consequences*. Lexington: University of Kentucky Press, 1994.

Kolodny, Annette. *The Land Before Her: Fantasy and Experience of the American Frontiers, 1630–1860*. Chapel Hill: University of North Carolina Press, 1984.

Langum, David J. *Law and Community on the Mexican California Frontier: Anglo-American Expatriates and the Clash of Legal Traditions, 1821–1846*. Norman: University of Oklahoma Press, 1987.

Lantz, Herman, Martin Schultz, and Mary O'Hara. "The Changing American Family from the Preindustrial to the Industrial Period: A Final Report," *American Sociological Review* 40 (February 1975): 21–36.

Lazerow, Jama. "Religion and the New England Mill Girl: A New Perspective on an Old Theme," *New England Quarterly* 60 (September 1987): 429–53.

Leavitt, Judith Walzer. "Under the Shadow of Maternity: American Women's Responses to Death and Debility Fears in Nineteenth-Century Childbirth," *Feminist Studies* 12 (Spring 1986): 129–54.

Lebsock, Suzanne. "Free Black Women and the Question of Matriarchy: Petersburg, Virginia, 1784–1820." *Feminist Studies* 8 (Summer 1982): 270–92.

———. *The Free Women of Petersburg: Status and Culture in a Southern Town, 1784–1860*. New York: W. W. Norton Co., Inc., 1983.

Lecompte, Janet. "The Independent Women of Hispanic New Mexico, 1821–1846," *Western Historical Quarterly* 12 (January 1981): 17–35.

Lerner, Gerda. "The Lady and the Mill Girl: Changes in the Status of Women in the Age of Jackson," *American Studies* 10 (Spring 1969): 5–15.

———, ed. *Black Women in White America: A Documentary History*. New York: Vintage Books, 1973.

Maestas, José Griego, and Rodolfo Anaya. *Cuentos: Tales from the Hispanic Southwest*. Santa Fe: Museum of New Mexico, 1980.

Malone, Ann Patton. *Women on the Texas Frontier: A Cross-Cultural Perspective*. El Paso: Texas Western Press, 1983.

Marín, Christine N. *The Chicano Experience in Arizona*. Tempe, AR: University Libraries, Arizona State University, 1991.

Matthews, Jane D. "'Woman's Place' and the Search for Identity in Antebellum America," *The Canadian Review of American Studies* 10 (Winter 1979): 289–304.

McMillen, Sally G. *Southern Women: Black and White in the Old South*. Wheeling, IL: Harlan Davidson, Inc., 1992.

Miranda, Gloria E. "Hispano-Mexican Childbearing Practices in Pre-American Santa Barbara," *Southern California Historical Quarterly* 65 (Winter 1983): 307–20.

Myres, Sandra L. *Westering Women and the Frontier Experience, 1800–1915*. Albuquerque: University of New Mexico Press, 1982.

———. "Mexican Americans and Westering Anglos: A Feminine Perspective," *New Mexico Historical Review* 57 (October 1982): 317–33.

Osterud, Nancy Grey. *Bonds of Community: The Lives of Farm Women in Nineteenth-Century New York*. Ithaca, NY: Cornell University Press, 1991.

Perdue, Theda. "Cherokee Women and the Trail of Tears," *Journal of Women's History* 1 (Spring 1989): 14–30.

Premo, Terri L. *Winter Friends: Women Growing Old in the New Republic, 1785–1835*. Champaign-Urbana: University of Illinois Press, 1990.

Ryan, Mary P. *Womanhood in America: From Colonial Times to the Present.* 3d ed. New York: New Viewpoints, 1983. Chapters 2 and 3.

Sachs, Carolyn E. *The Invisible Farmers: Women in Agricultural Production.* Totowa, NJ: Rowman and Allanheld, 1983.

Schweninger, Loren. "Property-Owning Free African-American Women in the South, 1800–70," *Journal of Women's History* 1 (Winter 1990): 13–44.

Sklar, Kathryn Kish, and Thomas Dublin. *Women and Power in American History: A Reader.* Vol. I. Englewood Cliffs, NJ: Prentice-Hall, Inc., 1991. Parts 7–15.

Spector, Janet D. *What This Awl Means: Feminist Archaeology at a Wahpeton Dakota Village.* St. Paul: Minnesota Historical Society Press, 1993.

Stansell, Christine. *City of Women: Sex and Class in New York, 1789–1860.* New York: Alfred A. Knopf, 1986.

Sterling, Dorothy. *We Are Your Sisters: Black Women in the Nineteenth-Century.* New York: W. W. Norton & Co., Inc., 1984.

Stevenson, Brenda K. "Slavery," 1055–70, in *Black Women in America: An Historical Encyclopedia,* edited by Darlene Clark Hine. Vol. II. Brooklyn, NY: Carlson Publishing, Inc., 1993.

Suitor, J. Jill. "Husbands' Participation in Childbirth: A Nineteenth-Century Phenomenon," *Journal of Family History* 6 (Fall 1981): 278–93.

Trulio, Beverly. "Anglo-American Attitudes Toward New Mexican Women," *Journal of the West* 12 (April 1973): 229–39.

Van de Watering, Maxine. "The Popular Concept of 'Home' in Nineteenth-Century America," *Journal of American Studies* 18 (April 1984): 5–28.

Welter, Barbara. *Dimity Convictions: The American Woman in the Nineteenth Century.* Athens, OH: Ohio University Press, 1976.

White, Deborah Gray. "Female Slaves: Sex Roles and Status in the Antebellum Plantation South," 20–31, in *Unequal Sisters: A Multicultural Reader in U.S. Women's History,* edited by Vicki L. Ruiz and Ellen Carol DuBois. 2d ed. New York: Routledge, Chapman, & Hall, Inc., 1994.

Wilson, Carol. *Freedom at Risk: The Kidnapping of Free Blacks in America, 1780–1865.* New York: W. W. Norton & Co., 1994.

Woloch, Nancy. *Women and the American Experience.* New York: Alfred A. Knopf, 1986. Chapters 5–6.

Reshaping American Life and Values
1837 to 1861

4

The nation fell upon hard times during the late 1830s. The Panic of 1837 brought an abrupt halt to the nation's economic boom and cast some doubt on the popular and widespread belief that America was the Promised Land. From the economic structure to the political system, American institutions demanded reshaping, while numerous aspects of American life also clearly required improvement. The term "reform" soon became common currency and women stood in the forefront, first to help their country and next to help themselves. Out of re-

form came the first feminist movement; by 1861, gender expectations would be well-shaken and the landscape set for future quakes.

MORAL GUARDIANSHIP

The Argument for Women as Moral Keepers

Throughout the late 1830s, 1840s, and 1850s, a wide variety of women's literature continued to preach that women must serve as the moral guardians of society. In *Godey's Lady's Book*, editor Sarah Josepha Hale repeatedly emphasized that while men engaged in necessary, and often compromising, business practices and public affairs, women acted as the moral keepers of home and family. In 1847, Hale expressed this principle in verse: "He must work—the world subduing/Till it blooms like Eden bright/She must watch—his faith renewing/From her urn of Eden light."

At the same time that Hale maintained that women's place was in the home, she promoted the expansion of women's activities by arguing for improved education, simplified clothing styles that would allow increased activity, and for women as teachers, authors of "moral" literature and poetry, missionaries, and medical practitioners. Hale's approach to widening women's sphere was so nonthreatening that generations of American readers of all ages revered both Hale and *Godey's Lady's Book.*

Many other editors and writers contributed their interpretations and perspectives to the concept of the moral American woman. Legions of women writers wrote books that became immediate bestsellers during the late 1830s, 1840s, and 1850s but have languished on library shelves ever since. Domestic novels, as they were called because of their homey themes, frequently went through multiple and world-wide editions.

One of the most eminent of these women writers was Caroline Lee Hentz. She published her first stories in *Godey's* during the 1830s, and, because of her husband's lack of business acumen, turned to writing full-time to support her family. By the 1850s, Hentz gained renown for such novels as *Ernest Linwood* (1856). While she seemed to uphold all the usual ideals of women's moral powers and domestic sphere, Hentz's story lines always revolved around strong, decisive, all-suffering, and highly moral female protagonists who rescued ill, mindless, or morally crippled men.

A contemporary of Hentz, E.D.E.N. Southworth, removed men from the scene entirely. In such novels as *The Deserted Wife* (1851) and *The Discarded Daughter* (1852), Hentz sent men off to war, the West, or in pursuit of pretty young women. The women they left behind proved self-dependent, energetic, and capable of supporting themselves and their siblings or children, often achieving fame and fortune in the process. When an abject father, suitor, or husband returned, his magnanimous daughter, fiancé, or wife always forgave him. That men could not function without the strength and morality of women formed Southworth's overriding message.

A less vitriolic writer was Lydia B. Sigourney, known as "the Sweet Singer of Hartford." Economic necessity also forced Sigourney to follow a literary career, which lasted over half a century and produced more than fifty works. Like other domestic writers, Sigourney lauded the traditional virtues of home and family in such works as *Whispers to a Bride* (1850) and *The Daily Counsellor* (1859), while flouting them in her own career and in her prowomen themes.

Eliza Leslie and Catherine M. Sedgwick, neither of whom ever married, also gained popularity by idealizing domesticity, even though they rejected it in their own lives. Leslie's works, such as *Mr. and Mrs. Woodbridge and Other Tales* (1841), reiterated homely and wifely virtues, but Sedgwick, especially in *Married or Single?* (1857), championed the cause of unmarried women.

Elizabeth Fries Lummis Ellet took yet another approach to women's roles. She reconstructed the history of women in a way that demonstrated that women had served as prominent nurturers and guardians of American democracy. Ellet also argued that women fulfilled a variety of social functions, did jobs considered to be "men's work," and contributed significantly to the settlement of the frontier. Her best-known work, *The Women of the American Revolution*, which appeared in two volumes in 1848, went into its fourth printing by 1850.

Implications of the "Morality" Argument

Clearly, these and other women writers achieved widespread popularity in their own day. At least on the surface, they preached all the fashionable beliefs regarding true womanhood and idealized the customary view of the family and women's place, especially as moral guardians of home and family. But, when read closely, their contradictory messages become apparent. Deep discontent riddled their portrayals of domesticity. On the one hand, these writers characterized men as sinful, obsessed with a desire for wealth and social position, and in need of reform. On the other, they presented women characters as superior beings, responsible for families, and increasingly capable of guarding society against evil.

This assignment of women as moral keepers had wide implications. For example, the moral guardian theory justified the argument that women must understand politics to influence male legislators wisely; that women rather than men must teach school to inculcate children with virtue; and that women must form charity organizations to implement their goodness on behalf of the poor and destitute. In short, morally superior women must dominate any function or social situation that would benefit from piety and righteousness.

This line of thought made it easier for women to stay in their own "sphere" because the sphere grew to accommodate more of the everyday world. Moreover, although American cultural values still promoted such "male" qualities as aggressiveness, economic achievement, and shrewdness, they also began to encompass such "female" values as flexibility, moral success, and lack of guile. This partial feminization of American cultural values gave women a measure of potency and prestige.

Usually, however, those who had the leisure and resources to pursue moral reform were middle- and upper-class white and black women. Only gradually would reformism draw in employed, poor, rural, and other types of women. The logical extension of Republican Motherhood, True Womanhood, and Moral Guardianship was that resulting beliefs regarding women virtually commanded them to assume the task of reforming society.

APPLYING MORAL POWERS TO SOCIAL PROBLEMS

Improved Female Education

Beginning in the 1840s, Catharine Beecher joined the ongoing debate in America regarding "proper" education. Beecher spoke and wrote for the improved education of women, and especially maintained that women teachers should be sent West to educate and morally improve native peoples, children, and unprincipled men. She also crusaded for the establishment of teaching-training, or normal, schools in western areas. Beecher personally organized missionary societies, which recruited and sent female teachers westward, and founded a number of women's schools, including the Dubuque Female Seminary (Iowa) and the Milwaukee Female College (Wisconsin), in the West.

Despite her active and vigorous campaign on women's behalf, Beecher never strayed from her conviction that women were by nature domestic creatures. Her schools trained women to work as teachers before marriage and to serve as homemakers after. Because she believed that such "higher" subjects as mathematics and philosophy would weaken the female constitution and interfere with a woman's desire and ability to bear children, Beecher's curriculum stressed health, home economics, and English. In her many books, including her popular *Treatise on Domestic Economy* (1841), Beecher offered household hints and recipes, always emphasizing that domesticity was an honorable and worthy profession.

Almira Lincoln Phelps took a different position, however, by trying to help women elude the limitations of women's sphere. In 1841, Phelps and her attorney husband took charge of the Patapsco Female Institute in Baltimore. Phelps included such subjects as science in the curriculum, wrote several standard botany textbooks, and became the second woman admitted to the American Association for the Advancement of Science. After her husband's death in 1849, Phelps ran the school by herself until her retirement at sixty-three.

Beecher and Phelps diverged in many ways, but both educators agreed that women should exercise. They encouraged women to abandon stays, corsets, and other fashionable, but unhealthy, practices. Arguing that women's roles demanded a robust physical condition, including stamina and endurance, Beecher and Phelps designed exercise programs for female students in their schools. They also regularly prescribed activities to improve posture, gracefulness, and general health.

Still, these and other reformers believed that women's bodies could sustain only a limited amount of moderate exercise. Women were, for example, encouraged to ride horses using a sidesaddle and wearing an appropriate riding habit. *Godey's Lady's Book* stressed this idea, urging women always to preserve their feminine grace and delicacy while riding. Racing and riding to the hounds were definitely frowned upon, but, by the 1850s, women began to compete in "female equestrian" events at county fairs.

Pedestrianism, or foot racing, constituted another acceptable sport for women during the 1840s and 1850s. In 1852, one American woman, Kate Irvine, competed in a British race in which she covered five hundred miles. Most women's magazines, however, only recommended moderate walking and sedate dancing as acceptable exercises. They advised women to proceed with caution, for as one counseled in 1858, when the body is "too much exercised, it is apt to produce ganglions on the ankle joints of delicate girls, as wind galls are produced on the legs of young horses who are too soon or too much worked."

Clearly, women reformers focused on white, middle- and upper-class women's education. They called for moderate changes, while their opponents clung to customary beliefs regarding women. Widely quoted in the United States, French commentator Jean Jacques Rousseau described the traditional ideal as follows:

> The whole education of women ought to be relative to men. To please them, to be useful to them, to make themselves loved and honored by them, to educate them when young, to care for them when grown, to counsel them, to console them, and to make life sweet and agreeable to them—these are the duties of women at all times, and what should be taught them from their infancy.

Only a few reformers concerned themselves with education for other types of American women. A few tried to help indigent and delinquent white women. The Lancaster (Pennsylvania) Industrial School for Girls offered moral instruction and vocational training for girls between the ages of seven and sixteen. The school also provided medical care, a temporary home, and an employment service.

A few reformers also tried to help educate black women. In 1837, the Society of Friends established the Institute for Colored Youth in Philadelphia. Grace Mapps taught at the school during its formative years. Later her daughter, abolitionist Sarah Mapps Douglass, a free woman of color in Philadelphia, became a teacher and an administrator at the Institute, where she trained black public school teachers.

Free black Fanny Jackson Coppin also joined the Institute. Coppin began her education while working as a domestic servant in Newport, Rhode Island. Coppin first hired a tutor, then attended the segregated Newport schools, and in 1859 completed the teacher training course at the Rhode Island State Normal School. In 1860, she enrolled in the only integrated college in the United States—Oberlin College in Ohio. After graduating, Coppin went to Philadelphia as principal of the Institute for Colored Youth.

In the South, "black codes" forbid the educating of slaves, but clandestine schools existed in many areas. Milla Granson of Natchez, Mississippi, for example, learned to read and write from her owners' children and then taught hundreds of other slaves late at night in what they called Milla's midnight school. Another, known only as Miss DeVeaux, opened a secret school in Savannah, Georgia, and operated it for twenty-five years without discovery.

Alcohol Abuse

Once Americans recognized the existence and extent of drunkenness, they also began to realize that numerous wives and daughters suffered mistreatment at the hands of intoxicated husbands and fathers. Also, because most women and children depended on men economically, alcoholic men could financially destroy families.

Soon, many people began to identify the problem of alcoholism as largely male and the solution as female. Women joined the Daughters of Temperance in unprecedented numbers; by 1848, it was one of the largest organizations for women, with a membership of thirty thousand. Members of Daughters of Temperance chapters held women's temperance meetings and organized such major gatherings as the Women's Temperance Convention, which met in New York in 1852. Women formed bands that prayed and sang hymns outside, or sometimes inside, saloons and petitioned legislatures for prohibition laws.

But women temperance reformers felt increasingly thwarted. Although they could indeed exercise their moral powers against alcoholism, they could not vote for or against prohibition laws. During the 1840s, when the American temperance movement rejected the use of moral suasion and began to urge legal prohibition of alcohol, women felt left out of the very cause that they increasingly saw as their own. Then, in 1846, Maine passed the first state law banning the manufacture and sale of alcoholic beverages, a move in which women had no direct hand.

Women temperance advocates initially responded to the change in policy by resisting the abandonment of moral suasion as a technique. Next, they maintained their influence in the temperance movement by resorting to the use of pressure, including personal confrontation and extralegal force. Between 1852 and 1859, groups of women entered saloons and physically destroyed the liquor stock. In essence, respectable and influential women became vigilantes who brandished weapons ranging from petitions to hatchets to protect their homes and families from what they called "Demon Rum."

The temperance cause also attracted black women. As early as the 1830s, they began working for temperance through their churches, clubs, and communities. During the 1840s, many joined with white women, especially in Utica, New York. During the 1840s and 1850s, black women also formed their own groups, particularly in Philadelphia, or joined black men's temperance societies, although the largest of these, The New England Colored Temperance Society, denied women membership.

Prison and Asylum Reform

Women also applied their moral powers to prison and asylum reform. In 1835, the Mount Pleasant Female Prison of New York became the nation's first women's prison but was not widely imitated.

During the 1840s, such reformers as Protestant missionaries Phoebe Palmer and Sarah Platt began to visit women prisoners in the Tombs, one of New York City's jails, while other women joined the Female Department, an auxiliary of the Prison Association of New York. Out of this and other women's groups came a concerted effort to reform prisons that held women as well as men and to establish separate women's prisons operated by women. In 1844, Eliza Burham Farnham became the matron of the women's prison at Sing Sing in New York, where she introduced inmate education.

Other women prison reformers worked on behalf of the mentally ill. In 1843, Dorothea Dix petitioned the Massachusetts legislature to construct enough buildings so that mentally ill and other disadvantaged people could be separated from felons and murderers. During the 1840s and 1850s, Dix continued her work on behalf of the indigent insane in the United States and Great Britain. During the 1850s, women's prison reform associations proliferated, while individual women accepted appointment to state prison boards, especially in Connecticut, New York, and Massachusetts.

Other Organized Reform Efforts

Thousands of other white and black women flocked to religious, moral reform, utopian, and benevolent groups. Although such organizations continued to maintain that women had domestic natures, they also argued that women's sphere should include neighborhoods and communities. They encouraged women to participate in shaping the cultural values of people outside their families and to attack social ills.

Evangelical religious sects especially granted women a measure of importance through religious conversion and membership in the women's auxiliaries of missionary, tract, and Bible societies. These sects also offered women an increased voice in church affairs and freed them from being simply obedient followers of authoritarian ministers. Moreover, in place of an emphasis on women's inherent evil as daughters of Eve, ministers now held out the hope of human perfectibility to women. Several sects, notably Shakerism, Spiritualism, Christian Science, and Theosophy, additionally deemphasized the masculine nature of God, denied the need for a traditional male clergy, and argued that other acceptable roles existed for women besides those of wife and mother. In 1853, the Congregational Church in South Butler, New York, ordained Antoinette Brown Blackwell, who had studied theology at Oberlin College. Although ordained only locally, Blackwell is regarded as the first female American minister.

Yet other women who wanted to improve American society participated in Utopian experiments dedicated to alternate forms of labor and products. Brook Farm, established in 1841 outside of Boston, drew the support of Transcendentalist Margaret Fuller. Other groups experimented with unconventional forms of marriage. Oneida, founded in upstate New York in 1848, practiced complex marriage in which all members cohabited with each other and cared for the children as a group. At the same time, the Shakers tried to free women from the handicaps of marriage and childcare by practicing celibacy.

Moral reform societies also attracted myriad women, many of whom formed auxiliaries to the parent group. In 1840, when the New York female reform group organized into the national American Female Moral Reform Society, its auxiliaries numbered 555. Women reformers employed the technique of "visiting," meaning they sang hymns and prayed at brothels, almshouses, and jails; talked with prostitutes, the ill, and the poverty-stricken; and solicited data and case histories relating to sexual abuse and other ills.

In addition to visiting, moral reformers petitioned state legislatures, lobbied for reform legislation, and opened refuges for women in need. In New York, this took the form of a House of Reception, a home for prostitutes, while in Boston, women reformers founded a Home for Unprotected Girls, a Refuge for Migrant Women, and an Asylum for the Repentant.

Moreover, by the 1850s benevolent organizations appeared in virtually every city and town. These groups dedicated their efforts to providing relief—or charity—for people in need. In New York, for example, the African Dorcas Society provided clothes for black school children, while in New Orleans, the Colored Female Benevolent Society promised to suppress vice and give its members insurance benefits.

Frequently, such groups became complex, influential institutions. Often turning into corporations, these organizations included boards of directors, treasurers and other officers, as well as public relations programs. Originally designed to help the bereft widows of seamen support themselves, Sarah Josepha Hale's Boston Seaman's Aid Society grew into a nonprofit business, vocational training program, school, and home. Similarly, the Providence (Rhode Island) Employment Society began in the 1830s by trying to help exploited seamstresses and soon turned into a small garment business that paid fair wages and provided good working conditions.

Family Size

A less organized reform movement examined the issue of family size. Clearly, many women desired to exercise control over their bodies and childbearing. In addition to marriage and motherhood, they wanted their lives to include other activities, or hoped to free themselves from economic dependence upon men. At the same time, changes in the American economy, especially the rising cost of living, and urban overcrowding increasingly made large families less desirable.

A few outspoken women, notably reformer Frances Wright, publicly advocated the practice of limiting family size, while others privately practiced abortion. By the 1840s, a dramatic rise in the abortion rate occurred, especially among married Anglo women. These trends culminated in the first explicit demand for information regarding contraception. During the mid-1840s, women's rights' leaders issued a call for "Voluntary Motherhood," arguing that women who chose to bear children would be better mothers than those who were denied a choice.

A decline in the white birth rate from an average of 7 children in 1800 to 5.4 in 1850 demonstrated women's willingness to use birth-control methods. Besides abortion, these included abstinence, coitus interruptus, pills, a pessary, and an improved rubber condom made possible by the 1843 discovery of the vulcanization of rubber. Regularly advertised were such products as "Preventive Powders" at five dollars a package; a rubber diaphragm called a "Family Regulator, or Wife's Protector," at five dollars each; and "Female Monthly Regulating Pills," supposedly abortants guaranteed to cure "all cases of suppression, irregularity, or stoppage of the mensus." Although religious and other leaders spoke against Voluntary Motherhood, no laws restricted the dispensing of such information or the providing of assistance to women.

Medicine

Also less organized than most reform movements were women's attempts to improve obstetrical and gynecologic care. In 1847, a twenty-six-year-old teacher in Kentucky, Elizabeth Blackwell, determined to enroll in medical school and eventually treat women patients. Although she applied to numerous schools, twenty-nine rejected her. Only at New York's Geneva College did students and faculty vote to accept Blackwell's application. Unaware that the College intended to use Blackwell as proof that women were incapable of medical practice, Blackwell entered Geneva in November 1847. After some ridicule and an unsuccessful attempt to bar her from classroom demonstrations involving human anatomy, Blackwell proved herself an exceptional student.

In 1849, Blackwell received her medical degree, then served a residency as a student midwife in Paris. In 1850, St. Bartholomew's Hospital in London admitted her to its residency program but barred her from practicing gynecology and pediatrics. The following year, Blackwell returned to New York and shortly wrote to her sister Emily that "a blank wall of social and professional antagonism faces a woman physician and forms a situation of singular and painful loneliness, leaving her without support, respect, or professional counsel."

Despite such discrimination, in 1850 the Woman's Medical College of Pennsylvania accepted forty women students and in 1857, Blackwell opened a private dispensary that incorporated as the New York Infirmary and College for Women. Conducted largely by women, the latter institution's staff included Blackwell's sister Emily and Maria Zakrzewska, both of whom Elizabeth had encouraged to pursue medical degrees.

As more women entered medical practice during the 1850s, they often chose women and children as their constituencies. They also differed from male doctors in their emphasis on holistic treatments and their sympathy for women's pleas for information regarding contraception.

Near the end of the decade, in 1859, Blackwell lectured in England on medicine as a profession for women. The British Medical Register placed her name on its rolls and the very hospitals that had earlier refused to admit her now welcomed her. Eventually, Blackwell settled in England, her place of birth. In 1871, she founded the National Health Society and in 1875 began to lecture on gynecology.

UNACKNOWLEDGED PROBLEMS

Employed Women

Despite their intense interest in change, middle- and upper-class women reformers seldom recognized the problems of white and black women who worked outside their homes for wages. These employed women labored behind factory walls, did piecework on their kitchen tables, roamed city streets as prostitutes, or ran other women's kitchens and sculleries. The problems of these employed women often remained unpublicized, while their predicaments often seemed self-inflicted. Even the campaign against prostitution was a moral issue for most reformers, rather than an attempt to help working women.

Consequently, workers themselves had to come to grips with the dilemmas of a recently industrialized society. During the mid-1830s, some women workers unsuccessfully devoted their energies to campaigns for higher wages, shorter hours, and improved working conditions. Despite the continuation of these ills, other women continued to flock to factory jobs, hoping for higher wages than they currently earned. Even during the Panic of 1837 and the ensuing economic depression, women left other occupations for factory employment. In 1839, mill worker Malenda Edwards lamented that "there are very many young ladies at work in the factories that have given up millinery dressmaking and school-keeping for to work in the mill."

When the depression extended into the late 1830s and early 1840s, wages fell and unemployment spread. In New York and other major cities, bread riots became the order of the day. By 1843, the panic had finally eased and most women had returned to work, but they earned under two dollars per week, which was hardly a living wage, even in the 1840s.

Unemployed and underpaid women workers sought assistance from benevolent women's societies and other charity organizations, such as the Mother Society in New York City, devoted to helping poor blacks and unemployed black women. But other employed women now argued that they needed some type of labor organization. In 1845, an operative in the Lowell mills, Sarah Bagley, acted on this idea by founding the Lowell Female Labor Reform Association, which advocated the ten-hour workday.

This group's journal, *Voice of Industry,* also complained about an increased work pace and asked Massachusetts legislators to investigate conditions in the mills.

Society in general, and male union members in particular, frowned upon women's participation in unions. Unwilling to accept the reality of women's employment, these people hoped that women workers would soon return to their "proper" places in the home. Working men also tended to fear women because women accepted low wages. These men did not yet realize that organizations of both women and men might establish fair wages for all workers.

Such prejudice did not prevent numerous women workers from joining men's unions, participating in strikes, and forming their own organizations. In 1845, the shoe-binders at Lynn, Massachusetts, established a Producers Cooperative. During the late 1840s and early 1850s, many of the 181,000 women workers in the clothing, shoe, wool, straw hat, printing, and other industries again attempted organization and walk-outs.

At the same time, household workers and home pieceworkers had little opportunity to organize, strike, or otherwise protect themselves from exploitation. Some made ends meet by taking aid from charitable societies or by hiring out their children. Others turned to prostitution. In 1858, an estimated six thousand prostitutes existed in New York City, one for every sixty-four adult males. Over half of these women had earned one to two dollars a week as seamstresses, dressmakers, hat-trimmers, milliners, tailors, servants, and factory workers before becoming prostitutes, and 63 percent of them had been born in other countries.

This latter statistic indicates the tremendous difficulty immigrant women faced in finding employment. Usually lacking industrial skills and, except for English immigrants, unable to speak the language of their new country, these women fell prey to unscrupulous and mercenary employers who forced them to accept less than subsistence wages and work in dreadful conditions. Others became pieceworkers or domestic servants at unbelievably low wages.

During the 1840s, one quarter of a million women, or one-tenth of the adult female population, worked as domestics. Irish immigrants constituted the majority of domestic workers, while other Irish women worked in the needle trades or as prostitutes. Stranded in urban areas by their lack of funds and kept at the bottom of the economic ladder by anti-Catholic and nativist sentiment, Irish and large numbers of other immigrant women were unable to migrate to rural areas where they might put their agricultural skills to use.

Among all these employed women, only factory women had the proximity, opportunity, and group consciousness to campaign for reform. During the late 1850s, they joined men's strikes or held their own walk-outs. A few even began to recognize that the success of the women's rights movement might facilitate labor reform. One early labor leader,

Harriet Farley, a former mill operative at Lowell, thus became an avowed women's rights advocate. In 1850, Farley wrote that "it has been impossible for me to consider so long the 'Rights and Duties of Mill-Girls' without opening my eyes to the vista just beyond the rights and duties of woman." Farley deplored the socialization of "masculine" men and "feminine" women that ignored the common ground between the two genders. In her view, women could support themselves without losing their womanhood: "I have seen that they do not become less worthy and interesting when they become more useful and independent."

Ten years later, in 1860, labor issues came to a head when five hundred men and one thousand women held a huge rally during a strike. In the middle of a terrible blizzard, the women cheered the reading of a special poem, "The Song of the Shoemakers Strike." Some twenty thousand more workers throughout New England joined this labor protest, known as "The Revolution in the North." From this came few actual gains, but workers felt newly experienced in labor disputes.

Farm Women

In rural areas in the Northeast, South, and West, numerous other women worked in agricultural pursuits. Despite land-holding policies that favored men, women could own land and participate in agriculture. Often the ones who did so were widows, women with disabled husbands, single women, and free women of color. By the early 1860s, one observer noted that "there are two sisters in Ohio who manage a farm of 300 acres: and two other sisters, near Media, Pennsylvania that conduct as large a farm. Mrs. D. owns a farm, and does not disdain to graft fruit trees, superintend their planting, gather fruit, send it to market, etc.: and she realizes a handsome profit."

Other women were less fortunate; they worked on farms as hired laborers during the late 1830s, 1840s, and 1850s. Often newly arrived immigrant or free black women, these hired hands did not disdain field work. They had performed heavy agricultural tasks in their countries of origin or in the South and were thus willing to join men in the fields.

The numbers of female farm hands increased as agricultural specialization developed. Wheat, corn, chicken, and dairy farms all demanded hired labor, both female and male. Immigrant women especially proved themselves invaluable as grain, dairy, and chicken farmers. In 1857, the *Illinois Farmer* pleaded: "We want a supply of young women from the butter regions of Eastern States to come here and also from the Dairy Districts of England, Scotland, Ireland, and Germany."

Still, although farmers usually recruited immigrant, free black, and poor women as field hands, it was considered appropriate work for all women during periods of labor shortages. Like their counterparts in domestic labor, these women had little opportunity to organize for their own sake and had to depend on outside forces for reform.

WOMEN IN THE SOUTH

Slave Women

Of course, black slave women who provided similar labor on the larger farms and plantations worked in even less enviable conditions. They usually had no right to choose their mates or the number of children they bore. They had no control over their bodies for sexual or breeding purposes. While they could not desert abusive husbands, they could be torn from loving husbands through sale. And, threat of physical punishment could force them to accept a new spouse after the sale or death of a mate in order to keep producing children.

One of the few considerations slave women received on some plantations was an occasional lightened workload while pregnant. One Virginia planter warned his overseers that "breeding wenches you must be Kind and Indulgent to, and not force them when with child upon any service or hardship that will be injurious to them." When not pregnant, however, slave women were expected to maintain an exhausting work schedule.

Some division of labor existed along gender lines, but many owners expect slave women to take part in all necessary tasks from plowing to building fences. In 1853, an observer in South Carolina saw male and female slaves carrying manure containers on their heads to fields where they applied it by hand to the earth around cotton plants. In North Carolina, he observed women hoeing, shoveling, and cutting down trees to create roadbeds. Slave women were also sometimes hired out to cotton and woolen mills, sugar refineries, and tobacco factories. In 1860, about five thousand slave women were so employed.

Only about 5 percent of black slave women attained the relatively privileged status of house servant, serving as cooks, personal attendants, nursemaids, and wet nurses. Aged slave women also worked hard at such tasks as sewing, weaving, spinning, canning, and caring for babies and young children whose mothers were in the fields. In addition, these aged "grannies" often served as nurses and midwives.

Slave women frequently rebelled against their heavy workloads. "She'd git stubborn like a mule and quit," one overseer complained. Another slave woman might strike an overseer across his head with her hoe or run away into the woods to hide as a "truant." One Florida woman even chopped her overseer to death after a reprimand. Rather than commit such violence, some women became concubines and mistresses to escape heavy labor. Others would "sham," that is, claim aches and disabilities due to their menstrual cycle or pregnancy.

Another more subtle rebellion involved slave women's adherence to traditional divisions of labor within their homes. By maintaining a modicum of true womanhood through the customary roles and tasks of wife and mother, slave women could mock their owners, who treated them as pseudo-men and beasts of burden in fields or foundry. Also, by acting as the force that held the family together in the face of daily adversity or that formed new kinship ties in times of crisis, slave women defied owners' casual attitudes toward the institutions of marriage and family among slaves. By preserving their families from the dehumanizing aspects of slavery, black women engaged in the ultimate revolt against the system.

By 1860, the population of the South included 7,033,973 whites, 258,000 free blacks, and 3,838,765 black slaves, with slaves at the bottom in every way. Although "black codes" prohibited slaves from learning to read or write, some did so and used their skills to reveal the desperate conditions in which they lived and worked. Harriet Brent Jacobs, who wrote her story, *Incidents in the Life of a Slave Girl*, under the pen name of Linda Brent, told a tale of cruelty and licentiousness. Edited and published by abolitionist Lydia Maria Child in 1861, the book included Jacobs's statement regarding her owner: "I was his property; that I must be subject to his will in all things."

White Southern Women

Anglo women in the South experienced a variety of reactions to the slave system. On the one hand, some women acted as harshly as any overseer, beating recalcitrant slaves themselves and ordering harsh punishments for others. On the other hand, many women felt outrage at the slave system and sometimes even publicly aired their opinions. Maria J. McIntosh, daughter of an illustrious Georgia family, created a scandal when in 1850 she published her antislavery views in a volume entitled *Woman in America*.

White southern women had good reasons to hate slavery. They feared revolt, resented their husbands' sexual liaisons with black women, disliked their own heavy workloads in supervising and training black workers, and experienced guilt about oppressing black people. At the same time, however, southern women's social status and financial security depended on the continuation of the slave system. Also, custom and economic dependence on planter husbands hedged in southern ladies, who seldom dared to voice antislavery sentiments for fear of reprisal or abandonment. In 1854, social theorist George Fitzhugh claimed that "Women, like children, have but one right, and that is the right to protection. . . . if she be obedient, she stands little danger of maltreatment."

Consequently, plantation mistresses confided their thoughts to their diaries rather than to spouses. Frances Kemble, a distinguished English actress who married Georgia planter Pierce Butler in 1834, recorded her emotions in her diary during the winter of 1838–1839, when she lived in the big-house of Butler's Sea Island plantation. When she later divorced Butler and released her diary under the title *Journal of Residence on a Georgian Plantation* (1863), Kemble's jottings divulged feelings that other women shared but were more hesitant to reveal. Of her time on a plantation, Kemble wrote: "It appears to me that the principal hardships fall to the lot of the [slave] women."

Black slave women continually appealed to Kemble to lighten their work, soften their punishments, and extend their time of rest after childbirth to the customary four weeks. Kemble felt overwhelmed by the women's stories, especially one involving a woman who had borne sixteen children, fourteen of whom were dead. According to the woman's own words, she had been lashed by "a man with a cowhide [who] stands and stripes" slaves. Kemble added, "and when I said: Did they do that to you when you were with child? she simply replied: Yes, missis." Incensed, Kemble wrote, "to all this I listen—I an Englishwoman, the wife of the man who owns these wretches, and I cannot say: That thing shall not be done again."

When other women's diaries finally came to light they also contained similar passion. In 1858, Georgian Ella Thomas had recorded her conviction that "Southern Women are all at heart abolitionists" in her journal. She added that "the institution of slavery degrades the white man more than the Negro. . . . The happiness of homes is destroyed but what is to be done?" Plantation mistress Mary Boykin Chestnut, whose husband later ranked high in the Confederate government, concurred; versions of her extensive diaries published in 1905 and 1981 indicate that numerous southern women condemned the slave system.

While such women appeared to support the pre–Civil War patriarchal system, they only tolerated it when necessary and strained against its dictates when possible. In fact, a rise in women's activism presaged an emerging women's rights movement in the South. Women generally developed a growing sense of self and of themselves as women.

Among the planter class, some young women employed the concept of True Womanhood to argue for improved educational opportunities. Their planter fathers and husbands concurred in the establishment of female academies because they believed that educating their women would help to maintain the "tone" of the planter class. Women cherished their right to better educations, yet recognized that intellectual development would end with marriage, casting them into roles much like those that their mothers filled.

Among the middle and lower classes, a different situation existed. Most women actively engaged in agricultural work. On small tobacco, cotton, and subsistence farms, women regularly joined men in planting crops, weeding, and harvesting. In addition, women transformed the raw materials of the fields into finished goods and provided cash income through the sale of their surplus products.

Women of the yeomanry (small landowners) class played an important economic role in the family and frequently participated in making economic decisions. A significant number worked outside their homes, especially as teachers and "exhorters," or lay preachers. They usually chose their own mates and often determined the number of children they would bear. Some abandoned abusive, negligent, or lazy husbands, while others bore children out of wedlock and headed their own households.

Such women were important economic and moral forces who, along with women of the planter class, challenged ideas when and where they could during the 1840s and 1850s. Southern women gained property rights in several states during the 1850s, and common practice often protected their ownership of land, looms, cattle, and furniture. In addition, women who sought divorces acted docile and submissive while substantiating their claim that adulterous, drunken, abusive, neglectful, or felonious husbands had wronged them. Often they gained judicial sympathy, followed by substantial alimony payments, property awards, and control of their children. Between 1800 and 1860, twenty-one women in Alabama sued for divorce as opposed to seven men. Eleven of the wives obtained final decrees, while only two of the husbands did so. In Louisiana, sixteen wives sought divorces as compared to six husbands. Seven of the women secured divorces, while only one man was able to do so. Because they functioned in a conservative agrarian society, southern women were not as effective in breaking down barriers as were their northern counterparts, who had the advantage of operating in an industrial, relatively progressive world.

ABOLITIONISM AND THE EMERGENCE OF WOMEN'S RIGHTS

Women in Abolitionism

Accordingly, an attack on the slave system had to come primarily from northern women. Of all the reform crusades, abolitionism affected black Americans the most directly and significantly. Consequently, black women, who by the 1830s constituted 52 percent of the total black population, energetically campaigned for the abolition of slavery. Sometimes these women worked alongside Anglo women, as in the Boston Female Anti-Slavery Society and the integrated Female Anti-Slavery Societies of Lynn, Massachusetts, and Rochester, New York. On other occasions, they formed their own antislavery groups.

The Forten family of Philadelphia was especially active. Sarah, Harriet, and Margaretta helped found the Philadelphia Female Anti-Slavery Society. After Sarah married Joseph Purvis in 1838, she continued to work on behalf of black Americans. In 1838 and 1839, Harriet served as a delegate to the Anti-Slavery Convention of American Women, while later both she and Margaretta combined abolitionist writing and speaking with extensive committee work.

Other black female abolitionists included Mary Ann Shadd Cary, a teacher, journalist, and lawyer; Sarah Parker Remond, a speaker and author; and Frances Ellen Watkins Harper, a lecturer, author, and poet. Of these, Harper gained the most public notice. Her books of poetry, *Forest Leaves* and *Poems on Miscellaneous Subjects*, sold thousands of copies. Harper also lectured throughout New Jersey, Pennsylvania, Ohio, and the South during the 1850s. In addition, the writings of Charlotte Forten appeared in *The Liberator* and the *National Anti-Slavery Standard*, while Harriet Wilson's novel, *Our Nig: or, Sketches from the Life of a Free Black* (1859) indicated that abolition of prejudice would have to follow the abolition of slavery.

The best-known black abolitionist of all, however, was Harriet Tubman. Born a slave in Maryland, Tubman fled to Philadelphia in 1849. In 1850, she returned to Maryland to guide her sister and her two children to freedom. The following year, Tubman helped a brother and his family to escape. Tubman made at least nineteen trips into slave territory and freed as many as three hundred people. Known as the "Moses of Her People," in 1860 Tubman had a price of forty thousand dollars on her head.

Of course, these black abolitionists faced numerous hurdles. Besides racial prejudice, they found themselves barred as women from speaking, writing, and organizing. The tale of Sojourner Truth is especially instructive. Born a slave in New York and originally named Isabella, she fled from her owner in 1827, a year before slaves were freed in that state. In 1829, she arrived in New York City with two of her children and obtained work as a domestic servant. She became a preacher and participated in the effort to turn prostitutes to religion.

In 1843, Isabella took the name Sojourner Truth and set out on foot to preach throughout New England. Three years later, she became an enthusiastic supporter of the abolitionist movement. She toured the Midwest lecturing against slavery in spite of threats and physical attacks. In Indiana, she bared her breast to disprove the allegations that she was a man in disguise.

Then, in 1850, after experiencing frequent discrimination as a female reformer, Sojourner Truth adopted the cause of women's rights. In 1852, at a women's rights meeting in Akron, Ohio, she delivered her famous "Ain't I A Woman" speech in which she pointed out that chivalry and True Womanhood were not very meaningful concepts to most women, especially black, laboring, and poor women. Truth argued adamantly for rights for black women because she believed that "if colored men get their rights and not colored women theirs . . . the colored men will be masters and it will be just as bad as it was before."

In addition to such black female abolitionists, white women also energetically championed the cause of antislavery. Because these women viewed slavery as a moral wrong, they felt compelled to exercise their moral powers against it. The Boston Female Anti-Slavery Society declared that "as wives and mothers, as daughters and sisters, we are deeply responsible for the influence we have on the human race. . . . We are bound to urge men to cease to do evil and learn how to do good."

White women also felt a growing sense of identification with black women. In 1837, abolitionist Angelina Grimké told a white women's antislavery convention that they were "sisters" to slave women. As women, she continued, slaves have a right to look to white women for "sympathy for their sorrows, and effort and prayer for their rescue." Others argued that if one woman suffered sexual degradation, it hurt womankind in general, and if one mother faced depreciation, then all mothers lost stature. Abolitionist women also hoped that if they helped free the slaves, liberation would be extended to white women as a logical and just outcome of their efforts.

At first, white women's abolitionist societies engaged in fund-raising and exhortation, but they soon adopted more aggressive tactics, including organizing petition campaigns, holding national conventions, and speaking on the public platform. They increasingly resented the limitations placed on their activities due to their gender. In 1837, one woman's convention proclaimed that "the time has come for woman to move in that sphere which providence has assigned her, and no longer remain satisfied in the circumscribed limits which corrupt custom and a perverted application of Scripture have encircled her."

Because not all Americans believed that women should actively engage in public controversy, women's involvement in abolitionism created its own contretemps. The Grimké sisters' lecturing and political reform activities especially led to a heated discussion of women's roles and responsibilities. In 1837, a group of Congregationalist ministers in Massachusetts issued a "Pastoral Letter" protesting the sisters' "unfeminine" conduct. The letter said in part: "We invite your attention to the dangers which at present seem to threaten the female character with widespread and permanent injury. The appropriate duties and influence of women are clearly stated in the New Testament. The power of woman is her dependence, flowing from the consciousness of that weakness which God has given her for her protection."

Abolitionist leaders feared that such invective and attendant controversy would jeopardize the antislavery crusade, so they begged the Grimké sisters to ignore it. But Sarah and Angelina replied that they could "not push abolitionism forward until we take the stumbling block out of the road." In other words, they were determined to exercise their moral powers and, if necessary, to fight for their rights so they could attack slavery.

Like Sojourner Truth, the Grimké sisters now espoused women's rights. In 1838, Sarah stated the sisters' position in her pamphlet, *Letters on the Equality of the Sexes, and the Condition of Woman*. She minced no words in presenting the case: "I ask no favors for my sex. I surrender not our claim to equality. All I ask of our brethren is that they take their feet from off our necks, and permit us to stand upright on the ground which God has designed us to occupy." Shortly thereafter, Angelina married abolitionist reformer Theodore Dwight Weld. The newly wed couple and Sarah settled in New Jersey, where they continued to work for the causes of antislavery and women's rights.

During the 1840s and 1850s, thousands of women followed the courageous example of Sarah and Angelina Grimké by joining the abolitionist movement. Because they could not vote, they chose instead to petition Congress to pass laws restricting slavery. Although gathering names on petitions entailed hard work, onerous travel, and frequent scorn, these women persevered and collected hundreds of thousands of signatures that Congress could not ignore. In addition to petitioning, abolitionist women lectured, helped slaves escape via a network known as the Underground Railroad, and wrote books and pamphlets.

One of the most eminent of the abolitionist writers was Harriet Beecher Stowe. Coming from a family of reformers and deeply interested in social reform herself, Stowe directed her early writings toward the issues of temperance, higher wages for seamstresses, and improved educational opportunities for women. Stowe later became involved in the abolitionist movement and wrote several antislavery novels. In 1852, she achieved acclaim with *Uncle Tom's Cabin*, and in 1856, published another slave novel, *Dred: A Tale of the Great Dismal Swamp*.

Women's Frustrations

Abolitionist and other voluntary organizations drew women out of their homes, trained them in a large variety of business positions, and helped turn women's morality into a paid vocation, yet few people seemed to appreciate women's efforts. Susan B. Anthony complained that American men simply left the dirty work of society to women: "Men like to see women pick up the drunk and falling. . . . That patching business is 'woman's proper sphere.'"

Other women reformers chafed at specific limitations they encountered. They wielded little political influence because they could not own property, vote, or hold office. They also endured censure for speaking in public and entering the halls of Congress with their petitions. Yet how were they to function as effective reformers without some weapons or power? And how were they to activate their moral force? If they were the moral guardians of society, then they had to have the freedom to exercise their salutary influence on American society.

In the temperance movement, numerous women became ardent women's rights' advocates in response to their lack of power. A temperance journal, *The Lily*, edited by Amelia Bloomer, began as a newspaper dedicated to "temperance and literature," but by 1852, its new masthead stated that it was "devoted to the interests of women." Thus, women who began their careers as reformers in the temperance crusade frequently ended them in the women's rights movement. Many of them also experienced an increasing enmity toward men, whom they saw as oppressors blocking them from their political rights, and often as morally weak alcoholics as well. At the same time, these women began to see themselves not as submissive domestic beings, but as aggressive, effective reformers. In general, the temperance movement caused large numbers of women to question their place and to challenge domestic ideology.

In the abolitionist movement a similar evolution occurred. Women abolitionists especially felt thwarted because they were trying to abolish what they defined as a huge moral wrong, slavery. Their encounters with an economic and political system in which they had little influence led to a widespread conviction that women must fight for their own rights. If they were to help free the slaves, women came to recognize that they had to free themselves first. Thus, during the 1840s, numerous abolitionists added the issue of women's rights to their platforms. For some, gaining rights seemed a practical matter; they simply wanted to proceed with their reforms. For others, achieving their rights constituted an ethical issue that would allow them to carry out their moral responsibilities to the nation.

The limits on women abolitionists became especially obvious in 1840, after the national antislavery organization split into male-only and male-female factions over the so-called woman question. The integrated group sent female delegates to a world antislavery convention in London in 1841, where male delegates seated the women behind a curtain and denied them the right to vote. When the women delegates walked out in indignation, a number of sympathetic black and white men joined them. As a result of this upsetting incident, delegates Lucretia Mott and Elizabeth Cady Stanton agreed that a women's protest meeting was needed in America. Mott, Stanton, and others recognized that their reform efforts would continue to confront obstacles until women had such rights as speaking, voting, and holding public office.

Seneca Falls

It was not until 19 July 1848 at Seneca Falls, New York, that the first women's rights meeting occurred. Although Elizabeth Cady Stanton's husband Henry fled town in embarrassment, Lucretia Mott's husband James agreed to chair the convention. The meeting attracted approximately three hundred people, including about forty men.

After many speeches, including one by black abolitionist Frederick Douglass on behalf of woman suffrage, delegates paraphrased the Declaration of Independence in a plea for equality and expanded rights for women, including the right to vote. It read in part: "We hold these truths to be self-evident: that all men and women are created equal: that they are endowed by their Creator with certain inalienable rights: that among these are life, liberty and the pursuit of happiness." It also condemned unfair practices of men: "The history of mankind is a history of repeated injuries and usurpations on the part of man toward woman, having in direct object the establishment of an absolute tyranny over her." Sixty-eight women and thirty-two men signed this Declaration of Sentiments and Resolutions, the first formal declaration regarding women's rights in the United States.

The press heaped unsparing ridicule on the Seneca Falls convention and its demands, but many other similar conventions followed in both eastern and western states. In 1850, James Gordon Bennett of the *New York Herald* asked "what do the leaders of the women's right conventions want? They want to be members of Congress, and in the heat of debate subject themselves to coarse jests and indecent language."

Other people expressed sincere dismay concerning women's rights, especially when, during the winter of 1850–1851, Amelia Bloomer, a temperance reformer, women's rights editor, and suffragist living in Seneca Falls, adopted a reform dress worn first by Elizabeth Smith Miller and composed of a short skirt and Turkish-style pantaloons. Women who became "Bloomer girls" expressed their desire for better health, freedom of movement, and even equality by freeing themselves from the dictates of fashion, but the Bloomer outfit created such controversy that most women abandoned it by the end of the decade.

Women's Rights Demands

Women's rights may have appeared a foolish and trivial issue to some people, but for its female and male advocates it held serious and far-reaching implications. For instance, married women's property rights meant a great deal to women who lost control of their property and were left destitute by mismanagement or death of a husband. Although several states discussed protective legislation during the 1830s and New York considered such a statute in 1836, the state of Mississippi passed the first Married Women's Property Law in 1839.

Soon, many women's rights advocates began to promote modification of women's property laws, notably a Jewish woman of Polish birth named Ernestine Rose. First a temperance and abolitionist reformer, Rose had become committed to women's rights by the 1840s. In New York, Rose circulated petitions and spoke for a newly introduced women's property bill. When the legislature finally passed the limited bill in 1848, it marked the beginning of alterations in women's ownership of property. Shortly afterward, Pennsylvania passed a similar bill, largely because of the urging of journalist and newspaper editor Jane Swisshelm. Other states soon followed.

Proponents of women's rights during the 1840s and 1850s also campaigned for political privileges for women. Outraged that the widely touted "democracy" that developed during the Age of Jackson applied only to white males, women came to believe that suffrage meant more than the right to cast a ballot. Suffragists saw women's entry into the political arena as the path to the ultimate goal of equality with men. In 1859, for example, Mary F. Thomas, M.D., addressed a special session of the Indiana General Assembly, convened to hear the grievances of Indiana women. Walker pleaded with her "brothers in the Senate and House of Representatives" to "remove the political disabilities" that retarded women's progress.

Women's Rights Ideology

In the process of defending their demands, women's rights leaders developed an intricate ideology during the 1840s and 1850s. First, doctrines established during the American Revolution contributed beliefs in equality, human perfectibility, and the right of citizens to participate in their own governance. Women's rights' leaders argued that if such rights belonged to Americans, then they certainly belonged to women who were also Americans.

Second, the philosophies of British reformers fed the American women's rights crusade by openly discussing women's issues and helping foster a climate that made reform thinkable and even possible. In the 1830s, for example, Scottish-born Frances Wright's lectures explored such topics as equality, improved education, divorce, and birth control. Also, English author Mary Wollstonecraft's *Vindication of the Rights of Woman* (1792), one of the earliest arguments for the equality of women, was widely read in America during the 1840s.

Third, American writers and speakers offered a variety of perspectives and philosophies. Margaret Fuller, known as the "high priestess" of the Transcendentalist movement, addressed the issue of equality. As editor of the Transcendentalist journal *The Dial* during the 1840s, Fuller maintained that women should be allowed to expand their strengths and interests, just as men did. In 1845, Fuller's *Woman in the Nineteenth Century* became the first American book to examine woman's place in society. It sold out within a week and created a spirited debate in the *New York Daily Tribune*, with editor Horace Greeley supporting Fuller.

Another American writer and speaker, Elizabeth Cady Stanton, concentrated her efforts on gaining the ballot for women. Because Stanton believed that liberation lay in political participation, she especially advocated woman suffrage. In 1850, Stanton met Susan B. Anthony, who soon became Stanton's closest collaborator. Henry Stanton reportedly told Elizabeth, "You stir up Susan and she stirs up the world." Anthony did indeed prove herself an effective orator and an efficient organizer for temperance, abolitionism, and women's rights during the 1840s and

1850s. A Quaker schoolteacher and manager of the family farm, Anthony never married and was thus free to travel and speak. Like Stanton, Anthony emphasized the right to vote: "Suffrage involves every basic principle of republican government, all our social, civil, religious, educational, and political rights."

Lucy Stone also contributed to the ideology of women's rights. After attending Oberlin College in the 1840s, Stone became an abolitionist speaker and soon came to deplore the idea of Civil Death and the limitations it placed on women. When she married Henry Blackwell (brother of physicians Elizabeth and Emily) in 1855, Stone kept her family name and entered into a well-publicized marriage contract which read in part: "we deem it a duty to declare that this act [marriage] implies no sanction of, nor promise of voluntary obedience to such of the present laws of marriage, as they refuse to recognize the wife as an independent, rational being, while they confer upon the husband an injurious and unnatural superiority."

Lucretia Mott also came to women's rights through abolitionism. As an official minister in the Society of Friends (Quakers), Mott had a deep religious belief in justice and equality for all people. During the 1850s, she turned her Philadelphia home into an Underground Railroad station and, in addition to caring for six children, traveled extensively to lecture on abolitionism and women's rights. She frequently employed Biblical evidence to argue that the inferior status of women was neither natural nor divinely ordained. Rather than promoting woman suffrage, Mott concentrated on a new view of women as responsible, self-sustaining individuals.

Black women contributed to the emerging ideology as well. Although many black women considered antislavery a more pressing cause, some espoused women's rights. For example, abolitionist and journalist Harriet Purvis and her sister Margaretta Forten, Sarah Remond, Mary Ann Shadd Cary, Harriet Tubman, and Sojourner Truth helped lay the groundwork for black feminism, advocating a humanistic community in which every individual would be encouraged to fulfill his or her potential.

The energy and ideas of these women's rights leaders helped create a dynamic and visible movement by the 1850s. Hundreds of women's rights meetings occurred each year, and the "woman question" was widely and hotly debated. Still, women's rights appealed primarily to white middle- and upper-class women. Thus, issues important to working, immigrant, poor, Native American, African American, and such other black women as those of Haitian and Jamaican heritage continued to receive short shrift. The existence and repercussions of classism and racism still eluded most of these reformers.

In addition, women's rights' leaders frequently identified men as the enemy rather than examining the economic and political structure of

American society. In scapegoating men, they underestimated an economic system that kept people of certain classes and races at the bottom of the economic ladder, and thus poor, uneducated, inarticulate, and seemingly inferior. Women's rights' leaders also typically failed to understand the impact of political power concentrated in the hands of a few. They believed that by gaining the right to vote for themselves, they would be able to equalize the American political system, but they limited their view to gender and ignored such other limiting factors as race, ethnicity, and social class that also demanded equalizing.

Still, issues had been pinpointed and discussed, while the public had been forced to increase its awareness of the ills afflicting women. Also, women had learned organizational and speaking skills, attracted a number of male supporters, and forced legislators to accept their petitions. As a result, the groundwork of an American feminist movement was in place.

WOMEN IN THE WEST

Native Women

As traders, missionaries, and settlers continued to cross the California and Oregon trails, they created near chaos among many native peoples. Indians who crossed the so-called Trail of Tears sometimes experienced a destructive transformation, while other American Indian women saw their influence and customs erode further. Missionary schools especially trained native women in customary white women's subjects, stressing homemaking and punishing them for speaking their native dialects or wearing traditional clothing.

Indian women agriculturalists also lost their work and status, for, even as early as the 1840s and 1850s, settlers effectively began to scatter such farming tribes as the Bannocks of Oregon and southern Idaho, the Utes of Utah and Nevada, and the Digger Indians of California. A ninety-year-old Chiuructo Indian living in Sonoma, California, commented that "before the whites arrived here we had much food and a very good life."

The U.S. government tried to compensate displaced Native Americans by giving them supplies and cash payments known as bounties and annuities. Beginning in 1841, however, a wave of Anglo migrants who intended to permanently settle and establish farms entered California by traveling overland. During the late 1840s and 1850s, the discovery of gold and silver in California, Colorado, Nevada, and Idaho dispossessed additional thousands of Native Americans with little restitution.

Rather than watch their families starve or disperse, native women often urged their bands and tribes to fight back. One much-publicized confrontation between U.S. soldiers and Native Americans occurred in Minnesota in 1861. Mass hangings of Sioux Indians who resisted U.S.

government land policies followed, leaving women and their children to fend for themselves.

As American settlers flooded into the Pacific Northwest, similar conflicts occurred. Although missionaries had gone to Oregon during the 1840s intending to educate Indians and convert them to Christianity, they had little success deflecting clashes between natives and settlers. A settler in the Nisqually Valley of present-day Washington State related a common scenario, the deterioration of good relations: "The Indians were very kind to us, protecting us from unfriendly tribes and doctoring us when sick. . . . but those times soon passed with the coming of other emigrants, who through mistreatment of the Indians caused hatred between the whites and the Indians."

Spanish-speaking women, who were also native to western areas inundated by settlers, similarly faced new dilemmas during the 1840s and 1850s. During the 1840s, for example, conflict escalated between Tejanos and the Americans who, since the Battle of the Alamo, ruled the Republic of Texas. In 1845, the United States annexed Texas as a slave state and the following year entered into war with Mexico, which still claimed ownership of Texas.

Texas and the Southwest soon fell into American hands. Colonel Stephen W. Kearney established American rule in Santa Fe in August 1846. Santa Fe native Marítza González recalled that the American soldiers' swearing, drinking, and brawling appalled and frightened her family and neighbors. They found it hard to believe that Kearney brashly seized the former Mexican governor's office and even sat in his chair. González added that many Mexicans talked heatedly of revolting against the conquering Americans and retrieving their former lands.

On 13 August 1846, explorer John C. Frémont and Commodore Robert F. Stockton similarly seized San Francisco and annexed California to the United States. When the U.S. Congress ratified the Treaty of Guadalupe Hidalgo on 10 March 1848, the United States acquired approximately one-half of Mexico's territory. According to the treaty, Texas now formally belonged to the United States, as did Arizona, California, and New Mexico.

Also in 1848, workers digging a mill race for John A. Sutter near Sacramento, California, discovered flecks of gold. Soon, especially during 1849 and 1850, hopeful Americans, Canadians, and Europeans flooded into California's goldfields. Here they appropriated *Chicano* (Mexican American) lands and warned Chicano miners, who accounted for 8 to 9 percent of all miners, to leave the mines. Thousands of Chicanas saw their lands confiscated, their livelihoods destroyed, their pastoral way of life eroded, and their families scattered.

In Texas, Tejanos also lost their land, both through legal and extralegal means, while in New Mexico, 80 percent of original residents eventually saw their lands confiscated or overrun. Despite a provision in the Treaty of Guadalupe Hidalgo guaranteeing New Mexicans all the rights and privileges of U.S. citizens, a number of social, economic, and legal provisions restricted them and their privileges. At least in part, negative beliefs regarding local peoples underlay such actions. Many Anglos characterized New Mexicans as lazy, immoral, and profligate.

In 1851, the U.S. Congress passed the Gwinn Land Act and appointed a land commission to provide a means for Spanish-speaking people to hold on to the land they claimed, but because the commission favored American claimants and the process consumed huge amounts of time and money, most *Californios* (native Californians) eventually lost their titles. One woman lamented her loss of three ranches to an American settler: "I find myself in the greatest poverty living by the favor of God, and them that give me a morsel to eat."

In addition to legislation, other factors mitigated against Chicanos. Luxurious living followed by drought years, high taxes, litigation regarding the division of *ranchos* among numerous heirs, and the inroads that shrewd American traders made into local commerce all contributed to their problems. As for Chicanas in particular, they found their lives drastically changed, for they were now subject to American laws, policies, and gender expectations.

By 1860, despite immigration from Mexico, Americans and others outnumbered Chicanos in Los Angeles, San Antonio, Santa Fe, and Tucson, previously the most populous Mexican towns in the Southwest. In all four cities, women held more paid employment and headed more households than they had before American conquest, yet continued to cling to patriarchal values. They also adhered to the concept of *la familia*, an extended kin network that could also include *compadres*, or friends, and demanded loyalty before an individual's own welfare or success.

Anglo Women

Across the California and Oregon trails coursed thousands of Anglo women. In 1843, 1,000 migrants assembled in Independence, Missouri, and then covered 2,000 miles to reach their final destination, Fort Vancouver on the Columbia River in Oregon country. In 1845, another 3,000 migrants entered Oregon. During the 1850s and early 1860s, settlers also began to inhabit the vast and arid Great Plains.

Of these migrants, perhaps as many as one-third to one-half were women, who soon discovered numerous freedoms and opportunities that had not existed in their former homes. For instance, schools throughout the West welcomed female students. When the first tax-supported university in Iowa, now the University of Iowa, opened its doors in 1856, it accepted 124 students—83 males and 41 females.

In addition, those western women who chose to marry—and not all did so—usually entered a monogamous union based upon an economic partnership. They offered their own experience, skills, and labors and, in turn, looked for good health, perseverance, and practical expertise in potential husbands. Still, couples often courted in haste. In a society where males far outnumbered females, matches frequently occurred without parental guidance or sufficient forethought.

Some women of the Latter-day Saints, or Mormons, constituted an exception to this process because they practiced polygamy. Only a small percentage of Mormons adhered to plural marriage and, among those families that did, the wife, or wives, had to grant a husband permission to marry another wife. Also, many of these Mormon women maintained that they preferred polygamy because it lightened their workloads, provided several "mothers" for their children, and supplied them with additional women in the household to share their emotional and psychological burdens. In 1857, one Mormon woman explained that plural marriage freed her to "work out her individual character as separate from her husband."

Western marriages and families, both monogamous and polygamous, experienced a huge number of stresses. Despite the positive aspects of western settlement, many factors exercised negative pressure: the demanding physical environment, financial worries, lack of support from kin and from religious institutions, and changing expectations of marriage. When marriages foundered, numerous western men and women deserted their mates or applied for a divorce. Because western divorce laws were generally more liberal than those in the Northeast and the South, the divorce rate in the West far outdistanced the divorce rate in other regions of the country. In fact, during the 1850s the then-western state of Indiana was widely known as a divorce mill—an early forerunner to Reno.

Female divorce petitioners increasingly complained that their husbands physically or verbally abused them, a grievance that more and more courts accepted as grounds for divorce. Male divorce petitioners frequently accused their wives of stepping out of bounds and of being strong-minded women. As these complaints suggest, the customary female ideal—that of an obedient, passive, docile, and quiet woman—began to break down in the West before the Civil War.

If western women asserted themselves it was because most recognized their own worth. Women working at home from sunup to sundown thought of themselves as crucial contributors to their families' western ventures. As one Illinois woman related, "While the men were learning to farm, the women and children actually supported the families. . . . The women were not unaware of this fact and were quite capable of scoring a point on occasion when masculine attitudes became too bumptious."

Growing numbers of western women also worked outside the home. Unlike the East, in the West more women taught school than did men. They also taught in missionary schools established for Native American pupils. Other women worked in an incredible variety of jobs, including boardinghouse keepers, domestics, doctors, editors, entrepreneurs, missionaries, milliners, ministers, nurses, shop clerks, and writers. Although they often met with prejudice and criticism, women continued to work. As a California book sales agent of the 1850s remarked, she had to steel herself daily to enter offices and restaurants to seek out potential customers—mostly men.

Western women also increasingly engaged in reform and club activities. Thousands of women, including rural women, joined church auxiliaries, book clubs, hospital aid associations, musical groups, and western chapters of the Women's Christian Temperance Union. As they battled to improve their communities and help less fortunate people, these women also discovered their own skills and abilities. They soon learned that they could capably run meetings, handle funds, and cast votes.

This expansion of women's roles and contributions encouraged many women to seek additional changes. During the 1850s and 1860s, the discussion of women's rights, including women's right to own property and to vote, gained momentum in western states and territories. Jane Grey Swisshelm, editor of the *St. Cloud Visiter* (Minnesota), also argued for women's rights, specifically improved education for women and woman suffrage, while Clarinda Nichols played a significant role in the constitutional convention that gave Kansas women the right to vote in school elections in 1861.

Black and Asian Women

Despite such advances, custom and law continued to prohibit many types of western women from seizing opportunities the West offered other women. Not all western women received the right to obtain a better education, hold a well-paid job, seek membership in a club, or exercise the right to vote in local elections. Black and Asian women often found themselves excluded from rights and privileges that Anglo women took for granted. Women's clubs accepted only members with the same skin color. Schools often barred nonwhite or non-English-speaking girls from attendance. Employers usually gave preference to white, English-speaking women. As a result, the western experience of a white woman could differ radically from that of a woman of color.

Still, a significant number of black settlers participated in the westward migration. Local manuscript census records indicate that slave women played an important part in settling the West. Even states that proclaimed themselves antislavery in sentiment had slaves in their population. Owners usually described these people as servants rather than slaves, although the terms of servitude were essentially the same as slavery. Frequently newspaper advertisements sought the return of a runaway "servant." One owner claimed that his black, thirteen-year-old servant had been "decoyed" away by a "meddling person." He declared that "it would be an act of charity to her could she be restored to him."

Unlike slaves, free women of color usually went west by choice and frequently settled in towns rather than rural areas. They often took jobs as unskilled laborers and domestic servants. They usually received less pay and worse treatment than did their white counterparts. Many employers refused to hire black women at all; businesspeople frequently denied them service; and landowners refused to rent their property to them.

Despite the difficulties, a sizable number of African Americans and black women of other backgrounds established themselves in the West. A Mississippi River steamboat cook nicknamed Black Ann not only supported herself but bought her children out of slavery during the 1830s. Another named Elizabeth Eakins bought land in Owen County, Indiana, in 1839, paying $1.25 per acre. Another free black family converted their home into a station on the Underground Railroad and worked with white abolitionists to help fugitive slaves escape to Canada. Other black women opened boardinghouses, restaurants, laundries, and similar businesses. Among these was Mary Ellen Pleasant, a boardinghouse owner, investor, and philanthropist in California. Black women also far outnumbered men in the teaching profession.

Like African Americans, Asian people also encountered problems in the American West. Asian women, including Chinese and Japanese, had long lived in Hawaii, but only a few settled on the mainland. Then war and poverty in China spurred a large number of Chinese, especially men, to migrate to the United States. In 1851 approximately twenty-seven hundred Chinese landed in the United States, many of them Cantonese from Guangdon (Kwangtung) Province on the southeastern coast of China; the following year over twenty thousand did so. Some 77 percent of Chinese immigrants permanently located in California, while others went to Idaho, Montana, Nevada, Oregon, and Washington.

A few of these immigrants were women, many of whom colonized the fishing villages of Monterey, California. Several other Chinese women went to rural areas as farm wives. But the majority of the early Chinese immigrants were single men, discouraged by low pay from bringing women as wives from China, and barred by miscegenation laws from marrying white American women. Other Chinese were married men who had left their wives and families in China. Employers, who viewed these men as temporary and migratory laborers, had little interest in attracting their wives and families to the United States. The low wages they paid also encouraged Chinese men to keep their families in China where the cost of living allowed their American wages to stretch farther.

These and other forces created a demand for Chinese prostitutes, and, after 1840, employers began to import Chinese women. Poverty-stricken families sold their daughters into indentured servitude, while other families were duped into parting with daughters. By the 1850s, Chinese societies known as *tongs* supplied West Coast brothels with Chinese women. Women who worked as prostitutes demonstrated a variety of responses to their situations: some died before the end of their four- or five-year term, while others became small entrepreneurs—such as shop or boardinghouse keepers catering primarily to the Chinese community—who made a profit and achieved influence in their communities. Yet others fled, especially to Protestant-sponsored mission rescue homes, or married and left the business.

In 1860, only 1,784 Chinese women lived in the United States, compared to 33,149 men. In such cities as San Francisco, approximately 85 percent of Chinese women were indentured servants working as prostitutes. Others were wives and daughters of men of the merchant class, who usually spent their cloistered lives caring for their families in segregated areas known as Chinatowns. Others worked for low wages sewing, washing clothes, rolling cigars, or making such goods as brooms and slippers. Yet others were farming wives and daughters, who, much like Anglo women, helped with agricultural and related tasks. One of these, a former prostitute turned homesteader in Idaho, Polly Bemis, became a legendary figure, known for her compassion and courage.

For many Americans, the age of reform meant little more than newspaper headlines or perhaps occasional annoyance with reformers' rantings. They were busy living their own lives, or perhaps they preferred to think of the United States in happier terms. During the 1850s, Frances Flora Palmer, a lithographer at the firm of Currier and Ives, captivated Americans with her cheerful and reassuring farm scenes, winter landscapes, railroad trains hurtling across the terrain, and pioneers trekking westward.

Other Americans, however, had had their awareness expanded. Even though economic panic and reformism had stimulated many changes for the better, including improved education, awareness of alcoholism, institutions to help the poor and ill, and the beginnings of married women's property rights, black slavery still blemished American democracy. In addition, women, who contributed heavily to the nation's economic system, received little in the way of rights. Other problems persisted as well. But by 1861 many Americans recognized the existence of injustice. What they would do to redress it further, however, was as yet unclear.

Suggestions for Further Reading

Albert, Judith Strong. "Margaret Fuller's Row at the Greene Street School: Early Female Education in Providence, 1837–1839," *Rhode Island History* 42 (May 1983): 43–55.

Aptheker, Herbert. *Abolitionism: A Revolutionary Movement.* Boston: Twayne Publishers, 1989.

Bardes, Barbara, and Suzanne Gossett. *Declarations of Independence: Women and Political Power in Nineteenth-Century American Fiction.* New Brunswick, NJ: Rutgers University Press, 1990.

Bartlett, Elizabeth Ann, ed. *Sarah Grimké: Letters on the Equality of the Sexes and Other Essays.* New Haven, CT: Yale University Press, 1988.

Basch, Françoise. "Women's Rights and the Wrongs of Marriage in Mid-Nineteenth Century America," *History Workshop Journal* 22 (Autumn 1986): 18–40.

Basch, Norma. "Invisible Women: The Legal Fiction of Marital Unity in Nineteenth-Century America," *Feminist Studies* 5 (Summer 1979): 346–66.

———. *In the Eyes of the Law: Women, Marriage, and Property in Nineteenth-Century New York.* Ithaca, NY: Cornell University Press, 1982.

———. "Equity vs. Equality: Emerging Concepts of Women's Political Status in the Age of Jackson," *Journal of the Early Republic* 3 (Fall 1983): 297–318.

Bean, Lee L., Geraldine P. Mineau, and Douglas L. Anderton. "High-Risk Childbearing: Fertility and Infant Mortality on the American Frontier," *Social Science History* 16 (Fall 1992): 337–63.

Bednarowski, Mary Farrell. "Outside the Mainstream: Women's Religion and Women Religious Leaders in Nineteenth-Century America," *Journal of the American Academy of Religion* 48 (June 1980): 207–31.

Beecher, Maureen Ursenbach. "Women's Work on the Mormon Frontier," *Utah Historical Quarterly* 49 (Summer 1981): 276–90.

Berg, Barbara J. *The Remembered Gate: Origins of American Feminism.* New York: Oxford University Press, 1978.

Berkin, Carol Ruth, and Mary Beth Norton, eds. *Women of America: A History.* Boston: Houghton Mifflin Company, 1979, Part III, section 7.

Blackett, R. J. M. *Building an Antislavery Wall: Black Americans in the Abolitionist Movement, 1830–1860.* Baton Rouge: Louisiana State University Press, 1983.

Bledsoe, Lucy Jane. "Adventuresome Women on the Oregon Trail, 1840–1867," *Frontiers* 7 (1984): 22–29.

Bleser, Carol, ed. *In Joy and in Sorrow: Women, Family, and Marriage in the Victorian South, 1830–1900.* New York: Oxford University Press, 1991.

Blocker, Jack S., Jr. *American Temperance Movements: Cycles of Reform.* Boston: Twayne Publishers, 1989.

Boylan, Anne M. "Women and Politics in the Era Before Seneca Falls," *Journal of the Early Republic* 10 (Fall 1990): 363–82.

Brenzel, Barbara. "Lancaster Industrial School for Girls: A Social Portrait of a Nineteenth-Century Reform School for Girls," *Feminist Studies* 3 (Fall 1975): 40–53.

Bunker, Gary L. "Antebellum Caricature and Woman's Sphere," *Journal of Women's History* 3 (Winter 1992): 6–43.

Burnham, Dorothy. "The Life of the Afro-American Woman in Slavery," *International Journal of Women's Studies* I (July/August 1978): 363–77.

Campbell, John. "Work, Pregnancy, and Infant Mortality Among Southern Slaves," *Journal of Interdisciplinary History* 14 (Spring 1984): 793–812.

Capper, Charles. *Margaret Fuller: An American Romantic Life.* Vol. I. *The Private Years.* New York: Oxford University Press, 1992.

Casper, Scott E. "An Uneasy Marriage of Sentiment and Scholarship: Elizabeth F. Ellet and the Domestic Origins of American Women's History," *Journal of Women's History* 4 (Fall 1992): 10–35.

Cazden, Elizabeth. *Antoinette Brown Blackwell.* Old Westbury, NY: Feminist Press, 1982.

Censer, Jane Turner. "'Smiling Through Her Tears': Ante-Bellum Southern Women and Divorce," *American Journal of Legal History* 25 (January 1981): 24–47.

Clinton, Catherine. "Equally Their Due: The Education of the Planter Daughter in the Early Republic," *Journal of the Early Republic* (Spring 1982): 39–60.

———. *The Other Civil War: American Women in the Nineteenth Century.* New York: Hill and Wang, 1984. Chapters 2–4, 6–8.

———. "Fanny Kemble's Journal: A Woman Confronts Slavery on a Georgia Plantation," *Frontiers* 9 (1987): 74–79.

Cohen, Sherrill. *The Evolution of Women's Asylums Since 1500: From Refuges for Ex-Prostitutes to Shelters for Battered Women*. New York: Oxford University Press, 1992.

Conrad, Susan P. *Perish the Thought: Intellectual Women in Romantic America, 1830–1860*. New York: Oxford University Press, 1976.

De León, Arnoldo. *The Tejano Community, 1836–1900*. Albuquerque: University of New Mexico Press, 1982.

———. *Mexican Americans in Texas: A Brief History*. Wheeling, IL: Harlan Davidson, Inc., 1993. Chapter 3.

Douglas, Ann. *The Feminization of American Culture*. New York: Alfred A. Knopf, 1979.

DuBois, Ellen Carol. *Feminism and Suffrage: The Emergence of an Independent Women's Movement in America, 1848–1869*. Ithaca, NY: Cornell University Press, 1978.

Dudden, Faye E. *Women in the American Theatre: Actresses and Audience, 1790–1870*. New Haven, CT: Yale University Press, 1994.

Dysart, Jane. "Mexican Women in San Antonio, 1830–1860: The Assimilation Process," *Western Historical Quarterly* 7 (October 1976): 365–75.

Eckhardt, Celia Morris. *Fanny Wright: Rebel in America*. Cambridge, MA: Harvard University Press, 1984.

Embry, Jessie L. "Effects of Polygamy on Mormon Women," *Frontiers* 7 (1984): 56–61.

———. "Mothers and Daughters in Polygamy," *Dialogue* 18 (Fall 1985): 99–107.

Evans, Sara M. *Born for Liberty: A History of Women in America*. New York: Free Press, 1989. Chapters 4–5.

Faust, Drew Gilpin. *The Ideology of Slavery: Proslavery Thought in the Antebellum South, 1830–1860*. Baton Rouge: Louisiana State University Press, 1981.

Foster, Lawrence. *Women, Family, and Utopia: Communal Experiments of the Shakers, the Oneida Community, and the Mormons*. Syracuse: Syracuse University Press, 1991.

Friedman, Jean E. *The Enclosed Garden: Women and Community in the Evangelical South, 1830–1900*. Chapel Hill: University of North Carolina Press, 1985.

Friedman, Jean E., William G. Shade, and Mary Jane Capozzoli, eds. *Our American Sisters: Women in American Life and Thought*. 4th ed. Lexington, MA: D.C. Heath and Company, 1987. Chapters 8–11.

Ginzberg, Lori D. "Moral Suasion Is Moral Balderdash: Women, Politics, and Social Activism in the 1850s," *Journal of American History* 73 (December 1986): 601–22.

———. *Women and the Work of Benevolence: Morality, Politics, and Class in the Nineteenth-Century United States*. New Haven, CT: Yale University Press, 1990.

González, Deena J. "La Tules of Image and Reality: Euro-American Attitudes and Legend Formation on a Spanish-Mexican Frontier," 57–69, in *Unequal Sisters: A Multicultural Reader in U.S. Women's History*, edited by Vicki L. Ruiz and Ellen Carol DuBois. 2d ed. New York: Routledge, Chapman, & Hall, 1994.

Greene, Dana. "'Quaker Feminism': The Case of Lucretia Mott," *Pennsylvania History* 48 (April 1981): 143–54.

Griswold del Castillo, Richard. *The Los Angeles Barrio, 1850–1890: A Social History*. Berkeley: University of California Press, 1979.

———. *La Familia: Chicano Families in the Urban Southwest, 1848 to the Present*. Notre Dame, IN: University of Notre Dame Press, 1984.

Groneman, Carol. "Working-Class Immigrant Women in Mid-Nineteenth Century New York: The Irish Woman's Experience," *Journal of Urban History* (May 1978): 255–73.

Hansen, Debra Gold, *Strained Sisterhood: Gender and Class in the Boston Female Anti-Slavery Society*. Amherst: University of Massachusetts Press, 1993.

Hardesty, Nancy A. *Women Called to Witness: Evangelical Feminism in the 19th Century*. Nashville: Abingdon Press, 1984.

Hersh, Blanche G. *The Slavery of Sex: Feminist-Abolitionists in Nineteenth-Century America.* Urbana: University of Illinois Press, 1978.

Hill, Marilynn Wood. *Their Sisters' Keepers: Prostitution in New York City, 1830–1870.* Berkeley: University of California Press, 1993.

Hirata, Lucie Cheng. "Free, Indentured, Enslaved: Chinese Prostitutes in Nineteenth-Century America," *Signs* 5 (Autumn 1979): 3–29.

Hoffman, Nancy. *Woman's "True" Profession: Voices from the History of Teaching.* Old Westbury, NY: Feminist Press, 1981.

Ireland, Robert M. "Frenzied and Fallen Females: Women and Sexual Dishonor in the Nineteenth-Century United States," *Journal of Women's History* 3 (Winter 1992): 95–117.

Jameson, Elizabeth. "Women as Workers, Women as Civilizers: True Womanhood in the American West," *Frontiers* 7 (1984): 1–8.

Jennings, Thelma. "'Us Colored Women Had to Go Through A Plenty': Sexual Exploitation of African-American Slave Women," *Journal of Women's History* 1 (Winter 1990): 45–76.

Jensen, Joan M. *Loosening the Bonds, Mid-Atlantic Farm Women, 1750–1850.* New Haven, CT: Yale University Press, 1986.

Jones, Jacqueline. "'My Mother Was Much of a Woman': Black Women, Work, and the Family under Slavery," *Feminist Studies* 8 (Summer 1982): 235–69.

———. *Labor of Love, Labor of Sorrow: Black Women, Work and the Family from Slavery to the Present.* New York: Basic Books, 1985.

Kaufman, Polly Welts. "A Wider Field of Usefulness: Pioneer Women Teachers in the West, 1848–1854," *Journal of the West* 22 (April 1982): 16–25.

———. *Women Teachers on the Frontier.* New Haven, CT: Yale University Press, 1984.

Kelley, Mary. "The Sentimentalists: Promise and Betrayal in the Home," *Signs* 4 (Spring 1979): 434–46.

———. *Private Woman, Public Stage: Literary Domesticity in Nineteenth-Century America.* New York: Oxford University Press, 1984.

Kerber, Linda K., and Jane DeHart Mathews, eds. *Women's America: Refocusing the Past.* New York: Oxford University Press, 1987. Part IIa.

Kolmerton, Carol A. *Women in Utopia: The Ideology of Gender in the American Owenite Communities.* Bloomington: Indiana University Press, 1990.

Lebsock, Suzanne. "Complicity and Contention: Women in the Plantation South," *Georgia Historical Quarterly* 74 (Spring 1990): 59–83.

Lerner, Gerda. *The Grimké Sisters from South Carolina: Pioneers for Woman's Rights and Abolition.* New York: Schocken Books, 1971.

———, ed. *Black Women in White America: A Documentary History.* New York: Random House, 1973.

———. "The Political Activities of Antislavery Women," 112–28, in *The Majority Finds Its Past,* edited by Gerda Lerner, New York: Oxford University Press, 1979.

Leslie, Kent Anderson. "Amanda America Dickson: An Elite Mulatto Lady in Nineteenth-Century Georgia," in *Southern Women: Histories and Identities,* edited by Virginia Bernhard, Betty Brandon, Elizabeth Fox-Genovese, and Theda Perdue. Columbia: University of Missouri Press, 1992.

Levy, Joann. *They Saw the Elephant: Women in the California Gold Rush.* Hamden, CT: Shoe String Press, 1990.

Malone, Ann Patton. *Sweet Chariot: Slave Family and Household Structure in Nineteenth-Century Louisiana.* Chapel Hill: University of North Carolina Press, 1992.

Matthews, Glenna. *The Rise of the Public Woman: Woman's Power and Woman's Place in the United States, 1630–1970.* New York: Oxford University Press, 1992.

Matthews, Jean V. "Consciousness of Self and Consciousness of Sex in Antebellum Feminism," *Journal of Women's History* 5 (Spring 1993): 61–78.

McCall, Laura. "'The Reign of Brute Force is Now Over': A Content Analysis of *Godey's Lady's Book,* 1830–1860," *Journal of the Early Republic* 9 (Summer 1989): 217–36.

―――. "'With All the Wild, Trembling, Rapturous Feelings of a Lover': Men, Women, and Sexuality in American Literature, 1820–1860," *Journal of the Early Republic* 14 (Spring 1994): 71–89.

McDannell, Colleen. *The Christian Home in Victorian America, 1840–1900.* Bloomington: Indiana University Press, 1986.

McLaurin, Melton A. *Celia, A Slave.* Athens: University of Georgia Press, 1991.

McMillen, Sally G. *Motherhood in the Old South: Pregnancy, Childbirth, and Infant Rearing.* Baton Rouge: Louisiana State University Press, 1990.

―――. *Southern Women: Black and White in the Old South.* Wheeling, IL: Harlan Davidson, Inc., 1992.

Mihesuah, Devon A. *Cultivating the Rosebuds: The Education of Women at the Cherokee Female Seminary, 1851–1909.* Urbana: University of Illinois Press, 1993.

Miller, Darlis A. "Cross-Cultural Marriages in the Southwest: The New Mexico Experience, 1846–1900," *New Mexico Historical Review* 57 (October 1982): 335–60.

Morantz, Regina Markell, and Sue Zschoche. "Professionalism, Feminism, and Gender Roles: A Comparative Study of Nineteenth-Century Medical Therapeutics," *Journal of American History* 67 (December 1980): 568–88.

Moss, Elizabeth. *Domestic Novelists in the Old South: Defenders of Southern Culture.* Baton Rouge: Louisiana State University Press, 1992.

Myres, Sandra L. "Mexican Americans and Westering Anglos: A Feminine Perspective," *New Mexico Historical Review* 57 (October 1982): 317–33.

Newcomer, Susan. "Out of Wedlock: Childbearing in an Ante-bellum Southern County," *Journal of Family History* 15 (1990): 357–68.

Osterud, Nancy Grey. "Gender and the Transition to Capitalism in Rural America," *Agricultural History* 67 (Spring 1993): 14–29.

Pease, Jane H., and William H. Pease. *Ladies, Women, and Wenches: Choice and Constraint in Antebellum Charleston and Boston.* Chapel Hill: University of North Carolina Press, 1990.

Perkins, Linda. *Fanny Jackson Coppin and the Institute for Colored Youth, 1837–1902.* New York: Garland, 1987.

Riley, Glenda. "'Not Gainfully Employed': Women on the Iowa Frontier, 1833–1870," *Pacific Historical Review* 49 (May 1980): 237–64.

Rosenberg, Rosalind. *Beyond Separate Spheres: Intellectual Roots of Modern Feminism.* New Haven, CT: Yale University Press, 1982.

Ryan, Mary P. "The Power of Women's Networks: A Case Study of Female Moral Reform in Antebellum America," *Feminist Studies* 5 (Spring 1979): 66–85.

Samuels, Shirley. *The Culture of Sentiment: Race, Gender, and Sentimentality in Nineteenth-Century America.* New York: Oxford University Press, 1992.

Schlissel, Lillian. "Family on the Western Frontier," 81–92, in *Western Women: Their Land, Their Lives,* edited by Lillian Schlissel, Vicki L. Ruiz, and Janice Monk. Albuquerque: University of New Mexico Press, 1988.

Scott, Anne Firor. "Almira Lincoln Phelps: The Self-Made Woman in the Nineteenth Century," *Maryland Historical Magazine* 75 (September 1980): 203–16.

Shammas, Carole. "Black Women's Work and the Evolution of Plantation Society in Virginia," *Labor History* 26 (Winter 1985): 5–28.

Sharpless, Rebecca. "Southern Women and the Land," *Agricultural History* 67 (Spring 1993): 30–42.

Sklar, Kathryn Kish. *Catharine Beecher: A Study in American Domesticity.* New York: W. W. Norton and Company, 1973.

―――. "The Founding of Mount Holyoke College," 177–202, in *Women of America: A History,* edited by Carol Ruth Berkin and Mary Beth Norton. Boston: Houghton Mifflin Company, 1979.

Sklar, Kathryn Kish, and Thomas Dublin. *Women and Power in American History: A Reader.* Vol. I. Englewood Cliffs, NJ: Prentice-Hall, 1991. Parts 16–18.

Sterling, Dorothy, ed. *We Are Your Sisters: Black Women in the Nineteenth Century*. New York: W. W. Norton, 1984.

———. *Abbey Kelley and the Politics of Antislavery*. Lexington: University Press of Kentucky, 1994.

Terborg-Penn, Rosalyn. "Discrimination Against Afro-American Women in the Women's Movement, 1830–1920," 17–27, in *The Afro-American Woman: Struggles and Images,* edited by Sharon Harley and Rosalyn Terborg-Penn. Port Washington, NY: Kennikat Press, 1978.

Thomas, Sr. M. Evangeline. "The Role of Women Religious in Kansas History, 1841–1981," *Kansas History* 4 (Spring 1981): 53–63.

Tong, Benson. *Unsubmissive Women: Chinese Prostitutes in Nineteenth-Century San Francisco*. Norman: University of Oklahoma Press, 1994.

Vertinsky, Patricia. "Sexual Equality and the Legacy of Catharine Beecher," *Journal of Sport History* 6 (Spring 1979): 38–49.

Walsh, Mary R. *"Doctor's Wanted: No Women Need Apply": Sexual Barriers in the Medical Profession, 1835–1975*. New Haven, CT: Yale University Press, 1977.

Walters, Ronald C. "The Erotic South: Civilization and Sexuality in American Abolitionism," 87–98, in *Procreation or Pleasure? Sexual Attitudes in American History*, edited by Thomas L. Altherr. Malabar, FL: Robert E. Kreiger Publishing Company, 1983.

Weiner, Nelia Fermi. "Of Feminism and Birth Control Propaganda, 1790–1840," *International Journal of Women's Studies* 3 (September/October 1980): 411–30.

Wellman, Judith. "The Seneca Falls Women's Rights Convention," *Journal of Women's History* 3 (Spring 1991): 9–37.

White, Deborah Gray. *Ar'n't I a Woman? Female Slaves in the Plantation South*. New York: W. W. Norton & Co., Inc., 1984.

Winter, Kari J. *Subjects of Slavery, Agents of Change: Women and Power in Gothic Novels and Slave Narratives, 1790–1865*. Athens: University of Georgia Press, 1994.

Woloch, Nancy. *Women and the American Experience*. New York: Alfred A. Knopf, 1984. Chapters 5–8.

Yasui, Barbara. "The Nissei in Oregon, 1834–1940," *Oregon Historical Quarterly* 76 (1975): 225–57.

Yee, Shirley J. *Black Women Abolitionists: A Study in Activism, 1828–1860*. Knoxville: University of Tennessee Press, 1992.

Yellin, Jean F. *Women and Sisters: Antislavery Feminists in American Culture*. New Haven, CT: Yale University Press, 1990.

IMAGES
AND
REALITIES

*Above: Pocahontas,
after the 1616
engraving by Simon
van de Passe.*

*Left: A Spanish
illustration of the
"heathens" who came
to the Jesuit missions
near the modern
Arizona-Mexico
border in the early
eighteenth century.*

Left: Mary Gibson
Tilghman and sons, 1789.

Below: Batting cotton.

Right: Phillis Wheatley (ca. 1753–1784), poet and first African American published author.

Below: The Market Plaza, by Thomas Allen.

The Wife, 1831.

The working women of
Lynn, Massachusetts,
protest, early 1840s.

Left: "Madonna of the
Prairie," painting by W.H.D.
Koerner, 1921.

Right: Ma-ke
and Kun-zan-ya,
St. Louis, 1848.

Bottom: Harriet Tubman.

Right: Engraving from Godey's Lady's Book, 1845, features a number of achievement-oriented women, including several popular authors.

Below: Sarah Josepha Hale, editor of Godey's Lady's Book.

*Above: A nineteenth-century
New England schoolroom,
painting by C. Bosworth.*

*Below: Sojourner Truth
(ca. 1797–1883),
abolitionist.*

Left: The water carriers,
ca. 1880.

Below: Southern women,
photographed around 1860.

Left: Indian woman with baby.

Below: Pawnee Indian Wind Lodge, ca. 1868–1870.

Opposite top: Apache camp, ca. 1885.

Opposite bottom: "Chicago Joe," Mary Josephine Welch Hensley, who established the Red Light Saloon in Montana before the state outlawed dance halls.

Left: Dancing girl, Virginia City, Nevada.

Below: Lithograph of a nineteenth-century revival meeting after a painting by A. Rider.

Right: Annie Oakley, early publicity photo.

Below: Hunting along the Red River, 1870s.

Left: Portrait of Old Crow and his wife, 1880.

Bottom left: Wedding picture, William and Anna Belle Steintemp, 1881.

Bottom right: Wedding portrait, Mr. and Mrs. James Sullivan, ca. 1870.

Opposite: Former slave, Tillie Brackenridge, in San Antonio, ca. 1900.

"Womanly Strength of the Nation"
The Civil War and Reconstruction, 1861 to 1877

5

In April 1861, the American nation split into warring factions, the United States of America and the Confederate States of America. During four years of hostilities lasting until 1865, the North lost some 364,000 lives and the South, 265,000. The Civil War and its aftermath not only shook American society and government to its foundations but caused important changes in the lives and roles of American women. The model of womanhood, already somewhat unstable as a result of reformers' attacks, experienced further blows during the years of war and reconstruction. Yet the resiliency of gender expectations and social constructs regarding women proved remarkable; although the invented American woman tottered a bit, the model staunchly resisted collapse.

WOMEN'S CONTRIBUTIONS TO THE WAR EFFORT, 1861–1865

Forsaking Women's Rights

As part of their contribution to the war effort, women's rights leaders disbanded their formal, organized campaign during the war years. Many women's rights advocates believed that abolishing slavery and bringing fighting to an end had to claim the nation's complete attention. Others took a more practical approach to the issue. In 1861, Martha Wright wrote to Susan B. Anthony that it was unwise to argue for women's rights "when the nation's whole heart and soul are engrossed with the momentous crisis and nobody will listen."

Women's rights' leaders turned instead to abolishing slavery at last. In 1863, Susan B. Anthony, Elizabeth Cady Stanton, Ernestine Rose, and

Lucy Stone issued a call for a women's meeting in New York City on 14 May. When thousands of women responded, the National Woman's Loyal League resulted. After Angelina Grimké Weld spoke eloquently for supporting a war for freedom, the delegates agreed to collect one million signatures on petitions supporting congressional approval of the Thirteenth Amendment, which would constitutionally abolish slavery.

Stanton as president and Anthony as secretary of the Loyal League led an organization of five thousand members. Of these, two thousand volunteers gathered 400,000 signatures by the time the League dissolved in 1864. Although the League had set aside women's rights, it trained thousands of women in speaking, organizing, and petitioning, skills that would later prove useful in the campaign for woman suffrage.

Sanitary Aid Societies

During the spring of 1861, women began to congregate in homes, hotels, and churches to preserve fruit, roll bandages, and sew shirts. They also organized charity fairs and other fund-raising events to collect money with which to buy supplies for ill-equipped troops and military hospitals.

As early as April of 1861, three thousand New Yorkers met in Cooper Union to form the New York Women's Central Association for Relief. Late in 1861, the U.S. Sanitary Commission began to coordinate the efforts of seven thousand Union aid societies. But in virtually every state, North and South, similar types of organizations soon appeared, in which women served as officers and members of finance committees and sat on boards of directors.

Such women's groups sent tremendous quantities of supplies to both the Union and Confederate fronts. Organized in 1862, the Weldon, Pennsylvania, society contributed seventeen thousand dollars worth of goods in one year. In one month in 1863, the Center Ridge, Alabama, group sent "422 shirts, 551 pairs of drawers, 80 pairs of socks, 3 pairs of gloves, 6 boxes and a bale of hospital stores, 128 pounds of tapioca and $18 for hospital use." Other local societies began to establish "refreshment saloons" in the North and "wayside homes" in the South to aid passing military personnel. Two Philadelphia saloons dispensed more than eighty thousand dollars in supplies and served more than 600,000 meals by 1864.

Frequently, representatives from women's groups who traveled to the front to assist in distributing supplies found that havoc prevailed. Some hospitals received far more goods than they needed while others received nothing, or troop movements shunted aside supply wagons that sat in the rain or sun until their cargo spoiled. These women thus acted as forwarding agents, regulating the efforts of women's groups to prevent duplicated deliveries in some cases and shortages in others, and routing supply wagons away from roads used by troops and munitions.

One of the most active and effective of these women was Annie Turner Wittenmyer of Keokuk, Iowa, who served as forwarding agent for aid societies throughout Iowa. In 1862, Iowa officials recognized Wittenmyer's efforts by appointing her a State Sanitary Agent. When one morning Wittenmyer walked into an overcrowded hospital and discovered her own wounded brother eating hardtack and greasy bacon from a metal tray, she began to campaign for "diet kitchens" that would serve patients healthful diets. In 1864, she established the first diet kitchen, but her cause was far from achieved. Wittenmyer frequently fought with hospital agents, cooks, and doctors who laced coffee grounds with sawdust or sand to make them last longer, and she tried to stop hospital cooks from preparing and serving tainted meat to wounded soldiers.

Even more renowned is Clara Barton, who assisted the efforts of the U.S. Sanitary Commission. A former schoolteacher, Barton soon earned the names "Angel of the Battlefield" and "American Nightingale" for her efforts. The Civil War taught her about corruption, lack of supplies, and carnage so great that, in her words, "I wrung the blood from the bottom of my clothing before I could step." Because Barton's wartime experiences convinced her of the need for a national, ongoing relief organization that would be able to offer aid during wars and other national disasters, she later founded the American Red Cross.

Throughout the war, women also helped contraband (runaway slaves) and slaves freed by the Emancipation Proclamation in 1863. The Contraband Relief Society of Washington, D.C., composed of forty black women, supplied food and clothing, while the Colored Ladies' Sanitary Commission of Boston sent five hundred dollars to help freed slaves in Savannah, Georgia. Other similar groups established schools, located housing for widows and orphans, and supplied bandages and medicine.

Nurses

In the years before the war's beginning, women had nursed family members; hospitals employed charwomen in a quasi-nursing capacity; and Catholic sisters provided nursing care. In 1850, the Massachusetts legislature had established the New England Medical College and urged potential nurses to attend lectures. But none of these resources could meet the demands of Civil War hospitals, so nurses were trained in short courses or at the front.

Dr. Elizabeth Blackwell, who quickly recognized the need for better instruction, established in 1861 a training program for nurses. Blackwell also applied for the position of Superintendent of Women Nurses, but as a "female doctor" she appeared suspect to many people and thus failed to gain appointment.

Dorothea Dix secured the position instead. As Superintendent of Women Nurses, Dix recruited only women who were at least thirty years of age and "plain in appearance," for she feared that young, attractive nurses might arouse their patients' interest and create chaos in the hospitals. This policy caused great bitterness among younger women who were eager to contribute their services to the war effort.

Among Union nurses, Mary Ann Bickerdyke was especially well known. Called "Mother" Bickerdyke, this Quaker woman gained a reputation as a tireless worker and a fearless administrator in nineteen battlefield hospitals between 1861 and 1865. A co-worker of Bickerdyke's claimed that she was not afraid of anybody, including the high-ranking generals. "But Lord, how she works!" she marveled.

A black woman from Georgia, Susie King Taylor, kept a diary of her remarkable service as a Union nurse. After first teaching black children at the behest of Union forces, she married Sgt. Edward King of the first South Carolina Volunteers and began to work as a nurse and laundress. Taylor served with Clara Barton on South Carolina's Sea Islands, bandaging the wounded and consoling the dying. Taylor also learned how to handle a musket and, although seriously hurt in a boat accident, she remained with her regiment until the fall of Charleston in 1865.

Another Civil War nurse, Hannah Ropes of Massachusetts, also kept a diary during her service in 1862–1863 in a Washington hospital. In August 1862, Ropes wrote: "We have just cleaned and dressed over a hundred men from the Harrison's Landing—poor, worn fellows!" A month later, she described a young man who was shot through the lungs yet survived the night: "We considered him the greatest sufferer in the house, as every breath was a pain." As a strong abolitionist, Ropes explained that she could endure the hardships associated with nursing because "this is God's war. . . . The cause is that of the human race, and must prevail."

Mary Livermore, also a Massachusetts war nurse, similarly revealed in letters the terrible conditions she found in military hospitals. After a tour of Union hospitals in 1863, Livermore instituted a letter-writing and canvassing campaign in Illinois to amass needed supplies. Her description of a hospital in which she served graphically reveals the horrible conditions: "It was a miserable place. . . . The cots were placed inside the tents, on unplanked ground. . . . The hospital swarmed with large green flies, and their buzzing was like that of a beehive. . . . Many of the patients did not lift their hands to brush away the flies that swarmed into eyes, ears, noses, and mouths."

The writings of Phoebe Yates Pember, a hospital matron near Richmond, Virginia, indicated that conditions were no better in Confederate hospitals. Railing especially against drunken surgeons, Pember also recorded incompetence, laziness, and discrimination against her as a woman administrator. By 1863, wartime prices were so high in Richmond and her salary so meager that, at night, she wrote articles for magazines or did copywork for the War Department to supplement it.

For their Herculean efforts, army nurses received compliments from people ranging from wounded soldiers to President Abraham Lincoln himself. But it was not until 1892 that the U.S. Congress finally granted nurses formal recognition for their invaluable services by giving them a pension of twelve dollars a month.

Doctors

At the outbreak of the Civil War, neither the Confederacy nor Union commissioned women physicians. Although such women as Elizabeth and Emily Blackwell and Maria Zakrzewska practiced in the North and Louisa Shepard and Elizabeth Cohen in the South, widespread resistance to women doctors continued.

During the war, however, people who began to recognize the medical competence of women and the nation's need for more physicians supported the idea that women should have access to medical training. Such arguments led to the founding of the Chicago Hospital for Women and Children and the New York Medical College for Women, both in 1863.

The following year, Mary Edwards Walker, M.D., who had graduated from Syracuse Medical College in 1855, received a commission from the Union as assistant surgeon, the first woman to perform such duties in the American armed services. The U.S. Congress awarded Walker the Congressional medal of honor, which it later rescinded, probably due to Walker's strident reform campaigns, especially for woman suffrage and women's health, and her propensity to wear male attire. Well after Walker's death in 1919, Congress restored the medal to her.

Also in 1864, only fifteen years after Elizabeth Blackwell became a doctor, Rebecca Lee, a black woman, earned an M.D. degree at the New England Medical College. She practiced in Boston, but at the end of the Civil War spent several years in Richmond, Virginia, helping newly freed women and men.

Propagandists

The demands of war also opened another previously banned activity to women; now female authors wrote on such previously taboo subjects as politics and war. Julia Ward Howe employed poetry to arouse her readers' love of country, the most famous of which was her poem "Battle Hymn of the Republic," written in 1861 and set to music in 1862. Mary Abigail Dodge composed many outspoken essays of opinion and propaganda under her pen name, Gail Hamilton. In "A Call to My Country-Women," written in 1863, she urged women to aid the war effort.

Other women authors were responsible for an outpouring of books, pamphlets, and tracts designed to raise funds or shape public opinion, while yet other women published personal diaries, reminiscences, and novels written during the war years. A few even served as newspaper correspondents who shared their wartime experiences and observations with thousands of interested readers. One of these was Charlotte Forten, a black teacher in Georgia, who contributed essays on "Life in the Sea Islands" to the *Atlantic Monthly* in 1864. Forten sketched a powerful portrait of southern black people that showed them ready to learn, work, and become citizens.

Soldiers

Women offered their talents in many other ways as well. On the home front, the absence of men necessitated women acting as guards and soldiers in defense of their families and farms. From Minnesota to Texas, women wielded weapons to repel attacks by unprincipled white men and dispossessed Native Americans. In 1864, Milly Durkin faced a group of Commanche Indians and died with her shotgun in her hands.

Nearer the front, black abolitionist Mary Ann Shadd Cary served as a Recruiting Army officer who enlisted black volunteers in the Union army. Meanwhile, other women went to the front as soldiers. Disguised as men, about four hundred women fought in the Civil War between 1861 and 1865. Sarah Emma Edmonds of Michigan claimed that she served as a male nurse, spy, mail carrier, and soldier for two years.

Also, a number of southern women fought for the Confederacy, especially during the first year of the war. Amy Clarke of Mississippi enlisted with her husband and continued to fight after he was killed at Shiloh. Some of these served under fictitious names, while others used names of deceased male relatives. When discovered, they were sent home without the formality of discharge papers.

But some women went unexposed for the duration of the war. Laura J. Williams disguised herself in a Confederate uniform, took the name "Henry Buford," and recruited a company which she led to Virginia. She fought at the Battle of Shiloh, and was later imprisoned. Annie Clark also served without discovery, both in Louisiana and the 11th Tennessee regiment. She too fought at Shiloh, saw her husband killed there, and was later taken prisoner in Richmond, Kentucky.

Spies to Saboteurs

Other women served as spies, couriers, guides, scouts, smugglers, informers, and saboteurs. Elizabeth Van Lew of Richmond posed as an eccentric known as "Crazy Bet." Under this guise, she rescued Union prisoners from the Richmond prison and operated as a spy. Harriet Tubman, the most notable black person to serve as Union scout and spy, was also known for her great fortitude and cleverness. Tubman's secret missions supplied the information that allowed Union troops to successfully raid arsenals, warehouses, and forts along the Combahee River in South Carolina. Less heralded was Elizabeth Bowser, a former slave who became a servant in Jefferson Davis's home. There Bowser memorized military plans and collected military information for the Union.

Female spies also assisted the Confederacy. The Washington society hostess, Rose Greenhow, effectively relayed intelligence to Confederate leaders in code until her house arrest in late 1861 and her subsequent dispatch to Richmond. Greenhow's efforts reportedly helped the South win the First Battle of Bull Run in July 1861. Belle Boyd also gained prominence as a Confederate spy and courier in Virginia before she was betrayed and arrested in July 1862.

Women were especially effective as couriers and smugglers because hoopskirts, bustles, and false hairpieces could conceal anything from messages to pistols. Both northern and southern soldiers soon overcame their modesty, however, and by late 1861 thoroughly searched these good Victorian ladies or hired matrons to do so. Louisa Buckner of Virginia was one of the many women arrested after such a search. She carried concealed in her skirt more than one hundred ounces of quinine intended for a Confederate hospital. Still, many ingenious women successfully slipped through the lines with goods hidden in crinolines, hoop skirts, parasols, and false-bottom trunks.

On the Home Front

Women were also important on the home front during the war years. They took jobs in arsenals and munitions factories, and were more visible than ever in mills and other industrial employment. They invaded the offices of the Union and Confederate governments to become clerks who were often called "Government Girls." Women also kept farms and plantations going. In addition, they often had to face the terror of war in their own backyards, especially in the South where most battles occurred.

In April 1861, when Lincoln's naval blockade cut off the primarily agrarian South from its sources of war supplies, Confederate women turned their homes into crude factories to produce what goods they could with limited materials. Moreover, they frequently pursued a "scorched earth policy," that is, they burned their own crops and killed their own stock to keep them out of Yankee hands.

Southern women also took up arms. They learned how to handle rifles so they could resist invasions. In several towns, southern women organized local defense units. In 1865, a group of women under the command of a Mrs. J. Brown Morgan lined up for battle when Union troops threatened their town of LaGrange, Georgia. Perhaps more important, women protected their families and southern culture. They also attempted to keep their plantations, farms, and slaves in place until their men returned.

Despite women's efforts, by 1864 and 1865 incredible want and poverty existed throughout the Confederacy. In 1864, a Virginia woman wrote to her soldier husband: "Chrismus is most here again, and things is worse and worse. . . . Everything me and the children's got is patched. . . . We haven't got nothing in the house to eat but a little bit of meal. I don't want you to stop fighten them Yankees till you kill the last one of them, but try and get off and come home and fix us all up some and then you can go back and fight them a heep harder. . . . We can't none of us hold out much longer down here . . . my dear, if you put off a-comin' 'twon't be no use to come, for we'll all hands of us be out in the garden in the old graveyard with your ma and mine."

To stave off the specter of starvation during the latter years of the war, some desperate southern women began pillaging and rioting for bread, especially in New Orleans and Atlanta. Many others supported themselves and their children by taking teaching positions in white schools or by joining the "missionary" teachers flocking in from the North to teach in schools that the Union established for freed blacks after the Emancipation Proclamation of January 1863. Others became sewing women or salespeople. Still others took jobs with the Confederate Army that ranged from clerk to engineer.

Many of these women were formerly members of a "genteel elite," but wartime conditions and economic need clearly took priority over the standards of womanhood that at one time would have prevented them from pursuing some means of sustenance and support. Still, not all southern women approved of the changes; expressions of discontent were numerous and vehement. Undoubtedly, many were pleased to see the war end in 1865, even though they were on the losing side.

Teachers

Women in both the North and South not only filled the void left by men as they deserted white classrooms for the battlefield, but began to provide education for black children as well. After the Union declared the education of black Americans a priority, a free black woman from Alexandria, Virginia, Mary Chase, established on 1 September 1861 the first day school for black contrabands. Later that month, the American Missionary Association (AMA) engaged Mary Kelsey Peake to begin teaching classes at Fortress Monroe in Virginia. At Port Royal, South Carolina, Charlotte Forten taught as a representative of the Pennsylvania Freeman's Relief Association. The African Civilization Society supported yet other black schools and teachers.

The number of both black and white women teachers grew during the war years. In 1864, Sara G. Stanley, a free black who had studied at Oberlin College, asked for the support of the American Missionary Association so she could teach in the South. "No thought of suffering, and privation, nor even death, should deter me from making every effort possible, for the moral and intellectual elevation of these degraded people," she asserted. Stanley would receive ten dollars a month plus board for her efforts. Another free black, Sallie Daffin, received fifteen dollars a month for teaching day, evening, and Sunday schools; visiting black families; assisting the ill; and helping at a nearby hospital.

Black Women

As the stories of specific black women mentioned above begin to demonstrate, black women fully participated in the war. In the South, they disrupted plantation work and initiated work stoppages in the fields. Others left farms and plantations, especially after the Emancipation Proclamation granted them freedom in 1863. Some joined communities on the Sea Islands of South Carolina and elsewhere that offered farms, education, and civil rights to former slaves. Moreover, black women, who urged their men to join the Union troops as soldiers, provided supplies, nursed the wounded, and kept families afloat. In the North, free black women joined the war effort as well, supplying sanitary goods, speaking against slavery, and gathering names on antislavery petitions.

WOMEN'S ROLES DURING RECONSTRUCTION

Freedwomen

On 9 April 1865, the Civil War finally came to a halt at Appomattox Courthouse, Virginia. For black women, who constituted the majority of the black population on the larger plantations and the minority on the smaller farms in the South, the war radically changed their lives. All black women were finally free of the shackles of slavery. Also, marriage was now a legal institution for former slaves. This resulted in a widespread move to formalize individual marriages and establish stable families that included both parents. Massive marriage ceremonies involved as many as sixty or seventy couples, while other former slaves worked diligently to locate spouses or children who had been sold away from them, some traveling from state-to-state and advertising in newspapers.

Marriage and the family might have gained legal recognition, but the economic insecurity of the black family remained. Consequently, a large number of newly freed black women labored for wages in order to supplement their families' inadequate incomes. Black men who viewed women's labor outside the home as a badge of slavery nonetheless had to watch their wives seek paid employment.

By 1877, half of adult black women held jobs, especially in such employment as washwomen, domestics, nursemaids, and seamstresses, jobs they had performed as slaves. Still others worked in the fields with their sharecropper husbands. Because sharecropping replaced slavery as the dominant mode of production in the postwar South, many black women, despite their desire to escape field work, continued to labor in the cotton, tobacco, and rice fields.

In addition, local codes and policies throughout the South restricted black women's personal lives. On railways, conductors ejected them from the "ladies" cars, forcing them to ride in baggage cars instead. Black women also still found themselves vulnerable to sexual aggression by both black and white men, as well as ridicule and abusive treatment by white women. When the Ku Klux Klan, the Knights of the White Camellia, and other white-supremacy groups formed, their members not only threatened and attacked black women, but sometimes raped them as well.

Helping Freedwomen and Freedmen

During the Civil War, the United States suffered tremendous property damage, extensive loss of lives, and a blow to its national spirit that would take generations to begin to heal. After the end of the war, black Americans especially needed immediate medical assistance, food, and housing, as well as eventual education, vocational training, and jobs.

Many women participated in the effort to aid newly freed slaves by working for the tax-supported Freedmen's Bureau, established in 1863 as a temporary method of assisting newly freed slaves by supplying food, medicine, housing, and education. The Freedman's Bureau provided $3 million to help give basic education to between 150,000 and 200,000 freed men and women. By 1869, the year the U.S. Congress terminated the Freedmen's Bureau, women accounted for half of the agency's nine thousand teachers.

Other women assisted freed women and men through charity organizations. One such advocate of relief work was Josephine Griffing, who served as the general agent for the Freedman's Relief Association in Washington between 1863 and 1872. This benevolent association differed from the government-funded Freedmen's Bureau in several ways. With contributed funds, Griffing established sewing and other vocational schools, and sought employment and housing for black families. She also argued that the U.S. Congress should relocate newly freed families in northern and western states at governmental expense. Although Griffing arranged jobs and housing for seven thousand black Americans in the Washington, D.C., area, her western relocation plan helped no more than a few thousand blacks resettle.

Many other women, especially educated black women, moved south as missionary teachers for black charity schools. Typically, they taught children during the day, adults at night, and held Sabbath schools on Sundays. In New Orleans and Charleston, freedmen's schools employed only black teachers. And in Savannah, Susie King Taylor extended her Civil War service by teaching black children. Such black teachers from the North often experienced discrimination in the South. They earned less than did white women teachers, but paid more for their lodgings. They often lived and dined separately, and in 1868 an AMA official prohibited Sara Stanley from marrying a white teacher.

Other institutions gave black women the opportunity to enter the professions. In 1864, Rebecca Lee graduated from the New England Female Medical College in Boston and became the nation's first black woman doctor. The Woman's Medical College of Pennsylvania, established in 1850, also began to recruit and train black female physicians during the 1860s and 1870s. In addition, Howard University Medical School and New York Medical College for Women provided medical training to black women.

Education

In 1860, women teachers accounted for 25 percent of the nation's teachers, but this figure grew rapidly, for many Americans believed that women's natures were especially suited to teaching impressionable children. For instance, in 1865, the *New York Times* commented that teaching was a work "to which intelligent women are preeminently adapted" and "a duty in which many more ought to be engaged." By the late 1870s, women composed 60 percent of the nation's teaching force.

Gradually, poorly trained women teachers began to demand admission to existing colleges and to request the founding of normal (teacher-training) schools and women's colleges. As early as 1865, Vassar College in Poughkeepsie, New York, opened its doors to a class of thirty-five women. The Vassar curriculum, trying to replicate that offered male students, offered philosophy, Greek, Latin, German, French, English, mathematics, astronomy, physics, chemistry, hygiene, art, and music. Although the Vassar faculty were largely men, a situation that led Sarah Josepha Hale to write many letters and *Godey's* editorials in protest, the college did hire Maria Mitchell, who in 1850 had been elected to the American Academy of Arts and Sciences for her discovery of the comet that bears her name. As professor of astronomy at Vassar, Mitchell trained the first group of women astronomers in the United States.

Smith College and Wellesley College offered similar programs when they opened in 1875, but Wellesley recruited primarily female faculty members. Wellesley thus provided the opportunity for young women to learn from the first generation of professionally trained women scholars in the United States, especially in botany and psychology.

In the South similar trends developed. Many middle- and upper-class women who now had to help to support their families entered the teaching profession. This movement of southern women into the classroom also resulted in a demand for teacher-training schools. In 1875, a normal school opened in Nashville with thirteen women in its student body and two women on its faculty. Several fine southern women's colleges were also established during the postwar years, including Agnes Scott, Goucher, Randolph-Macon, and Sophie Newcomb.

Women also eagerly enrolled in western land-grant colleges, which had been coeducational since their underwriting by the Morrill Act in 1862. The presence of female students often created confusion at such schools as Iowa State College (present-day Iowa State University), which tried to integrate women into a male-oriented curriculum. The school's "equality" policy resulted in uniformed women toting rifles and drilling in military science programs. Not until 1869 did Iowa State design a domestic science program for its female students.

Sports

Changes in women's sports accompanied these educational developments. Vassar College furnished facilities for gymnastics, bowling, horseback riding, swimming, skating, and gardening. In 1866, several Vassar women formed a baseball club that played every Saturday afternoon. One young woman commented that "the public so far as it knew of our playing was shocked."

Numerous other fashionable activities developed for women. Ice and roller skating were favorites. Bowling became popular, and in 1868, *The New York Clipper* reported that a woman bowled 290- and 300-point games in the same evening. Later, in 1874, Mary E. Outerbridge of New York introduced tennis into the United States. Hampered by long skirts, corsets, and large hats, women played tennis with ladylike grace but little agility. Also in the mid-1870s, archery tournaments provided the first organized sport for women, while croquet allowed women and men to compete in the same game.

During these years, hundreds of handbooks on diet, appearance, hygiene, digestion, and female health rolled off the presses in an attempt to convince wan, corseted women to begin self-improvement programs. One type suggested mechanical aids such as nose pinchers, shoulder braces, and massage rollers. In addition, intellectual exercises such as hobbies, reading, and "character development" were advised. Others recommended a variety of cosmetics or medicine. Of these, Lydia E. Pinkham's Vegetable Compound, produced by a family business founded in 1875, achieved great renown.

Women's Organizations

Thousands of women also turned to clubs as an outlet for their energies and interests. The women's club movement originated with such women as reformer Caroline Severence and poet Julia Ward Howe, co-founders of the New England Woman's Club (NEWC) in Boston in 1868, and Jane Cunningham Croly, a journalist who founded Sorosis in New York in the same year.

These and other early women's clubs pursued a wide range of activities, including reading and discussing books, establishing libraries, performing plays, collecting and studying plant specimens, raising money for the needy, and undertaking community improvement projects. Although such organizations seemed innocuous, they would eventually provide a solid foundation for a full-blown and well-organized reform effort by women.

In 1867, young working women in Boston founded the Young Women's Christian Association (YWCA) to assist young, single working women. During its early years, the YWCA focused its efforts on "white, native-born women dispossessed of their status by the need or desire to work." As the YWCA grew it also established boardinghouses with matrons and curfews for "respectable" working women.

Besides creating and expressing themselves in women's organizations, women stepped to the fore in male groups as well. When a new farm organization called the Patrons of Husbandry, or Grange, organized in 1867, its local units welcomed women members. Women not only seized but broadened this opportunity. As early as the 1870s, women held local leadership positions and began to pressure local Granges to add woman suffrage planks to their platforms. At its first national convention in 1873, the Grange passed a resolution admitting women to the national unit on a limited basis. The following year, the Grange's Declaration of Purposes charged members with developing "proper appreciation of the abilities and sphere of women."

Women Writers

Women also became writers in growing numbers. During the 1860s and 1870s, Emily Dickinson of Amherst, Massachusetts, wrote many of the 1,775 poems she produced in her lifetime. Dickinson took as her motif such topics as death, immortality, love, nature, and passion. Although she published only six poems while alive, Dickinson was later hailed as the first "serious" American woman poet.

Another well-known woman writer of the era was Louisa May Alcott, daughter of Transcendentalist Bronson Alcott and reformer Abigail Alcott. Although Alcott wrote several novels, dozens of thrillers and short stories, and a diary of the time she spent as a Civil War nurse, she is best known for *Little Women*, published in two parts in 1868 and 1869. Alcott used a family, domestic tale to chronicle the passage of four sisters from girlhood to True Womanhood. Interested herself in alternative roles for women, Alcott put the following advice into the mouth of one of her characters: "Don't shut yourself up in a bandbox because you are a woman, but understand what is going on, and educate yourself to take part in the world's work, for it all affects you and yours." Alcott also portrayed Jo, the central character, as a restless, searching feminist; in the end, however, Jo failed to escape marriage and domesticity.

Art

Women continued to produce a tremendous amount of folk art in their homes during this era. Quilts especially recalled recent events through such designs as the Underground Railroad, the Slave Chain, and Sherman's March to the Sea. At the same time, Americans increasingly perceived art as "feminine." Some claimed that a woman's delicate and sensitive nature lent itself to artistic production, while others, who thought of art as embellishment and refinement, identified it as part of woman's sphere.

This new attitude underwrote several important changes for aspiring women artists. Gradually, art schools admitted women to life drawing classes with nude models. Women could also move to cities and other countries for art training, as well as frequently relocating in search of commissions. And in 1874, when the Art Students' League organized in New York City, it routinely admitted women.

One example of the "new" woman artist was Harriet Hosmer of Watertown, Massachusetts, who had studied in Rome with respected sculptor John Gibson during the 1850s. Far from being an ardent feminist, Hosmer maintained that "every woman should have the opportunity of cultivating her talents to the fullest extent, for they were not given her for nothing." By the late 1860s and early 1870s, Hosmer's commissions ranged from San Francisco to London.

As a sculptor of international repute, Hosmer enjoyed a rich social life, yet declined to accept any of her suitors. At the age of twenty-four, she had written to a friend, "an artist has no business to marry." She added that male artists might marry, but not a woman "on whom matrimonial duties and cares weigh more heavily . . . for she must either neglect her profession or her family, becoming neither a good wife and mother nor a good artist." Hosmer's decision was consistent with that of other women, for more than half of mid-nineteenth century women artists chose to remain single rather than attempt to combine their demanding careers with marriage.

Hosmer also encouraged the work of Edmonia Lewis, a New Yorker of black and Chippewa Indian parentage. Lewis studied briefly with a Boston sculptor in the early 1860s, then went to study in Rome in 1865. By the 1870s, Lewis had established a solid reputation in both the United States and Europe. Her works enjoyed quite a success at the Centennial Exposition of 1876 in Philadelphia. Because women had been denied exhibit space in the main exhibition hall, they collected money for a woman's pavilion, where they displayed women's art, including Lewis's sculptures.

Music

In the field of music, women composers similarly demonstrated that despite such obstacles as prejudice against publishing their compositions women could produce fine work. During the 1860s, Faustina Hassae Hodges, daughter of organist Edward Hodges and an organist herself, composed ballads, sacred songs, and piano pieces. One of her songs, "Rose Bush," reportedly sold 100,000 copies. Frances Raymond Ritter, a composer, music historian, and music professor at Vassar, included among her work *Some Famous Songs: An Art-Historical Sketch* (1878) and *Ballads* (1887). Few American female composers of symphonies and concertos have been identified, but neither were there many American male composers since classical music in America concentrated on European repertory well into the late nineteenth century.

Technology

Because the Civil War stimulated industrial development, including the mass production of paper patterns, the production of clothing became easier. Employing treadle-powered sewing machines, women could make their own stylish clothes at will. In 1867, Ebenezer Butterick, who borrowed the idea for paper patterns from those his wife made from newspaper on her kitchen table, began his business with 12 workers; three years later he employed 140 people.

Technology also offered women such new contrivances for the home as improved lamps and stoves. At first, domestic ideology impeded the adoption of home technology; it preached that only unfeminine, lazy, or incompetent women would use newfangled, mechanical instruments to care for their families. Catharine Beecher was the first to urge women to embrace technology, especially in the kitchen, where, according to her, women spent over 50 percent of their time. In 1869, Beecher even designed a model kitchen, which incorporated flour and grain bins, a built-in dishdrainer, a cast-iron stove set in an alcove with glass doors to block the heat, and an indoor sink with two pumps, one for rain water and one for well water.

Other women besides Beecher took an interest in technology and its applications. Before the Civil War, only fifty-five women had obtained patents, but between 1860 and 1888 nearly three thousand women applied for patents. Many other female inventions were patented under men's names, as were Butterick's clothing patterns.

Revising Domestic Ideals

To many advocates of enlarged roles for women, a major revision of the stereotyped American woman seemed to be at hand after the war's end. Some even thought that women might be granted the right to vote at the same time that former black male slaves received citizenship and suffrage.

During Reconstruction, ideas about American women would indeed undergo many modifications but not drastic ones. When Catharine Beecher and Harriet Beecher Stowe collaborated in writing their *Principles of Domestic Science* in 1870, they revealed typical attitudes of the era. They outlined the American woman's "profession" as "the care and nursing of the body in the critical periods of infancy and sickness, the training of the human mind in the most impressible period of childhood, the instruction and control of servants, and most of the government and economies of the family state."

Beecher and Stowe added that, although they sympathized with "every honest effort to relieve the disabilities and sufferings of their sex," they believed that most of women's problems stemmed from the disregard in which most Americans held domestic endeavors. If, they argued, women received training for their duties just as men did for their trades and professions, family labor would no longer be "poorly done, poorly paid, and regarded as menial and disgraceful." The sisters' rationale for domestic training would soon help underwrite the development of the science of home economics.

Numerous other Americans also believed that women should return happily to their homes after the war and focus their full attention on domestic matters, but several factors subverted this return to domestic ideals. Because of their work with such groups as women's aid societies, sanitary commissions, and the National Women's Loyal League, women could effectively speak in public, raise money, handle finances, and serve as executive officers of large organizations. Those whose husbands died in the war now acted as the arbiters, decision makers, and disciplinarians in their families. Although many women physically returned to their homes after the war's end, they found it difficult to resume submissive roles.

Women's Problems During Reconstruction

Women as Paid Workers

During the late 1860s and the 1870s, women not only entered the arts and professions, but all types of paid employment as well. Women continued to dominate the needle trades and were now present in growing numbers in retail sales, office work, cigar making, typography, commercial laundries, and various types of mills. In the latter venue they toiled in an atmosphere that one operative described as inundated by smoke: "it rolls sullenly in slow folds from the great chimneys of the iron-foundries, and settles down in black, slimy pools on the muddy streets . . . smoke on the wharves, smoke on the dingy boats, on the yellow river."

Many of these women filled new jobs—that is, ones that had not been held by men but were created by the growing economy. Whether in new jobs or old, whenever women were hired, wages fell. This occurred because employers believed that women's place was in the home; thus, women who worked outside the home must be occasional workers interested in "pin money." Actually, numerous women worked to support their families because their husbands had been disabled or killed during the Civil War. In other cases male workers did not receive a living wage, so their wives and daughters had to work. Furthermore, the number of single women who had to support themselves was rising.

Several reformers attempted to alert the American public to the problems facing paid women workers. For instance, Caroline Wells Dall, a feminist author and lecturer, repeatedly argued that relegating women to only a few kinds of jobs created low pay and competition. Dall also pointed out that thousands of underpaid or unemployed women turned to prostitution. In her best-known work, *The College, the Market, and the Court: or, Woman's Relation to Education, Politics, and Law* (1867), Dall criticized middle-class women for lives of frivolity, while their sisters labored in sweatshops and lived in poverty.

Female workers tried to rectify their low pay, long hours, and terrible working conditions. A number of female workers, like many male workers, came to believe that some form of labor organization might help to improve their situation. At first, women turned to men's labor organizations but soon learned that men's unions seldom welcomed women. In fact, when the National Labor Union (NLU) formed in 1866, no women were present. Two years later, under pressure from such suffragists as Stanton and Anthony, the NLU began to admit women members. In 1870, the NLU elected a Mrs. E. O. G. Willard of the Sewing Girls' Union of Chicago as second vice-president, but overall, women were barely represented in the thirty-two unions that existed in the United States. In 1873, a major economic panic brought hard times to workers and an accompanying decline in union membership, especially among underpaid women workers.

Employed women responded to their exclusion from male unions by forming their own organizations. Although women cigar makers accounted for close to 10 percent of all cigar makers, they were denied membership in the national union. Thus, the Lady Cigar Makers of Providence, Rhode Island, organized in 1864. Another woman's union, the Collar Laundry Union of Troy, New York, also organized in 1864. This group's efforts proved remarkably successful in raising its women members' wages to a level near that of working men.

Middle- and upper-class women who continued to be interested in reform after the war began to found other types of groups to help working women. Called working women's protective societies, these associations offered services such as legal aid, medical treatment, and advice to employed women.

Black Women

Unarguably, freedom offered definite advantages to black women workers. Many could now define their working hours to some extent or could change employers. They could marry and bear children without fearing the loss of family members through sale. They also had the right to appeal to authority when dissatisfied.

Formal complaints to agents of the Freedmen's Bureau indicated widespread problems, but they were different from those that arose under slavery. Employers commonly withheld pay to control black women workers and sometimes reacted to them with violence, but women now resisted, filed complaints, moved to other plantations, or took different jobs. Wages remained low and conditions difficult, but black women were no longer chattel.

The lives of black women, however, remained circumscribed in many ways. Free black women lacked access to vocational training and the right to hold certain jobs. While black men received the right to vote and to hold office in the late 1860s, black women acquired no political rights. Black men could also own land, but black women seldom had the means to do so.

A large number of rural black women tried to improve their lot by migrating to southern cities. Here they found poor housing, limited job openings, and low wages. In Jackson, Mississippi, and Galveston, Texas, black washwomen went on strike to boost their wages to $1.50 per day. Anglo officials arrested the leaders and threatened to require license fees of all washwomen. Domestic servants fared even worse. They worked long hours, seven days a week, for which they received low pay supplemented by castoff clothing and leftover food.

Some urban black women escaped these evils by selling such goods as spruce beer, peanuts, blueberries, strawberries, and vegetables in local markets. Those women who could raise the necessary capital opened restaurants, grocery stores, and boardinghouses. Despite independence, these urban black women found that their lives were still harsh.

Nor did black women who migrated to northern cities after the Civil War find the opportunities for which they had hoped. Like their southern counterparts, they were usually limited to domestic, menial, and service jobs with long hours and poor pay. In 1871, a northern black woman complained in the Philadelphia Post: "Why is it that when respectable women answer an advertisement for a dressmaker, they are invariably refused, or offered a place to cook or scrub, or to do housework: and when application is made to manufactories immediately after having seen an advertisement for operators or finishers, meet with the same reply."

These women expressed further dismay when they learned that, although they paid taxes, their children were denied admission to tax-supported schools because of their race.

Southern Women

Southern white women also faced difficult conditions after the Civil War. Highborn ladies now learned to perform domestic tasks without the help of servants and to run plantations without the aid of their men who had been disabled or killed during the war. Southern women of all classes had to take jobs as clerks, teachers, and industrial laborers to help support their families. The thousands who failed to find employment had to depend on rations from northern-based charity groups. Already bitter over the war's destruction of their plantations and other businesses, southern women lived in fear of the black patrols picketing their towns or regions. When black males obtained the right to vote in 1866, many disenfranchised white females felt additional resentment and outrage.

Because their labor and any cash income that they produced were now in demand to help keep agricultural enterprises afloat, southern women gained more respect as farmers after the war. As they moved into the fields and various aspects of farm operations, women proved themselves as workers and managers. One notable female farmer was Frances Butler, the daughter of British actress Frances Kemble and Georgia planter Pierce Butler. When her father died shortly after the war, Butler took over the management of his rice and cotton fields on the Sea Islands of Georgia. She negotiated labor contracts with black workers, acted as her own overseer, and paid wages without resorting to sharecropping.

Controlling Childbearing

North or South, many women expressed a desire to gain control over their bodies, especially in the matter of reproduction. Birth control by abortion had increased during the war years, which alarmed many people who believed it was woman's responsibility to bear many children. Others thought that the population of the United States would be depleted if women practiced birth control.

Accordingly, medical practitioners and concerned citizens accelerated their opposition to planned parenthood and birth control. In 1862, an Ohio obstetrician introduced the first statute prohibiting contraception and abortion. By 1865, Americans worried about the number of lives lost during the Civil War and how long it would take to repopulate the United States.

Thus, the American Medical Association launched a full-scale campaign headed by Anthony Comstock against birth control and abortion. In 1873, these events culminated in the U.S. Congress passing the Comstock Law, which made it a federal crime to send obscene materials, defined to include birth control information and devices, through the U.S. mail. Because manufacturers could not mail their products to customers, this restriction also ended the widespread publication of birth-control advertisements in newspapers, and it effectively dampened public discussion of birth control.

Still, thousands of women continued to seek abortions and birth-control information despite the Comstock Law and similar state laws that followed. Such feminists as Elizabeth Cady Stanton encouraged women to do so, arguing that women were entitled to choose how many children they would bear. At the same time, an industrial, urban economy made the rearing of large numbers of children more expensive and difficult than it had been on farms. Although technology had not yet offered dependable birth-control devices, it had helped motivate women to search for them.

Alcohol Abuse and Temperance

Because alcohol and family abuse continued to pose a problem for women and children, the temperance movement attracted thousands of female supporters. Out of local bands of women who either prayed in saloons or destroyed stocks of whiskey came the National Women's Christian Temperance Union, founded in 1874, with Annie Turner Wittenmyer of Iowa as its first president. To Wittenmyer, the crusade offered women the opportunity to fulfill their moral obligations by liberating humankind from alcohol. In an 1877 address Wittenmyer stated her position: "The drink system is the common enemy of women the world over, and the plans we inaugurate, will be eagerly sought after by the women of all civilized nations, and as the success of all moral reforms depends largely upon women, the world will halt, or move in its onward march toward millennial glory, as we halt or march." The WCTU soon became the largest woman's organization in the nineteenth century.

Women Prisoners

The situation of female inmates in prisons and reform schools also continued to demand improvement. During the late 1860s, Clara Temple Leonard, a reformer who worked with the Dedham home for Discharged Female Prisoners in Massachusetts, visited female prisoners and observed the horrible conditions in which they lived. In 1869, Leonard called for a separate women's prison under female supervision, but she soon discovered that unenfranchised women had little influence on penal theory and practice. It was not until 1874 that the Massachusetts legislature appropriated $300,000 for a women's prison at Sherborn. When the prison opened in 1877, its superintendent assured the public that prison officials now taught women inmates "how to work, how to read and write, and how to apply themselves industriously to their given tasks," but it seemed clear to most reformers that far more change was needed.

Science

During the postwar years, widespread prejudice and discrimination deterred women from entering technological and scientific fields and from admitting their interest in such matters. A mid-nineteenth-century editor remarked that "if an unfortunate female should happen to possess a lurking fondness for any special scientific pursuit she is careful (if of any social position) to hide it as she would some deformity."

In spite of such a disheartening climate of opinion, some women continued to pursue their scientific interests. A number of women formed scientific study groups during the mid 1860s, while others promoted the introduction of more science courses into women's curricula. During the 1870s, women even approached male scientific societies requesting membership. Women were, however, granted only the status of corresponding members who were neither expected to attend the meetings nor allowed to vote.

Law

The field of law also spurned women's participation during the 1860s and 1870s. Thus, state licensing bodies uniformly barred women from taking the required examinations. In 1869, Arabella Babb Mansfield applied for admission to the bar in Iowa. An Iowa judge sympathetic to women's rights ordered that Mansfield be allowed to take the examinations. One of her examiners noted that Mansfield passed with high honors, giving "the very best rebuke possible to the imputation that ladies cannot qualify for the practice of law." Mansfield never practiced law, however, choosing instead to teach at Iowa Wesleyan and later at DePauw University in Indiana.

In the same year that Mansfield became the first licensed woman lawyer in the United States, Myra Bradwell applied to the Illinois Supreme Court for a law license. Bradwell had studied law with her husband while founding and editing the very successful *Chicago Legal News*. An avowed suffragist, Bradwell had also drafted several bills to expand women's property rights. In 1869, Bradwell took the licensing examination and passed it with honors, but Illinois denied her a license because she was a woman. Bradwell appealed her case to the United States Supreme Court, which tossed the matter back to the state of Illinois. Bradwell would not obtain a license until 1890, four years before her death.

Other women, however, soon became "firsts" in the legal field. In 1871, Phoebe Couzins became the first woman to receive a formal law degree when she graduated from Washington University in St. Louis. The state of Missouri licensed Couzins, but she never practiced law. Instead, she became a leading figure in the national woman suffrage movement. A year after Couzins's graduation, Charlotte E. Ray graduated from Howard University in law and was admitted to the Washington, D.C., bar. She was the first black woman lawyer in the United States and the first woman admitted to practice in the District of Columbia.

During these years, Clara Shortridge Foltz helped open law to women in the Southwest. Foltz waged a campaign to open the bar exam to women and, after gaining admission to the California bar, she successfully sued Hastings Law School for admission. As an attorney, Foltz later helped devise the California parole system and instigated a public defenders' bill.

Religion

Most sects had long since feminized their membership and messages, but they still barred women from voting and holding congregational offices. Beginning in 1861, women in thirty-three denominations began to form segregated missionary societies. These women-only groups met to pray, study, and raise funds for domestic and foreign mission work. By the 1870s, hundreds of missionary societies existed and proved themselves highly effective in fund-raising and in training women in leadership positions.

Some women, however, wanted more: to defy the widespread prohibition of women as ministers. In 1863, Olympia Brown graduated from St. Lawrence University's theological school in Canton, New York, as a Universalist minister, the first woman ordained by full ecclesiastical jurisdiction. In 1867, Brown left her pulpit to campaign for woman suffrage in Kansas. Although she soon returned to parish work, married, and bore two children, Brown continued to work on behalf of woman suffrage for almost sixty years.

Martha White McWhirter asserted her leadership rights in a very different manner. Probably in 1867, McWhirter helped found the Woman's Commonwealth in Belton, Texas. Under McWhirter's guidance, this Christian socialist, feminist, and celibate community achieved financial success but drew searing criticism and disdain from clergy, family members, and neighbors. The woman-only community later moved to Washington, D.C., where it remained until the 1980s.

Women's Rights Renewed

Given the lack of gains from the Civil War, it is little wonder that the women's rights movement soon reappeared. As early as 1865, women's rights' leaders who had hoped for great changes as an immediate result of the war met with disappointment. They were stunned to learn that abolitionists were far more concerned about insuring the freedom of former slaves than with improving the status of women. Abolitionist leaders feared that raising women's rights issues in 1865 would complicate, or even prevent, the passage of legislation to protect blacks. Although the United States ratified the Thirteenth Amendment abolishing slavery in December 1865, additional protective and civil rights legislation for blacks was under consideration. Its supporters argued that one step should be taken at a time and that women's turn would come eventually. Even black leader Frederick Douglass, who had been sympathetic to women's rights, stated in 1865: "This is the Negro's hour."

In 1866, the U.S. Congress passed the Fourteenth Amendment which would, when ratified, extend political privileges to white and black men but not to white or black women. The amendment supported the continued disenfranchisement of women by specifically defining citizenship rights as "male," the first time that this word had appeared in the U.S. Constitution. Women's rights leader Frances Gage scathingly wrote, "can any one tell us why the great advocates of Human Equality . . . forget that when they were a weak party and needed all the womanly strength of the nation to help them on, they always united the words 'without regard to sex, race, or color?' Who ever hears of sex now from any of these champions of freedom!"

Elizabeth Cady Stanton direly predicted, "If that word 'male' be inserted, it will take us a century at least to get it out." Stanton's and other leaders' concern over women's political exclusion erupted at the first major women's rights convention held since the beginning of the war. Meeting in New York City in 1866, delegates listened to a number of speakers, including forty-one-year-old black poet and antislavery lecturer Frances Ellen Watkins Harper. Along with others such as Mary Ann Shadd Cary and Sojourner Truth, Harper saw the need for black and white women to work together. Convention members agreed and unanimously decided to approve the pursuit of suffrage for black American men and for women as their primary goals.

After the convention, leaders duly organized the American Equal Rights Association (AERA) to work toward these objectives. In 1866 and 1867, the new organization lobbied and petitioned to have race and gender restrictions deleted from state constitutions. In 1867, the association supported two suffrage bills in Kansas, one for black men and one for women. When abolitionist leaders failed to support the Kansas woman-suffrage bill, the association decided that it was time to part company with their former allies. The following year, the ratification of the Fourteenth Amendment enfranchised black men; suffrage was now a woman's issue.

Suffrage leaders found, however, that many disagreements existed in their own ranks regarding how woman suffrage might best be achieved. As a consequence, two opposing groups emerged. In 1869, Stanton and

Anthony formed the National Woman Suffrage Association (NWSA) in Washington. It excluded men from membership and concentrated its efforts on getting the U.S. Congress to pass an amendment granting women the right to vote. The NWSA published a newspaper coedited by Stanton and Anthony called *The Revolution*. The newspaper's masthead read: "Men, Their Rights and Nothing More, Women, Their Rights and Nothing Less." In addition to working for the immediate enfranchisement of women, the NWSA supported equal pay for equal work, childcare centers for working mothers, and more equitable divorce laws.

Also in 1869, Lucy Stone, Mary Livermore, and Julia Ward Howe, author of the "Battle Hymn of the Republic," organized the American Woman Suffrage Association (AWSA) in Boston. Unlike the NWSA, the AWSA encouraged men to join and focused members' efforts on gaining woman suffrage state-by-state. The AWSA published a newspaper called *The Woman's Journal*, designed to counteract what AWSA leaders called the "radicalism" of *The Revolution*.

When these two rival organizations formed in 1869, public opinion on the issue of extended rights for women was mixed. In 1867 and 1868, Kansas woman-suffrage amendments had failed. In 1868, a woman-suffrage amendment introduced in Congress had also floundered. But, in 1869, Wyoming Territory granted women the right to vote, followed in 1870 by Utah Territory. Although these latter actions were encouraging, they did not precipitate a landslide toward woman suffrage. Rather, in 1870 the Fifteenth Amendment stipulated that a citizen's right to vote could not be denied on the basis of race or color; the amendment ignored the issue of gender.

Other voices soon supported the call for woman suffrage, however. In 1869, two years after he failed to secure woman suffrage in the British Reform Bill of 1867, English philosopher and politician John Stuart Mill published *The Subjection of Women* in England. When Mill's book reached the United States, American readers discovered that Mill believed true social satisfaction depended upon the happiness of women, including their equal access to education and legal rights.

The Quaker lecturer and suffragist, Anna Dickinson, also called for women's rights. During the Civil War, Dickinson had lectured eloquently not only on antislavery but on political and military affairs. She had further shocked people by campaigning on behalf of political candidates in 1863. After the war, dressed in elegant gowns accented by extravagant jewelry, Dickinson lectured on injustices to women. Known as the "Queen of the Rostrum" to some, Dickinson exhibited the "worst possible taste" in the eyes of others.

Also somewhat embarrassing to suffrage leaders were the activities of an articulate and dramatic woman, Victoria Claflin Woodhull, who became the nation's first female stockbroker in 1870, ran for President in

1872, and frequently lectured on women's rights. Along with her equally colorful sister, Tennessee Claflin, Woodhull attracted a good deal of attention to the suffrage movement but also convinced a lot of people that woman suffragists were highly eccentric. Yet, in spite of the controversy that continually swirled around them, Woodhull and Claflin successfully drew attention to the cause of woman suffrage while demonstrating that women could effectively enter such male-only areas as finance and politics.

Another determined woman, Virginia Minor, took a different tack; she sued the state of Missouri in 1872 for refusing to let her vote. Because married women were unable to bring suit on their own, Minor worked in conjunction with her attorney husband. They carried the case to the Missouri Supreme Court and the U.S. Supreme Court. In the case of *Minor v. Happersett* in 1874, Chief Justice Morrison R. Waite ruled that the state had the power to grant or deny suffrage, and that the U.S. Constitution "does not confer the right of suffrage upon any one." Eight other male justices concurred and wrote: "If the courts can consider any question settled, this is one."

Southern women were also interested in women's rights during the postwar years. In 1869, Louisa Rollin, a black woman of Haitian descent, spoke to the South Carolina legislature on behalf of woman suffrage, while a year later her sister, Charlotte (Lottie) Rollin, chaired the organizational meeting of the South Carolina Woman's Rights Association in Columbia.

White southern women such as Sarah Ida Fowler Morgan of South Carolina also publicly declared their advocacy of women's rights. Through editorials in the Charleston *News* and *Courier* during the 1870s, Morgan examined the woman question in great detail. Writing under the pseudonym "Mr. Fowler," Morgan supported employment, singlehood, and equality for women. Instead of focusing on woman suffrage, however, Morgan believed that the women's movement should pursue economic independence for women.

WESTERN WOMEN DURING RECONSTRUCTION

Native Women

American Indian women continued to face numerous problems during the postwar era. By the 1860s and 1870s, white settlement had disrupted Native American communities, wars had torn apart their families, and government imposition of white values further reduced the status of native women. Along with native men, women were increasingly confined to reservations where malnutrition, famine, and disease further decimated them, while their children attended reservation schools which attempted to erase both their culture and their pride in it.

Still, American Indian women of the Plains and in some far western tribes still exercised a measure of choice and control over their lives. White observers often thought that native women were degraded because they performed all domestic and most agricultural labor while men engaged in hunting and warfare. Actually, this division of labor extended respect and the right of decision making to both women and men. Also, because many Indian women were not required to resume sexual relations until they had finished nursing their most recent child and reportedly used herbal birth control, they had a degree of control over childbearing. In addition, most Indian cultures stressed the need for both partners to derive satisfaction from marriage. Because divorce was usually simple to obtain, native women could escape abusive, lazy, or intemperate mates without losing their children and personal property.

Furthermore, some American Indian women continued to wield a degree of power within their tribes. Occasionally, Plains Indian women served as shamans, medicine people, and warriors. Matrilineal tribes such as the Mandans of the Dakotas and Tlingits of the Pacific Northwest vested land in the eldest female of the family. Ownership of lands, fields, gardens, houses, and stock passed through female descendants. American Indian women also frequently functioned as decision makers and sat on the council of elders, participating in decisions that concerned both wars and hunts.

A Sioux named Eagle Woman well demonstrated such influence and ability. Uprooted in 1868 from her home near Fort Rice in the Dakota Territory, Eagle Woman decided to help her family and her people adjust to life on a reservation. For the next twenty years, the widowed Eagle Woman, also known as Mrs. Picotte-Galpin, ran a trading post, supported her children, helped others in need, and acted as a liaison between the Sioux people and U.S. government agents.

Another example of a woman who asserted herself was Buffalo Calf Road of the Cheyenne Indians. Although the Cheyenne expected women to act docile and deferential to men, numerous Cheyenne women broke and rode horses, hunted, and fought in battles. They also formed women's associations, including quillers' societies and a secret military society. Buffalo Calf Road distinguished herself by fighting at the Battle on the Rosebud River in June 1876, and by rescuing her brother Comes-in-Sight from enemy fire. Buffalo Calf Road fought a week later against General George Armstrong Custer and his troops at the Little Bighorn River, where she earned the honorary name Brave Woman. Two years later, Buffalo Calf Road led Cheyenne women against the U.S. Army in Nebraska; she died in 1879 of diphtheria.

Still, as lines of forts and increasing numbers of government officials, settlers, and miners arrived on the Great Plains and the Far West, it became clear that native women would share a fate similar to that of the

Algonquian tribes along the East Coast. Moreover, few reformers recognized the plight of Indian women or spoke on their behalf. Even though thousands of Anglo families employed these women as cooks, nursemaids, and washwomen, most seemed oblivious to their problems.

A similar situation existed between Spanish-speaking and Anglo women. Brought together by such situations as an Anglo woman employing a *Latina* or by intermarriage, Latinas and Anglo women shared recipes, childcare ideas, and fashions but lived separate lives in other respects. Apparently, gender did not provide a strong enough bond to overcome racist and nativist sentiments. Thus, Latinas were left to confront major social changes on their own.

By 1870, people of Spanish heritage lived on ranches, farms, or in segregated urban areas called *barrios*. In Los Angeles, for example, they increasingly lived in a barrio called Sonora Town. Because the birthrate began to stabilize after 1860, the population grew primarily from immigration, which remained relatively low during the post–Civil War period. By 1870, residents with Spanish backgrounds accounted for only 28.5 percent of the city's total population (down from 30.9 percent in 1860).

In addition, the developing western economy increasingly colonized Latinos as a manual, low-paid workforce. Numbers of property holders declined, while those working at manual jobs increased to 80 percent in 1870 (up from 62 percent in 1860). This decline in the middle and upper classes, accompanied by a growth in the working classes, created a changed situation for many women. Because male workers often earned inadequate wages, women had to take paid employment as well, usually as domestic servants, nursemaids, laundresses, and prostitutes. Some even broke with tradition by becoming actresses and theater impresarios.

Moreover, a growing number of women headed households. Before the Mexican War, only 13 percent had done so, but after the Civil War, approximately 25 percent did so. Because of religious restrictions, divorce was atypical. Rather, the change probably resulted from men seeking jobs away from home and a higher death rate for men than women. As a result, the female-centered family was now an important institution in the Spanish-speaking community in Los Angeles.

The Latino family altered in other ways as well. Women escaped arranged marriages by forming more common-law marriages, which California began to recognize in 1862. In 1861 and 1864, other state laws undercut the community property provisions that had passed from Mexican law into California law. As a consequence of the new stipulations, wives's property at their death no longer passed to their children but reverted to their husbands. Nor was all of a husband's property subject to inheritance by his survivors.

At the same time, intermarriage with Anglo settlers increased. Before the Civil War, only one Latino marriage in ten involved an Anglo spouse;

after the war nearly one in three did so. Unlike earlier settlers, most of these Anglos had little interest in adapting to local culture and customs. Latinas, who often hoped to improve their social and economic status through intermarriage, adapted to Anglo ways instead, including bearing fewer children than they might have in earlier decades and sending their children to English-language public schools.

Clearly, Latinas, especially those of the working and lower classes, were losing the support of extended kinship family systems, forfeiting a network of godparents and *compadres*, and working outside the home for low wages in greater numbers. Fewer women had time to serve their communities as low-paid or volunteer teachers, *parteras* (midwives), and *curanderas* (healers). Increasingly, they also saw their traditional culture attacked by a state "Sunday law" which prohibited bullfights, horse races, cockfights, and other *Californio* pastimes, as well as fearing for their fathers, brothers, husbands, and sons who were now subject to local vagrancy laws that could result in the imprisonment of unemployed men. Moreover, women lived with the fear of Anglos lynching their men, a practice deplored in the Spanish-language press as *"los linchamientos."*

Similar changes occurred in other Latino centers such as Tucson, Santa Fe, and San Antonio. Especially in San Antonio, the largest Spanish-heritage city in the United States, urban industrialization drew women out of their homes into paid employment and changed the structure of the traditional family. A growing number of Tejanas sought paid employment, working primarily as unskilled laborers or as *vendedoras* in local markets. Others turned their homes into restaurants or boardinghouses.

By the 1860s, women headed over 30 percent of Latino families in San Antonio. This often occurred because men had to seek employment as migrant field hands or return to Mexico to work, thus leaving family authority in the hands of the women. Tejano families usually lived in *jacales* (timber dwellings), or, in west Texas, in adobes. Women continued to use a *mano* (grinding stone) to grind corn in a *metate* (stone vessel). From this they prepared staples of their diet, *tortillas* and *tamales,* to which they added *frijoles, chiles*, meat, and fish.

From Los Angeles to San Antonio, Latinas generally proved themselves able to maintain their families in the face of numerous difficulties, to preserve traditional culture, and to perpetuate a semblance of the extended kinship system. They paid the price, however, of working an extended day, often toiling for wages outside the home and performing extensive domestic labor in poor quality housing and communities neglected by municipal officials.

Anglo Women

During the same era, Anglo women in the West began to participate more fully in cattle ranching, especially in Texas, and in farming and homesteading throughout the West. On the Great Plains, wives often managed isolated claims by themselves while their husbands worked elsewhere to raise the necessary capital for seed, equipment, and building materials. Other women worked alongside their fathers or husbands in "breaking" the claim for cultivation. During the 1870s, one Dakota woman graphically described the demands placed on women settlers: "I had lived on a homestead long enough to learn some fundamental things: that while a woman had more here than in any other part of the world, she was expected to contribute as much as a man—not in the same way, it is true, but to the same degree . . . the person who wasn't willing to try anything once wasn't equipped to be a settler."

Growing numbers of single women also began to take up western land. The Homestead Act, passed by the U.S. Congress in 1862, offered a settler a free quarter-section of land on the condition that she or he cultivate it for a period of five years. A sample of land office data for Colorado and Wyoming indicates that the number of female homestead entrants ranged from 11.9 to 18.2 percent of the total. The data further indicate that 42.4 percent of women succeeded in placing final claims—or "proving up"—on their homestead as opposed to only 37 percent of men. One Dakotan judged these "girl homesteaders" an "interesting segment of the population."

Female migrants also entered the mining, lumbering, farming, and ranching areas of the Far West. Some traveled across the Isthmus of Panama or "around the horn" of South America, but most journeyed across overland trails. In many cases, women found the hardships of the overland trip less severe than they had feared. Female travelers traded with American Indians, who often were not as fierce and savage as women had been led to believe. As one woman later wrote: "We suffered vastly more from fear of the Indians before starting than we did on the plains." Yet other women raved about the beauty of the prairies, plains, and mountains, and extolled the "wonders of travel." In some cases, however, women became discouraged, frightened, and determined to return to their former homes as soon as possible.

Some plains and far western women had lifestyles similar to those of earlier frontierswomen on agrarian frontiers, while others lived more novel lives. An army wife of the 1860s enjoyed her rough and erratic life in frontier forts. She traveled around Kansas and Oklahoma in an army ambulance without much discomfort, or any danger from Indians. She basked in the attention paid her as one of the few women in camp and decided that "there is considerable romance in my manner of living." Some army women, however, found themselves thrust into unexpected situations. In 1874, an Arizona army wife wrote: "I concluded that my New England bringing up had been too serious. . . . young army wives should stay at home with their mothers and fathers, and not go into such wild and uncouth places."

Other western women with unusual lifestyles included those who took jobs in service industries, including dance halls, saloons, and brothels. Many "soiled doves" who provided companionship and sexual services were hardworking laborers and business entrepreneurs. Irish immigrant Mary Josephine Welch, for example, settled in Helena, Montana, in 1867, where she established the Red Light Saloon. Soon known as "Chicago Joe" after her last hometown, Welch hired women as dollar-a-dance workers in her saloon. These women, known as "hurdy-gurdy girls" after the popular stringed instrument of the day, earned up to fifty dollars an evening. In 1873, however, Montana passed legislation against dance halls in an attempt to attract a stable family population.

Apparently, women's adaptation depended to a great extent on their backgrounds, personalities, philosophies, and occupations. Certainly by the 1860s and 1870s, all types of women lived in the West. Some resided in the raw western towns that composed the urban frontier. In towns and countryside, single women sought employment, husbands, or both. In cattle towns and gold camps, prostitutes waited for men to complete a trail drive or strike ore. Some women, like the popular trail guide, Mountain Charley, even donned male clothing and assumed male roles. Other women immigrated from Canada, Mexico, Germany, Holland, England, Ireland, Sweden, Norway, and the Orient. Yet others came as members of such religious groups as the Presentation Sisters in the Dakotas, or the Church of Jesus Christ of Latter-day Saints (or Mormons) in Utah. Others, like Abigail Scott Duniway of Oregon, ardently advocated woman suffrage.

Frontierswomen were not only a diverse group but often a politically privileged one as well. In 1869, Wyoming Territory gave women the right to vote. Supposedly, this occurred because of the urging of Esther Morris and others, who argued that woman suffrage would attract women to Wyoming, thus helping to balance the current population ratio of six men to one woman and introducing a "law and order" faction into unbridled Wyoming society. Utah followed with its own woman suffrage law in 1870. Some believe that leaders of the Church of Latter-day Saints wished to insure their political power over the influx of male non-Mormons, or Gentiles, to the area, and hoped that Mormon women would vote in favor of polygamy, the extremely controversial institution of plural marriage practiced by some Mormons at the time.

Black Women

Black women, disillusioned with southern plantations or the urban areas in the South and North, also turned their faces westward during the late 1860s and 1870s. As pioneers and Exodusters (communities of black immigrants, especially in Kansas), they soon discovered that they could not escape racial prejudice. It followed them even into the most progressive of western communities. Once again they were relegated to farm labor and domestic service. In one Iowa town, a black woman who worked as a washwoman for many of the community's white women lived by herself in poverty despite continuous labor and was patronizingly called "Nigger Ellen" by townspeople.

Still, a number of black women achieved economic success in the West. One of the most renowned of these was Mary Ellen Pleasant, who arrived in San Francisco during the Gold Rush, probably in 1849. She claimed to have been born in Philadelphia in 1814, the daughter of a free black woman and a wealthy white planter. She married Alexander Smith, an abolitionist and prosperous Cuban planter, who willed his estate to her. She later married John James Pleasant, worked for abolitionism in Canada during the 1850s, and returned to San Francisco during the 1860s, where she became a restaurateur and investor. Pleasant ran elegant restaurants and boardinghouses, as well as laundries that employed black women and men. She used her wealth to build a striking mansion, but she also helped black Americans find jobs and gain civil rights.

Another similar case was "Aunt" Clara Brown, who purchased her freedom during the 1850s. In 1859, Brown convinced a group of gold seekers to hire her as a cook; she accompanied them across the Great Plains to Denver then moved to Central City where she established a laundry, worked as a nurse, invested in mining claims, and organized a Sunday school. Brown earned ten thousand dollars by 1866, which she used to bring relatives and others to Colorado.

Asians and Asian Americans

In 1868, China and the United States signed the Burlingame Treaty, which established reciprocal trade, travel, and immigration but did not provide citizenship for Chinese who remained in the United States. Despite this lack, between 1870 and 1877, over 100,000 Chinese arrived in the continental United States. More than 90 percent were men who worked as miners, railroad builders, factory workers, entrepreneurs, vendors, fishermen, and agriculturalists. By the late 1870s, California contained more than 70,000 Chinese men and less than 4,000 Chinese women. In other parts of the country, Chinese men totaled approximately 30,000 and women fewer than 1,000.

Chinese women ranged from a growing number of middle- and upper-class wives, usually living in Chinatowns and sometimes assisting in family businesses, to a declining number of prostitutes in such urban areas as San Francisco, farm women in rural areas, and fishing village women along the West Coast. In 1870, a small number of Chinese women also worked as unskilled laborers, especially as domestic servants, laundresses, and seamstresses. Ah Yuen of Evanston, Wyoming, for example, worked as a cook in mining and railroad camps during the 1860s and 1870s. She also outlived three husbands and, in later years, made it a point to participate in Evanston's annual Cowboy Days celebration.

Single Chinese men occasionally married Native American, African American, or Spanish-heritage women, or, in New York, sometimes, Irish women. Most, however, established split households by marrying Chinese women still living in China. To insure their daughters a source of income, families willingly married their daughters to Chinese men living in the United States. For years afterward, husbands worked in the United States while wives existed, and even raised families, in Chinese villages without the aid of men and with only the meager financial assistance that their men working in the United States sent to them. Consequently, the primary goal of many Chinese couples was to reunite and establish whole families.

During this era, the U.S. Asian population diversified, for Japanese immigration to the United States began. In 1868, 148 laborers migrated to Hawaii's sugar cane fields. The following year a Japanese band performed in San Francisco's Woodward Gardens, perhaps as goodwill ambassadors. Those Japanese who followed usually settled in urban areas called Little Tokyos. This early migration included some female Issei (Japanese born in Japan), who eventually bore Nisei offspring (Japanese born in the United States). Besides being wives and mothers, Issei women also helped establish and run family businesses. Because they lived in segregated areas, however, few learned English or interacted with Americans.

By 1877, when President Rutherford B. Hayes issued the order that removed the army of occupation from the South and technically brought Reconstruction to a close, women clamored for all manner of modifications in American society. Women's rights, civil rights, temperance, and American Indian rights constituted some of the issues. Other women initiated modifications in the prevailing social system by pushing into jobs, professions, and endeavors previously dominated by men. Women of all backgrounds had a long list of changes they wanted implemented in post-Reconstruction American society.

Suggestions for Further Reading

Abram, Ruth J. *"Send Us a Lady Doctor"*: *Women Doctors in America, 1835–1920*. New York: W. W. Norton, 1985.

Adreadis, A. Harriette. "The Woman's Commonwealth: A Study in Coalescence of Social Forms," *Frontiers* 7 (1984): 79–86.

Agonito, Rosemary, and Joseph Agonito. "Resurrecting History's Forgotten Women: A Case Study from the Cheyenne Indians, *Frontiers* 6 (Fall 1981): 8–16.

Alber, Patricia, and Beatrice Medicine. *The Hidden Half: Studies of Plains Indian Women.* Washington, DC: University Press of America, 1983.

Andrews, William D., and Deborah C. Andrews. "Technology and the House-wife in Nineteenth-Century America," *Women's Studies* (1974): 109–28.

Ardis, Cameron. *Radicals of the Worst Sort: Laboring Women in Lawrence, Massachusetts, 1860–1912*. Urbana. University of Illinois Press, 1993.

Aron, Cindy S. "'To Barter Their Souls for Gold': Female Clerks in Federal Government Offices, 1862–1890," *Journal of American History* 67 (March 1981): 835–53.

Babcock, Barbara Allen, "Clara Shortridge Foltz: 'First Women,'" *Arizona Law Review* 30 (1988): 673–717.

Bacon, Margaret Hope. "'One Great Bundle of Humanity': Frances Ellen Watkins Harper," *Pennsylvania Magazine of History and Biography* 113 (January 1989): 21–43.

Bakken, Gordon Morris. *Rocky Mountain Constitution Making*. Westport, CT: Greenwood Press, 1987. Chapter 8.

Banner, Lois W. *Elizabeth Cady Stanton: A Radical for Women's Rights*. Boston: Little, Brown and Company, 1980.

Bargo, Michael. "Women's Occupations in the West in 1870," *Journal of the West* 32 (January 1993): 30–45.

Barnhart, Jacqueline Baker. *The Fair but Frail: Prostitution in San Francisco, 1849–1900*. Reno: University of Nevada Press, 1986.

Barry, Kathleen. *Susan B. Anthony—A Biography: A Singular Feminist*. New York: New York University Press, 1988.

Basch, Norma. "Invisible Women: The Legal Fiction of Marital Unity in Nineteenth-Century America," *Feminist Study* 5 (Summer 1979): 346–66.

———. "'Relief in the Premises': Divorce as a Woman's Remedy in New York and Indiana, 1815–1870," *Law and History Review* (Spring 1990): 1–24.

Beesley, David. "From Chinese to Chinese American: Chinese Women and Families in a Sierra Nevada Town," *California History* 67 (September 1988): 168–79.

Beeton, Beverly. *Women Vote in the West: The Woman Suffrage Movement, 1869–1896*. New York: Garland Publishing, Inc., 1986.

Beezley, William H., and Joseph P. Hobbs. "'Nice Girls Don't Sweat': Women in American Sport," *Journal of Popular Culture* 16 (Spring 1983): 42–53.

Berch, Bettina. *The Endless Day: The Political Economy of Women and Work*. New York: Harcourt Brace Jovanovich, Inc., 1982.

Berkeley, Kathleen C. "'The Ladies Want to Bring About Reform in the Public Schools': Public Education and Women's Rights in the Post–Civil War South," *History of Education Quarterly* 24 (Spring 1984): 45–58.

Berkin, Carol Ruth, and Mary Beth Norton, eds. *Women of America: A History*. Boston: Houghton Mifflin Company, 1979. Part III, except section 7.

Blanton, DeAnne. "Cathay Williams: Black Woman Soldier, 1866–1868," *Minerva: Quarterly Report on Women and the Military* 10 (Fall/Winter 1992): 1–12.

———. "Women Soldiers of the Civil War," *Prologue* 25 (Spring 1993): 27–34.

Blocker, Jr., Jack S., ed. "Annie Wittenmyer and the Women's Crusade," *Ohio History* 88 (Autumn 1979): 419–22.

Bookspan, Shelley. *A Germ of Goodness: The California State Prison System, 1851–1944*. Lincoln: University of Nebraska Press, 1991.

Boydston, Jeanne, Mary Kelley, and Anne Margolis. *The Limits of Sisterhood: The Beecher Sisters on Women's Rights and Women's Sphere*. Chapel Hill: University of North Carolina Press, 1988.

Brown, Minnie Miller. "Black Women in American Agriculture," *Agricultural History* 50 (January 1976): 202–12.

Bulger, Margery A. "American Sportswomen in the 19th Century," *Journal of Popular Culture* 16 (Fall 1982): 1–16.

Butler, Anne M. *Daughters of Joy, Sisters of Misery: Prostitutes in the American West, 1865–1890*. Champaign: University of Illinois Press, 1985.

———. "Still in Chains: Black Women in Western Prisons, 1865–1910," *Western Historical Quarterly* 20 (February 1989): 19–35.

Bynum, Victoria E. *Unruly Women: The Politics of Social and Sexual Control in the Old South*. Chapel Hill: University of North Carolina Press, 1992.

Carrell, Kimberley W. "The Industrial Revolution Comes to the Home: Kitchen Design Reform and Middle-Class Women," *Journal of American Culture* 2 (Fall 1979): 488–99.

Cayleff, Susan E. *Wash and Be Healed: The Water-Cure Movement and Women's Health*. Philadelphia: Temple University Press, 1987.

Chan, Sucheng. "Chinese Livelihood in Rural California: The Impact of Economic Change," *Pacific Historical Review* 53 (August 1984): 273–307.

Chaudhuri, Nupur. "'We All Seem Like Brothers and Sisters': The African-American Community in Manhattan, Kansas, 1865–1940," *Kansas History* 14 (Winter 1991–92): 270–88.

Clinton, Catherine. *The Other Civil War: American Women in the Nineteenth Century*. New York: Hill and Wang, 1984. Chapter 5.

Clinton, Catherine, and Nina Silber, eds. *Divided Houses: Gender and the Civil War*. New York: Oxford University Press, 1992.

Cogan, Frances B. *All-American Girl: The Ideal of Real Womanhood in Mid-Nineteenth-Century America*. Athens: University of Georgia Press, 1989.

Collier-Thomas, Bettye. "The Impact of Black Women in Education: An Historical Overview," *Journal of Negro Education* 51 (Summer 1982): 173–80.

Cowan, Ruth Schwartz. "From Virginia Dare to Virginia Slims: Women and Technology in American Life," *Technology and Culture* 20 (January 1979): 51–63.

Culpepper, Marilyn Mayer. *Trials and Triumphs: Women of the American Civil War*. East Lansing: Michigan State University Press, 1991.

de Graaf, Lawrence. "Race, Sex, and Region: Black Women in the American West, 1850–1920," *Pacific Historical Review* 49 (May 1980): 285–314.

Dill, Bonnie T. "Our Mothers' Grief: Racial Ethnic Women and the Maintenance of Families," *Journal of Family History* 13 (1988): 415–31.

Diner, Hasia R. *Erin's Daughters in America: Irish Immigrant Women in the Nineteenth Century*. Baltimore: Johns Hopkins University Press, 1983.

DuBois, Ellen C. *Feminism and Suffrage: The Emergence of an Independent Women's Movement in America, 1848–1869*. Ithaca, NY: Cornell University Press, 1978. Pages 53–78.

———. "Outgrowing the Compact of the Fathers: Equal Rights, Woman Suffrage, and the United States Constitution, 1826–1878," *Journal of American History* 74 (December 1987): 836–62.

Dunfey, Julie. "'Living the Principle' of Plural Marriage: Mormon Women, Utopia, and Female Sexuality in the Nineteenth Century," *Feminist Studies* 10 (Fall 1984): 523–36.

Edwards, G. Thomas. *Sowing Good Seeds: The Northwest Suffrage Campaigns of Susan B. Anthony*. Portland: Oregon Historical Society Press, 1990.

Elbert, Sarah. *A Hunger for Home: Louisa May Alcott and Little Women*. Philadelphia: Temple University Press, 1984.

Embry, Jessie L. "Effects of Polygamy on Mormon Women," *Frontiers* 7 (1984): 56–61.

Endres, Kathleen L. "The Women's Press in the Civil War: A Portrait of Patriotism, Propaganda, and Prodding," *Civil War History* 30 (March 1984): 30–53.

———. "'Strictly Confidential': Birth Control Advertising in a 19th-Century City," *Journalism Quarterly* 63 (Winter 1986): 748–51.

Epstein, Barbara Leslie. *The Politics of Domesticity: Women, Evangelism, and Temperance in Nineteenth-Century America*. Middletown, CT: Wesleyan University Press, 1981.

Faragher, John Mack. *Women and Men on the Overland Trail*. New Haven, CT: Yale University Press, 1979.

Faust, Drew Gilpin. "Altars of Sacrifice: Confederate Women and the Narratives of War," *Journal of American History* 76 (March 1990): 1200–28.

Foote, Cheryl J. *Women of the New Mexico Frontiers, 1846–1912*. Niwot: University Press of Colorado, 1990.

Foster, Lawrence. "Polygamy and the Frontier: Mormon Women in Early Utah," *Utah Historical Quarterly* 50 (Summer 1982): 268–89.

Freedman, Estelle B. *Their Sister's Keepers: Women's Prison Reform in America, 1830–1930.* Ann Arbor: University of Michigan Press, 1981.

Godfrey, Kenneth W., Audrey M. Godfrey, and Jill Mulvay Derr. *Women's Voices: An Untold History of the Latter-Day Saints, 1830–1900.* Salt Lake City: Deseret Book Company, 1982.

Gollaher, David L. *A Voice for the Mad: The Life of Dorothea Dix.* New York: Free Press, 1994.

Gordon, Jean. "Early American Women Artists and the Social Context in Which They Worked," *American Quarterly* 30 (Spring 1978): 54–69.

Gordon, Linda. "The Long Struggle for Reproductive Rights," *Radical America* 15 (Spring 1981): 74–88.

———. "Voluntary Motherhood: The Beginnings of the Birth-Control Movement," 131–47, in *Family Life in America, 1620–2000,* edited by Mel Albin and Dominick Cavaloo. New York: Revisionary Press, 1981.

Gray, Barbara L. "Organizational Struggles of Working Women in the Nineteenth Century," *Labor Studies Journal* 16 (Summer 1991): 16–34.

Gray, John S. "The Story of Mrs. Picotte-Galpin, a Sioux Heroine," *Montana the Magazine of Western History* 36 (Summer 1986): 2–21.

Gutman, Herbert G. "Persistent Myths about the Afro-American Family," *Journal of Interdisciplinary History* 6 (Autumn 1975): 181–210.

Hall, Richard. *Patriots in Disguise: Women Warriors of the Civil War.* New York: Paragon Books, 1993.

———. "Women in Battle in the Civil War," *Social Education* 58 (February 1994): 80–82. Special edition of *Social Education* on "Women in Wartime"; includes articles and lesson plans regarding women in this and other wars.

Hamand, Wendy F. "The Woman's National Loyal League: Feminist Abolitionists and the Civil War," *Civil War History* 35 (May 1989): 39–58.

Harris, Barbara J. *Beyond Her Sphere: Women and the Professions in American History.* Westport, CT: Greenwood Press, 1978.

Harris, Katherine. *Long Vistas: Women and Families on Colorado Homesteads.* Niwot: University Press of Colorado, 1993.

Hedges, Elaine. "The Nineteenth-Century Diarist and Her Quilts," *Feminist Studies* 8 (Summer 1982): 293–308.

Hewitt, Nancy A., ed. *Women, Families, and Communities: Readings in American History.* Vols. I and II. Glenview, IL: Scott, Foresman, 1990. Part 5 and Part 1.

Hinckley, Ted C. "Glimpses of Societal Change Among Nineteenth-Century Tlingit Women," *Journal of the West* 32 (July 1993): 12–24.

Hoffert, Sylvia D. "Childbearing on the Trans-Mississippi Frontier, 1830–1900," *Western Historical Quarterly* 22 (August 1991): 273–88.

Horton, James O. "Freedom's Yoke: Gender Conventions among Antebellum Free Blacks," *Feminist Studies* 12 (Spring 1986): 51–76.

Hudson, Lynn M. "A New Look, or 'I'm Not Mammy to Everybody in California': Mary Ellen Pleasant, a Black Entrepreneur," *Journal of the West* 32 (July 1993): 35–40.

Jeffrey, Julie Roy. *Frontier Women: The Trans-Mississippi West, 1840–1880.* New York: Hill and Wang, 1979.

Johnson, Michael P., and James L. Roark. *No Chariot Let Down: Charleston's Free People of Color on the Eve of the Civil War.* Chapel Hill: University of North Carolina Press, 1984.

Johnson, Susan L. "Sharing Bed and Board: Cohabitation and Cultural Difference in Central Arizona Mining Towns, 1863–1873," *Frontiers* 7 (1984): 36–42.

Jones, Jacqueline. *Soldiers of Light and Love: Northern Teachers and Georgia Blacks, 1865–1873.* Chapel Hill: University of North Carolina Press, 1980.

Kasson, Joy S. *Marble Queens and Captives: Women in Nineteenth-Century American Sculpture.* New Haven, CT: Yale University Press, 1990.

Kaufman, Janet E. "'Under the Petticoat Flag': Women Soldiers in the Confederate Army," *Southern Studies* 23 (Winter 1984): 363–75.

Kessler-Harris, Alice. *Out to Work: A History of Wage-Earning Women in the United States.* New York: Oxford University Press, 1982.

Kitch, Sally L. *This Strange Society of Women: Reading the Letters and Lives of the Woman's Commonwealth.* Columbus: Ohio State University Press, 1993.

Kohlstedt, Sally Gregory. "In From the Periphery: American Women in Science, 1830–1880," *Signs* 4 (Autumn 1978): 81–96.

Kugler, Israel. *From Ladies to Women: The Organized Struggle for Women's Rights in the Reconstruction Era.* Westport, CT: Greenwood Press, 1987.

Kunkle, Camille. "'It is What it Does to the Souls': Women's Views of the Civil War," *Atlanta History* 33 (Summer 1989): 56–70.

Lerner, Gerda, ed. *Black Women in White America: A Documentary History.* New York: Random House, 1973.

Lupton, Mary Jane. "Ladies Entrance: Women and Bars," *Feminist Studies* 5 (Fall 1979): 571–88.

Madsen, Carol C. "At Their Peril: Utah Law and the Case of Plural Wives," *Western Historical Quarterly* 21 (November 1990): 425–43.

Maret, Elizabeth. *Women of the Range: Women's Role in the Texas Beef Cattle Industry.* College Station: Texas A & M University Press, 1993.

Marti, Donald B. *Women of the Grange: Mutuality and Sisterhood in Rural America, 1866–1920.* Westport, CT: Greenwood, 1991.

Massey, Mary Elizabeth. *Bonnet Brigades: American Women and the Civil War.* New York: Alfred A. Knopf, 1966.

McBridge, Mary G., and Ann M. McLaurin, "Sarah G. Humphreys: Antebellum Belle to Equal Rights Activist, 1830–1907," *Filson Club Historical Quarterly* 65 (April 1991): 231–51.

Melville, Margarita B., ed. *Twice a Minority: Mexican-American Women.* St. Louis: C. V. Mosby Co., 1980).

Morantz, Regina Markell. "Feminism, Professionalism, and Germs: The Thought of Mary Putnam Jacobi and Elizabeth Blackwell," *American Quarterly* 5 (Winter 1982): 459–78.

———. *Sympathy and Science: Women Physicians in American Medicine.* New York: Oxford University Press, 1985.

Morello, Karen Burger. *The Invisible Bar: The Woman Lawyer in America, 1638 to the Present.* New York: Random House, 1986.

Morris, Robert C. "Freedmen's Education," 462–68, in *Black Women in America: An Historical Encyclopedia*, edited by Darlene Clark Hine. Brooklyn: Carlson Publishing Inc., 1993.

Moynihan, Ruth Barnes. *Rebel for Rights: Abigail Scott Duniway.* New Haven, CT: Yale University Press, 1983.

Murphy, Lucy Eldersveld. "Business Ladies: Midwestern Women and Enterprise, 1850–1880," *Journal of Women's History* 3 (Spring 1991): 65–89.

Myres, Sandra L. *Westering Women and the Frontier Experience, 1800–1915.* Albuquerque: University of New Mexico Press, 1982.

Nomura, Gail M. "Significant Lives: Asians and Asian Americans in the History of the United States West," *Western Historical Quarterly* 25 (Spring 1994): 69–88.

Oates, Stephen B. *A Woman of Valor: Clara Barton and the Civil War.* New York: Free Press, 1994.

Ong, Paul M. "Chinese Labor in Early San Francisco: Racial Segmentation and Industrial Expansion," *Amerasia* 8 (1981): 69–92.

Painter, Nell. *Black Migration to Kansas After Reconstruction.* New York: Alfred A. Knopf, 1977.

———. "Sojourner Truth in Memory and History: Writing the History of an American Exotic," *Gender and History* 2 (Spring 1990): 3–16.

Pickle, Linda Schelbitki. "Rural German-Speaking Women in Early Nebraska and Kansas," *Great Plains Quarterly* 9 (Fall 1989): 239–51.

Pleck, Elizabeth H. "The Two-Parent Household: Black Family Structure in Late Nineteenth-Century Boston," *Journal of Social History* 6 (Fall 1972): 3–31.

Pursell, Carroll. "Women Inventors in America," *Technology and Culture* 22 (July 1981): 545–49.

Reverby, Susan M. *Ordered to Care: The Dilemma of American Nursing, 1850–1945.* Cambridge: Cambridge University Press, 1987.

Riley, Glenda. *Women and Indians on the Frontier, 1825–1915.* Albuquerque: University of New Mexico Press, 1984.

Rogers, Gayle J. "The Changing Image of the Southern Woman: A Performer on a Pedestal," *Journal of Popular Culture* 16 (Winter 1982): 60–67.

Russett, Cynthia Eagle. *Sexual Science: The Victorian Construction of Womanhood.* Cambridge: Harvard University Press, 1989.

Ryan, Mary P. *Womanhood in America from Colonial Times to the Present.* New York: New Viewpoints, 1979. Chapter 4.

———. *Women in Public: Between Banners and Ballots, 1825–1880.* Baltimore: Johns Hopkins University Press, 1990.

Schlissel, Lillian. *Women's Diaries of the Westward Journey.* 2d ed. New York: Schocken Books, 1993.

Schultz, Jane E. "Race, Gender, and Bureaucracy: Civil War Army Nurses and the Pension Bureau," *Journal of Women's History* 6 (Summer 1994): 45–69.

Scott, Anne Firor. *The Southern Lady: From Pedestal to Politics, 1830–1930.* Chicago: University of Chicago Press, 1970.

Shover, Michele. "The Blockhead Factor: Marriage and the Fate of California Daughters," *The Californians* 7 (September/October 1989): 32–39.

Sklar, Kathryn Kish, and Thomas Dublin, eds. *Women and Power in American History: A Reader.* Vol. 1. Englewood Cliffs, NJ: Prentice-Hall, 1991. Parts 16–18.

Smith-Rosenberg, Carroll. *Disorderly Conduct: Visions of Gender in Victorian America.* New York: Oxford University Press, 1985.

Special Issue. "19th-Century Women on the Frontier," *Montana the Magazine of Western History* 32 (Summer 1982).

Stage, Sarah. *Female Complaints: Lydia Pinkham and the Business of Women's Medicine.* New York: W. W. Norton & Company, 1979.

Stanley, Amy Dru. "Conjugal Bonds and Wage Labor: Rights of Contract in the Age of Emancipation," *Journal of American History* 75 (September 1988): 471–500.

Sterling, Dorothy, ed. *We Are Your Sisters: Black Women in the Nineteenth Century.* New York: W. W. Norton & Company, 1984.

Streitmatter, Rodger. *Raising Her Voice: African-American Women Journalists Who Changed History.* Lexington: University Press of Kentucky, 1994.

Turbin, Carole. *Working Women of Collar City: Gender, Class, and Community in Troy, New York, 1864–1886.* Urbana: University of Illinois Press, 1993.

Venet, Wendy H. *Neither Ballots nor Bullets: Women Abolitionists and the Civil War.* Charlottesville: University Press of Virginia, 1991.

Walsh, Margaret. "The Democratization of Fashion: The Emergence of the Women's Dress Pattern Industry," *Journal of American History* 66 (September 1979): 299–313.

Wertheimer, Barbara Mayer. *We Were There: The Story of Working Women in America.* New York: Pantheon Books, 1977.

Wertsch, Douglas. "Iowa's Daughters: The First Thirty Years of the Girl's Reform School of Iowa, 1869–1899," *Annals of Iowa* 49 (Summer/Fall 1987): 77–100.

Woloch, Nancy. *Women and the American Experience.* New York: Alfred A. Knopf, 1984. Chapters 9–10.

INDEX

This is a combined index for Volume 1 and Volume 2.
Volume 2 begins with page 173.

Credits in full
Volume 1

Opening illustrations:

Photoessay for Volume 1
Sixteen pages, A–P, following p. 134

Page A

Top: Pocahontas, after the 1616 engraving of her by Simon van de Passe. *National Portrait Gallery, Smithsonian Institution*

Bottom: An early Spanish illustration of the "heathens" who came to the Jesuit missions near the modern Arizona-Mexico border in the early eighteenth century. *Newberry Library*

Page B

Top: Mary Gibson Tilghman and sons (see p. 33, above)

Bottom: Batting cotton. *Joseph E. Taulman Collection, The Center for American History, The University of Texas at Austin*, 3166, CN 00939

Page C

Top: Phillis Wheatley (ca. 1753–1784), poet and first African American published author. *Library of Congress*

Bottom: The Market Plaza, by Thomas Allen. Courtesy of *The Witte Museum*, San Antonio, Texas

Page D

The Wife (see p. ix, above)

Page E

The working women of Lynn, Massachusetts, protest, early 1840s. *Wayne State University, the Archives of Labor and Urban Affairs*

Page F

Top left: "Madonna of the Prairie" (see p. 65 above)

Top right: Ma-ke and Kun-zan-ya, St. Louis, 1848. *Newberry Library*

Bottom: Harriet Tubman. *Library of Congress*

Page G

Top: Engraving from *Godey's Lady's Book*, 1845

Bottom: Sarah Josepha Hale, editor of *Godey's Lady's Book*. From *Godey's Lady's Book*

Page H

Top: A nineteenth-century New England schoolroom, painting by C. Bosworth. *Massachusetts Historical Society*

Bottom: Sojourner Truth (ca. 1797–1883), abolitionist. *Library of Congress*

Page I

Top: The water carriers, ca. 1880. Photo by John K. Hillers. *Museum of New Mexico,* Neg. #102081

Bottom: Southern women, photographed around 1860. *The Western Reserve Historical Society*, Cleveland

Page J

Top: Indian woman with baby. Photo by Keystone View Co. *Museum of New Mexico,* Neg. #91528

Bottom: Pawnee Indian Wind Lodge, ca. 1868–70. Photo by Wm. H. Jackson. *Museum of New Mexico,* Neg. #58632

Page K

Top: Apache camp, ca. 1885. Photo by Ben Wittick. *Museum of New Mexico,* Neg. #102038

Bottom: "Chicago Joe," Mary Josephine Welch Hensley, who established the Red Light Saloon in Montana before the state outlawed dance halls. *Montana Historical Society,* Helena

Page L

Top: Dancing girl, Virginia City, Nevada. *Montana Historical Society,* Helena

Bottom: Lithograph of a nineteenth-century revival meeting after a painting by A. Rider. *Library of Congress*

Page M

Top: Annie Oakley, early publicity photo, mid-1800s. *Annie Oakley Foundation,* Greenville, Ohio

Bottom: Hunting along the Red River, 1870s. *State Historical Society of North Dakota,* Bismarck

Page N

Top: Portrait of Old Crow and his wife, 1880. *Newberry Library*

Bottom left: Wedding picture, William and Anna Belle Steintemp, 1881. *Minnesota Historical Society*, from the Dorothy St. Arnold papers

Bottom right: Wedding portrait, Mr. and Mrs. James Sullivan, ca. 1870. *Montana Historical Society*, Helena

Page O

Former slave, Tillie Brackenridge, in San Antonio, ca. 1900. *Mrs. Charles Bush III, copy from the Institute of Texan Cultures,* San Antonio

Page P

Top: Na-tu-ende (see p. iii, above)

Bottom: Mormon settlers, Arizona, ca. 1885. Photo by Ben Wittick. *Museum of New Mexico,* Neg. #15615

Glenda Riley is Alexander M. Bracken Professor of History at Ball State University. Formerly, she was professor of history and director of the Women's Studies Program at the University of Northern Iowa. Professor Riley has also served as visiting endowed professor at University College, Dublin; Marquette University; and Mesa State College. In addition to authoring two editions of *Inventing the American Woman*, Professor Riley has written *The Life and Legacy of Annie Oakley* (1994), *A Place to Grow: Women in the American West* (1992), *Divorce: An American Tradition* (1991); *The Female Frontier: A Comparative View of Women on the Prairie and Plains* (1988); *Women and Indians on the Frontier, 1825-1915* (1984); and *Frontierswomen: The Iowa Experience* (1981; 2nd ed., 1994), as well as numerous published articles, reviews, and chapters in edited volumes.

Inventing the American Woman: An Inclusive History, Second Edition

The publisher's editorial and production team for this text consisted of Maureen Hewitt, Lucy Herz, and Andrew Davidson.

Index: Scholars Editorial Services
Typesetting: Bruce Leckie
Cover design: DePinto Graphic Design
Printing and binding: BookCrafters, Inc.